# Quivering on the Brink

# Quivering on the Brink

## REVEALING HIGHER SPIRITUAL TRUTHS

By Mary Ebben Livingston

**Quivering on the Brink**

Copyright ©2011, 2014, 2017, 2019, by Mary Ebben Livingston
All rights reserved.
No part of this book may be reproduced in any manner without
prior written permission from the author
except for quotations embodied in critical articles or reviews.

ISBN: 978-0-9638726-6-1 (e-book)
ISBN: 978-1-7982957-9-3 (paperback)
Imprint: Independently published

Also by
Mary Ebben Livingston

The Urantia Book Basics (revised)
Copyright ©2003 by Mary Ebben Livingston
ISBN 978-0-9638726-5-4 (e-book)
Translated and published with permission:
French by Father Louis, Guinea, Africa, 2012
Korean by Wan Park, Korea, 2010
Portuguese by Elyr Silva, Brazil, 2009
Spanish by Agustin Arellano, Mexico, 2007

The Urantia Book Basics
Copyright ©1994 by Mary Ebben
First Printing ISBN 978-0-9638726-1-6
Library of Congress Catalog Card Number 94-094235

A Young Child's Guide to The Urantia Book
Copyright ©1993 by Mary Ebben
First Printing ISBN 978-0-9638726-0-9
(Spanish translation done with permission)

Quivering on the Brink
Cover Design by Larry Hensel of Hensel Graphics

Dedicated To:

my daughter, Christina Marie,
my son, Michael Thomas,

and all who seek to expand
their spiritual horizons.

# Acknowledgements

*The Urantia Book* changed me; it gave me the desire to be my spiritual best. However, it is a book and not to be considered sacred. It is the people that helped me understand more of the UB, those who live the teachings, people who had a profound impact on my life, those that encouraged me to write this book, and those who played a part in *Quivering on the Brink* reaching publication, that I wish to thank.

Archie and Rusti Lowe, you literally introduced me to *The Urantia Book* in 1975. I have never forgotten how you treated me with such regard, gentleness, and patience, as you shared the teachings and answered my questions. It was the first deep and meaningful dialog I ever had. It is with sincere gratitude that I thank you both.

About 25 years ago, I went to my first UB study group at Mo and Jen Siegel's home. I was fearful and extremely shy. Mo, you were incredibly thoughtful and perceptive. Through your patience and encouragement, you coaxed me out of my shell and got me to open-up to ask questions and participate. Jen, you have always impressed me with your problem-solving abilities and community service. I loved that our daughters were friends and how you and Mo treated her like family. (And, what wonderful women they turned out to be!) Thank you both for being instrumental in creating a village for our children and adding to my personal growth.

John Hay, I will never forget the first time I tried to tell you 'my story'—I was angry at God... You simply stopped me with, "God isn't angry with you," and tried to get away from me. I learned that you are really a 'softie' (very compassionate and loving) and I thank you for telling me what I needed to hear. I greatly appreciate how supportive you and Carol were while I was creating my first UB children's book and 'Basics'. John, I have utmost respect for the work you do behind the scenes. It will always have a tremendous impact on the furtherance of the Revelation, thank you!

Paula Thompson, you were the best boss I ever had. Working with you at Jesusonian was the opportunity of a lifetime and I always felt I should pay to work there. You taught me how to introduce *The Urantia Book* to people at expos and shows. By example, you showed me how to integrate the teachings into ordinary life circumstances. Thank you for always being supportive, loving, and a spiritual light in my life.

David (Llama Karuna Seva), your experiences and understandings of the UB have kept me sharp, or at least questioning. You are extraordinarily talented in many areas with a willingness to help others. Thank you for the beautiful healing website and most recently, for the promo videos for this book. You certainly are unique and I thank you for a long and meaningful friendship.

Jim Cleveland, you are one amazing dynamo and your productivity is contagious. I very much appreciated the experience of co-chairing the TM Network with you. I am thankful for the support you have given me on various projects but especially for sharing your publishing expertise with me.

JJ Johnson, you were a Godsend. Thank you for sharing your Position Paper on Personality that helped enhance this book. Your knowledge of the UB, combined with your gracious offer to edit *Quivering on the Brink*, added precise clarity, for which I am grateful.

My Aunt Pat McDougle once told me that we have biological family, and then we have a family we create. I love my aunt and her wisdom. JoiLin Johnson, you are my created sister and best friend. I love your openness and all the adventures and experiences we have shared. You would have been an awesome English teacher—a talent you applied to editing this book. I thank you for enriching my life.

Steve Livingston, if it wasn't for you, the original 'Basics' would have died in obscurity. Thank you for encouraging me to improve it many times. I am grateful for your IT expertise and willingness to help others. Thank you for teaching me the skills needed to produce a quality publication. I appreciate what a good friend, listener, and natural teacher you are.

Christina Ebben, both you and Michael are incredible children but I owe you special thanks for editing parts of this book. You are a remarkable mathematician, researcher, and writer; actually, you are a remarkable person. I am honored you are my daughter.

Urantia is now quivering on the very brink
of one of its most amazing and enthralling epochs
of social readjustment, moral quickening, and
spiritual enlightenment.
Urantia Book 195:9.2


My beloved,
you must always make a difference in teaching
so as to suit your presentation of truth
to the minds and hearts before you.
Jesus to his apostles,
Urantia Book 151:3.1

# Table of Contents

## PART TWO - The Unfolding of Events that Shaped Our World

# Author's Notes

Every book has a back-story and this one is no exception.

I had more than my fair share of childhood trauma and by age ten, I had "fallen away" from God. Actually, I had a huge fight with God and told Him in a fit of rage that I would never, never, *ever* speak to Him again. On many levels, I feared God. I believed God could *make* my life better but was either mean or uncaring for not doing so. With child-like ignorance, I felt it was best to keep a low profile, to live under God's radar.

I lived like this for a very long time and in 1975, I found *The Urantia Book* (pronounced you-ran'-chah). For the most part, the huge book sat on a bookshelf. It claimed to be a revelation, the fifth major revelation to our world. Little parts that I read were interesting but no one around me thought it made sense. I was not yet ready to take on such a huge endeavor and back then, I was not a very deep thinker.

Today, I understand that revelation is a method used to save ages upon ages of time. It sorts and shifts the errors of evolution from the truths of spiritual attainment. Revelation fills in the gaps and eliminates error as it restores lost knowledge of past revelations. These past revelations are called epochal (ep'-ek-al) revelations where the term epochal is used to denote an important and often long period of time.

Revelation is like looking through a divine lens. With each epochal revelation, the lens widens to give us a broader picture of the truth and the reality of our spiritual existence.

The newest revelation, the one offered by *The Urantia Book*, serves to fill in the gaps in our planet's history and to detail a destiny of eternal adventure. Unlike other revelations, this one was given to our world in the form of a book published in only 1955. The book is sometimes referred to as The Fifth Epochal Revelation but that is indicative of an experienced reader. The five major revelations are covered in chronological order in this book.

If you are wondering why you have only recently heard of *The Urantia Book*, it is probably because there are no churches or temples; there are no clergy; there are no doctrines. And, there are no human authors.

*The Urantia Book* is also commonly referred to as the UB or the Urantia Papers, because, rather than chapters, the teachings are presented as 196 Papers. There are now two Publishers of *The Urantia Book*. The Urantia Foundation is the original organization responsible for publishing. Their editions are referenced by page numbers. The Urantia Book Fellowship began publishing in 1996 with the exact wording and punctuation but has two columns and references Paper, section, and paragraph, as well as the original page numbers. Both organizations publish beautiful books so it is a matter of which format you prefer. This may seem like an intimidating amount of material to cover, but that is why I am writing *this* book. You can experience the revelation, *The Urantia Book*, without intimidation or years of study.

As a child, I wanted a mother more than anything in the world; as an adult, I wanted to be a mother more than anything in the world. December of 1985, at age 34, I had my first child, a daughter. My world exploded with joy. Motherhood was everything I had imagined. I was so happy I even liked God again. My son was born in November 1987. I had two healthy, wonderful babies—I finally felt blessed and was talking to God after years of stubborn silence.

It was at this time, in the bliss of motherhood, that I was drawn to the Urantia Papers again. Though, given the complexity of *The Urantia Book*, I could never read even one page without looking up words in the dictionary. But something drove me. I became determined to read the complicated, 2,097-page book cover-to-cover! My children were preschool age when I dedicated myself to reading the Urantia Papers. I would wait until after my children were put to bed, and I would read alone late at night. At this pace, it took me somewhere between three to five years to read, absorb, and integrate the teachings of the Urantia Papers.

Though I knew I had found something important, I did not know *The Urantia Book* would forever change my life. If I had known, I would have taken note of the date that I began my cover-to-cover reading.

At one point along my journey, towards the end of the book, I was struggling to understand God's will. I had just 50 pages left to read in *The Urantia Book*. It did not help me to read about the horrible deaths of some of Jesus' disciples that were near the end of *The Urantia Book*. Just what was God going to ask me? How could I commit to something I did not understand?

While confused about God's will, I saw a notice in the newspaper about a group that met weekly to study the book. I had never participated in group gatherings. Before I thought about it too much, I asked my husband to watch the children and I went. I admit I was nervous. I even had a silly idea that they might be strange hippies studying the book with candles and incense burning.

About twenty-five people gathered in a well-lit basement of a large home to read and discuss the book. It was their practice to begin reading where they had stopped the previous week. Someone volunteered to read the next small section on page 1,221 titled, "The Consecration of Choice." I was not exactly sure what the word consecration meant. Before I could give it further thought the group reading began. I heard, "The doing of the will of God is nothing more or less than an exhibition of creature willingness to share the inner life with God—with the very God who has made such a creature life of inner meaning-value possible. Sharing is Godlike—divine." (UB 111:5.1) My whole body began to tremble. I looked around, embarrassed, but everyone had their eyes on their books.

I had read that passage long before, almost nine hundred pages before, but had forgotten it. I was feeling lost and confused, but through that reading God was answering my questions about what it meant to follow his will. He was asking me to share my inner life with him. I believe that meant I was to become more aware of his Presence, more aware of his indwelling Spirit. Perhaps my trembling was the Spirit of Truth.

The people in the study group were all warm and genuine so I returned week after week. Families attended, and this pleased me. The children played while the adults read and discussed *The Urantia Book*. I would not read aloud and I turned beet-red when I did speak up to ask a question. But I was as comfortable as a severely shy person could be in a group setting.

Reading alone is very different from reading with others in a study group, and the experiences of group discussion can be priceless. For years, alone, I had pronounced the name of our planet as "You-ran-tee-ah." I also mispronounced, in my own mind, many other names. While I understood many of the concepts, a lot became clearer through study group discussions.

After only a few weeks attendance I shared my aspirations of writing a book that would introduce *The Urantia Book* concepts to young children, specifically my children. If only some of what I had learned had been known to me as a child, on a child's level, my entire life might have been quite different. As an adult, I had a solid understanding of the major concepts of the

Urantia Papers, and, I had passion; I passionately wanted to do this for my own children as well as others. Although I was compelled, I did not know anything about writing a book, much less getting a book published. In 1993, I was encouraged by another mom to write *A Young Child's Guild to The Urantia Book*, while keeping our children in mind.

My days were filled with the responsibilities of a wife and mother. So, late each night I worked on what would become my first book. It would be a guide for young children to explore the very basics, such as the spiritual Thought Adjuster and Jesus' early childhood. There was no market for such a book outside of scattered Urantia Book readers. I decided I had to find a bookbinder and do it myself. The mom who had encouraged me was a long-time UB reader who helped me by verifying the book for content accuracy.

In 1994, I wrote and self-published *The Urantia Book Basics*. I wrote it as a study aid for new readers. I had very limited exposure and a small audience. Nevertheless, the 1,000 copies sold within two years. In spite of the books' (embarrassingly) amateurish publishing quality, Urantia reader's thirst for *any* materials was so great, the books sold.

In 2003, almost a decade later, my new husband encouraged me to rewrite *The Urantia Book Basics*. Again, I had it reviewed by long-time readers, and this time I also had it professionally edited. My husband formatted it as an e-book, but *The Urantia Book Basics* remained obscure and largely unknown; thus, not reaching those who might benefit the most from its message.

For years, my book was simply referred to as "Basics." I am honored to say that it has been published in several other languages by UB readers across the world. But I believe that the time has come to republish a new, revised "Basics" in English. I have grown as an author, studied more, and researched more, so that I could present the clearest teachings of *The Urantia Book* that I possibly can. I also did another rewrite, added more information, more visuals, and renamed it *Quivering on the Brink*.

In time, I want to see *Quivering on the Brink* in libraries and bookstores. I want it available to those struggling to understand life. It is meant for those people not yet ready to invest the time it takes to read the magnificent, but very large Urantia Book, which is over a million words long and complex. The run-on sentences alone can be mind-boggling. But I have spent years studying the book. I believe people need the teachings and they need them now. The world is changing rapidly and we need information as to what is happening and why. With understanding, we can make better choices. With a broader perspective, we can move through fear and turmoil to make choices from a secure place of love. This is my motive.

Many people want to read a book written by an authority figure. They want an expert. But, when it comes to your relationship with God, no one is an expert or an authority except you. *Quivering on the Brink*, in its evolved form, has been read by many long-time UB readers and is considered an accurate condensed work. But I claim no authority. I only want to share the message of *The Urantia Book* in an easy to read format so that those who are ready to broaden their spiritual perspectives can receive the basic teachings of the Urantia Papers.

Paper 12, Section 7, Paragraph 9 of *The Urantia Book*, (denoted as UB 12:7.9) states, "The love of the Father absolutely individualizes each personality as a unique child of the Universal Father, a child without duplicate in infinity, a will creature irreplaceable in all eternity." This quote is at a reading level of someone with over twelve years of college. But it can be written in easier language. We are *each* valued as unique. There are no duplicate copies of *you*. No one can *ever* replace you. And, all of this is made true because of God's love for *you*.

Humanity is now quivering on the very brink of one of its most amazing ages. We are in the midst of a new revelation and a time of social readjustment. It is a time of moral quickening and spiritual enlightenment. Mankind is at the threshold. We are headed toward a higher evolving destiny. There is a global need for truth and deeper understanding.

We are a confused world! You do not need a book to know this. But, knowing more about the universe can assist all of us through the maze of confusion. We have little knowledge beyond God and man with angels in between. We know little about our evolving souls and who is "out there" guiding us, much less who is inside us helping us to become the best we can be. We have thought, if we gave it thought, like an 'only' child and many haven't recognized that we are cosmic citizens within a friendly universe teeming with life.

For the sake of understanding, *Quivering on the Brink* contains much of the details of *The Urantia Book* but uses more common language and shorter sentences. It also provides pronunciations as you encounter new words. It includes a brief glossary, also with pronunciations that you can refer to if you forget how to say something or what it means. *Quivering on the Brink* also includes diagrams and a well laid out format that has been divided into two parts.

Part One is about the personalities and organization of Creation. This helps us to understand where we fit into Creation. Part One also explains what happens after death and details eternal life. This part of the book tracks our eternal career as a son or daughter of God. In general, Part One is about God, celestials, and our destiny. It is a sort of who's who of the various orders of beings and their natures and roles. You need this information in order to understand Part Two. You do not need to memorize the information but you should be familiar with the material to move forward in understanding.

Part Two is a time-line of activities. It gives an account of the events that took place on our world and, at the same time, gives the known activities of the spirit world. Part Two covers our history, our origins. It includes a condensed account of Jesus and his teachings. One-third of *The Urantia Book* is devoted to the "Life and Teachings of Jesus," presented in chronological order. This part of the UB covers the missing years not documented in the New Testament of the Bible. It explains what happened to Joseph and covers how Jesus helped his mother raise his brothers and sisters after Joseph's death and many other of Jesus' experiences.

Within *Quivering on the Brink* are concepts and explanations that may fit nicely into your current religious beliefs. Some concepts may expand or clarify your beliefs. However, some concepts might not find a place in your belief system and initially feel uncomfortable. *There is no penalty for not believing all or part of these teachings.* The Urantia Papers teach that faith in God, not faith in a religious practice or set of beliefs, is what assures eternal life.

There is one concept, one teaching from the UB, that I believe is essential. It is the teaching that a fragment of God lives within each morally conscious person. This "Divine Spark" or Spirit within us is termed the Thought Adjuster and is called such because he adjusts our thoughts Godward. This explains how God has an intimate and personal relationship with each of us if we desire it.

*The Urantia Book* taught me about the Thought Adjuster and once that knowledge entered my consciousness, my life began to change. I began to *feel* the presence of God in my life like never before. Some Eastern religions teach that the Divine is within us and Christians teach that "The Kingdom of God is within." But I never understood that to mean, "God is within." No matter what religious background you may have, my greatest hope for you is that you find the very God that lives within you. It is the journey and exploring of new ideas and concepts that might assist you in expanding your understandings.

I am ordinary and I have written *Quivering on the Brink* for ordinary people. My intention is not to convert or convince, but simply to aid you in your journey.

The key to getting something meaningful from this book is to read with curiosity and an open mind. Again, you do not have to believe everything you read. There are no penalties, no threats, no punishments, and no withheld blessings. God and his ministering spirits truly love us as if we are small children. Nevertheless, truths have a way of staying with us. Truths will crowd out errors over time. So, allow these new teachings and ideas to enlighten you, to help you feel closer to God, and to experience more brotherly love in your daily life.

I sincerely hope you enjoy *Quivering on the Brink;* I hope you find it life changing. May you experience more love in your life and may you more strongly feel the divine presence of God Within.

# Part One

## Personalities, Organization, And Eternal Life

# 1. Spiritual Thought Adjusters

*[Understanding of the spiritual Thought Adjuster that dwells within you is one of the most valuable teachings I can share with you. This concept can be integrated within nearly any religion. It will assist you in experiencing the presence of God more fully in your life. However, many new terms and personalities are introduced that may seem confusing in the beginning. It will all come together as you read this book. Please allow it to unfold. —Mary Ebben Livingston]*

God the Father dwells on Paradise but he also lives in the minds of his mortal children. An actual fragment of the Paradise Father lives inside the normal mind of every morally conscious person. The term "Thought Adjusters" was used because these fragments of God work with our spiritual thoughts to guide us Godward.

It is the mission of each Thought Adjuster to represent, to be, the Paradise Father. They are from the Father, and, they **are** the Father. They work to transform and raise the immortal souls of men up to the spiritual heights of Paradise perfection. They are vital to the mortal Paradise ascension plan. The Adjuster is the divine reality that God is man's Father. The Adjuster is man's perfect cosmic compass. The Thought Adjuster always and perfectly points the soul Godward. He adjusts our spiritual thoughts Godward, yet never violates our free will. He is the Divine Presence in man. He is the indwelling Spirit, the Light that dwells within.

The mission and influence of the Adjuster should not be confused with your conscience. They are not directly related. Conscience is a human reaction. It is hardly the voice of God to the soul. Conscience, rightly, cautions you to do right. The Adjuster attempts to tell you what truly *is* right, when you are able to perceive his leading.

It is the Adjuster who creates the desire in man to be like God. Our Adjusters encourage us to ascend to Paradise and to worship the source of such a divine gift. The Adjusters are the living presence that links the mortal sons and daughters with their Paradise Father. The Thought Adjusters compensate for our distance from God.

Before the arrival of an Adjuster, the ancestry and patterns of life of a mortal are reviewed. What you inherit from your parents and ancestors goes into a forecast. Intellect and spiritual capacity are also considered. Before the Adjusters volunteer to indwell a mortal mind, they have full knowledge of the mortal's potentials.

The Adjuster is very much interested in three areas:
- *Intellectual capacity.* Is the mind normal? Can the individual develop into a free will creature? Will wisdom have an opportunity to function?
- *Spiritual perception.* This concerns the birth and growth of the religious nature. What is the likely spiritual capacity of receptivity? What is the potential of soul?
- *Combined intellectual and spiritual powers.* To what degree do these two qualities combine to produce strength of human character? Combined, will they lead to the evolution of an immortal soul of survival value?

Probably more than one Adjuster volunteers and the one best suited is selected. The job is to assist the mortal mind in becoming spiritual and eternal. The time between volunteering and actual dispatch is spent in the Adjuster schools. A working pattern of the waiting mortal mind is used to instruct the Adjuster. The Adjuster will plan the best approach for spiritualizing the mind.

Adjusters cannot enter the mortal mind until it has been prepared. The mortal mind must be connected with the seven adjutant mind-spirits (pages 39, 40) and the Holy Spirit (pages 15, 150). When the Spirit of Truth (Chapter 42) is present on a world, an Adjuster comes the instant the seventh adjutant mind-spirit begins to work in a human's mind. (More is described in future chapters.) Thus, the stage is set for the human mind to receive his or her Adjuster. However, the Adjusters cannot enter the mortal mind before he or she makes their first moral decision. This is usually around the age of five. The Adjuster accepts his mission when the mortal mind is ready.

## DIVINE GIFTS

| AGE | SPIRITUAL ACTIVITY | OUTCOME | UB REFERENCES | ADDITIONAL INFORMATION |
|---|---|---|---|---|
| Conception | Living mind develops | Life begins | 36:5.15, 103:2.1, 108:2.1 | Thought Adjusters study potentials |
| Birth | Receives 7 Adjutant Mind-Spirits | Universe identity | 1:7.5, 12:8.16, 12:9.6, 36:5.5-14, 37:3.7 | |
| Approx. 2 years-old | Attains 7 Adjutant Mind-Spirits (superminded) & Universe level of moral discernment | Personality Bestowed & child encircuited. Receives Holy Spirit & child encircuited. Capacity to receive the Spirit of Truth | 2:2.6, 5:6.3-6, 16:8.1-19, 36:5.12-15, 103:0.1, 108:2.2-3, 112:0.12, 194:2.3 | |
| Approx. 5 years-old | Makes 1st moral decision | Adjuster arrives! | 108:2.4 | Thus, "God and man are directly related" |

Special thanks to JJ Johnson of AZ. His "Position Paper on Personality Bestowal", Oct. 2018, gave me clarity, making this chart possible. (He may be contacted at JJ_6062003@yahoo.com )

God and man are *directly* related. There are no powers or authorities functioning between the Adjusters and their human subjects.

The average child on Urantia makes his or her first moral decision during the fifth year of life. That first moral choice is recorded at once. This fact is passed through the local universe and over the mind gravity circuit of the Infinite Spirit. (See "circuit" in the Glossary.) Then, the Adjuster takes authority right away. He will actually arrive to live inside the mortal mind. Transit time of an Adjuster to Urantia is just under four days and twenty-two hours. Most of that time is spent registering on Uversa, our superuniverse capital. (UB 108:1.9)

Thought Adjusters are not personalities. However, they are real entities, spirit entities, rather than beings. They plan, work, love, and have the ability to communicate with each other. They are subservient to mortal will. Human will functions on the personality level of reality. Thought Adjusters are pre-personal. That means they are responsive to the will and acts of existing personality.

Personality is one of the mysteries of the universes. It is designed and bestowed by the Paradise Father. It is the exclusive function of the Father. It is the personalization of the living energy systems, to which he gives free will and consciousness. Personality is self-consciousness and free willed.

God the Father bestows personality upon the living energies of matter, mind, and spirit. It is superimposed upon living energy systems. Personality is changeless in the presence of change. It is not a progressive achievement. Either there is personality or there is no personality. That which changes—grows—becomes the moral character of a person. Personality is that cosmic gift that can coexist with change. At the same time, it keeps its identity through all changes.

Personality depends upon the identity of selfhood. This can only be achieved through the medium of mind. Selfhood persists in spite of continuous change in self. In the physical life, the change is gradual. At death and upon re-personalization, the change is sudden. Human life is endless change unified by the stability of the unchanging personality.

Personality is always diverse and original. Personalities may be a lot alike, but they are never the same. Even though we see groups or types of people with common patterns, no two beings are identical. Personality is unique. There are no duplicates.

Personality is potential in creatures. A creature must have a mind ranging from self-consciousness to God-consciousness. But mind alone is not personality. Mind can think even when deprived of all power of choice, as in the lower types of animals. However, animals are not persons. They cannot know God and strive to be Godlike. Animals do not have free will such as humans have.

"The relative free will which characterizes the self-consciousness of human personality is involved in: (UB 16:8.7)

1. Moral decision, highest wisdom
2. Spiritual choice, truth discernment
3. Unselfish love, brotherhood service
4. Purposeful co-operation, group loyalty
5. Cosmic insight, the grasp of universe meanings
6. Personality dedication, wholehearted devotion to doing the Father's will
7. Worship, the sincere pursuit of divine values and the wholehearted love of the divine Value-Giver"

Personality continues with the survival of the soul. But, mortal personality is not body, mind, nor spirit. Neither is personality the soul. Personality is the changeless essence of a being. Loved ones will know who you are even when you have a spirit form. This is because you have the Father's gift—a unique personality.

Thought Adjusters are a fragment of the Paradise Father—the source of personality. The physical self has personality but it has brief identity. The pre-personal Thought Adjuster has eternal identity. The mortal personality and the Adjuster's pre-personality can unite. Together they can bring to life the identity of the immortal soul.

You, as a personal creature, have mind and will. The Adjuster, as a pre-personal creature, has pre-mind and pre-will. If you and your Adjuster align your minds so that you see eye-to-eye, then your minds become one. You receive the support of the Adjuster's mind. Then, if your free will carries out the decisions of this stronger combined mind, the Adjuster's pre-personal will attains personality expression. As far as that particular thought-choice is concerned, you and your Adjuster are one. Your mind has reached divine attunement. The Adjuster's will has achieved personality expression. And, every mortal who is following the leading of his indwelling Adjuster is living God's will.

The Thought Adjuster makes eternity possible for man. Man makes personality possible for the Thought Adjuster. Your Thought Adjuster is the potential of your new and next order of existence. With the consent of your will, the Adjuster works with your material mind. Your Adjuster will build a new mind for your future life.

Adjusters are heavenly helpers. They are not earthly helpers. They are not interested in making the mortal life easier. They are concerned with making your life challenging so that decisions will be stimulated and multiplied.

*The soul of man is acquired through experience.* It is only through experience that you create your soul. As you choose to do the will of the Father, the Adjuster becomes the father of a new reality. Your mind is the mother of this same budding reality. And this new creation is called the soul. The Adjuster is the Father and your mind is the mother of your soul.

As you achieve higher levels of spirituality, your Adjuster is provided an increased range of function. When you reach perfection of alignment, when your will becomes God's will, your Adjuster can complete the unity of your identity and soul. This provides for immediate fusion.

Fusion is the merging of the soul and the Adjuster. Your soul and your Adjuster are destined to become one. All the experiences and values of one become the possession of the other so that the two are actually one. This new being, this fused being, is of the eternal past as well as of the eternal future.

Eternal survival is dependent on the choosing of the mortal mind. Mind decisions determine the survival potential of the immortal soul. When the mind believes God, the soul knows God, and they *desire* God, then is survival assured. We could never do it alone. However, God our Father has provided for all our needs.

Poor intellect or a poor education is a handicap. Lack of culture or social status is a disadvantage. Low morals because of harsh conditions, are difficult to overcome. Nevertheless, the presence of the Adjuster in a *believing* individual conquers human flaws. The indwelling of the Father's Adjuster makes eternal life possible for each of his children.

God has not set an imaginary bar that everyone must reach. There are no standardized tests for us to take. Growth is mandatory but growth is based on individual capacity. God never gives you more than you can handle. Your Adjuster wants you to succeed.

"Mind is your ship, the Adjuster is your pilot, the human will is captain." (UB 111:1.9) With your permission, your faithful pilot will safely carry you across the troubles of time. He will carry you through the limitations of space. He will take you to the very source of the divine mind and on beyond, even to the Paradise Father of Adjusters.

The success of your Adjuster in piloting you through the mortal life and bringing about your survival depends upon your decisions, resolve, and *faith.* All these efforts of growth become powerful influences. They aid in your advancement because they help you to cooperate with your Adjuster. They assist you in ceasing to resist. Adjusters succeed or fail in their task just as far as mortals succeed or fail to cooperate with the Adjuster. The Adjuster's plan is to move you along the ascension path. This is the path of perfection attainment. "The secret of survival is wrapped up in the supreme human desire to be Godlike..." (UB 110:3.2)

**Suggested Reading**

There are 196 papers presented in *The Urantia Book*. Papers 107 through 111 cover the "Origin and Nature of Thought Adjusters," their mission and ministry, and their relationship to individuals and the soul. Also of interest is a beautiful passage in Paper 110, Section 7, Paragraph 10, (UB 110:7.10) that conveys the desires of an Adjuster for his human partner.

A small but powerful book, *The Call of The Spirit*, by Merritt Horn is outstanding. [Seraphic Publishing, Boulder, Colorado, ©1984, 2008] While this book makes no claims, it feels as if an Adjuster is speaking to the reader.

"God has embarked upon the eternal adventure with man." UB 5:1.12) If you embrace the leadings of the spiritual forces in you and around you, then you cannot fail. You will attain the high destiny provided by our loving Paradise Father.

"...love is the dominant characteristic of all God's personal dealings with his creatures." (UB 2:5.12) Through the presence of the Father's spirit, the indwelling Adjuster, he keeps direct and loving contact with his children.

# 2. God, the Paradise Father

| GOD THE FATHER |
| --- |
| First Source and Center |
| Absolute I AM, reality, free will |
| Creator, then Controller |
| Upholder—Infinite in love, will, spiritual thought, and purpose. |
| Thought |
| Expresses Love as a father |
| Loves mankind |
| Draws all personality to himself. Personality-Gravity Circuit |
| Attainment Plan: Evolutionary ascension—progressive attainment (eternal life) |
| Father's Spirit Lives In Us. He sends a small piece, fragment of himself, to live inside of us |
| The Father IS our eternal destination |

God is the First Source and Center of all things and beings. The name God is most often used on our world, Urantia (you-ran'-chah), which is God's name for our planet. But God is known by many, many names throughout the universes.

The First Source and Center has never revealed himself by name. To those who know God, the Father is an expressive term frequently used. The name used is not important although the name suggests the creature's concept of the Creator. What is important is that you should know him and desire to be like him.

God is the great and only I AM. He is infinite—never beginning and never ending. He is forever changeless. To God there is no time—no past, present or future.

It is said we are made in God's image. The Father is not like us in form or physique. The Father is spirit. He is a universal spiritual presence. However, the Father lives at the center of all things. He is really on the Isle of Paradise. He also lives in each of his mortal children through his bestowed fragments.

God is not an accident; he is not a man, a machine, or nature. God is eternal truth, infinite reality, and father personality. God *is* personality. He is a person. "Man might fear a great God, but he trusts and loves only a good God. This goodness of God is a part of the personality of God..." (UB 2:6.1) Personality is the unique bestowal of the Paradise Father. How the Father gifts personality and what exactly it is, remains a great mystery.

The Father somehow places personality over living energies, mind, and spirit. Personality unites these factors. Two characteristics of personality are self-consciousness and relative free will. But they alone do not explain what makes us a unique personality.

Personality is changeless. What changes or grows is the moral character of man. Personality separates us from the animals. Because of personality, we have morality, scientific curiosity, and spiritual insight. Only a personality has insight in advance of experience. We can know what we are going to do before we do it. A personality can look before he leaps. He can learn from looking as well as from leaping. An animal ordinarily learns only by leaping.

Because personality is unique, no two persons are the same. Logically, no two people can exactly interpret the guidance of the spirit that lives within each of them. We vary in our understandings of religious thought and spiritual experiences. Therefore, each person's relationship with God is unique as well.

The divine personality of the First Source and Center, the Paradise Father, reveals himself to the universes as love. God is always and consistently a loving spirit Father. God is a Father in the highest sense of the word. He is eternally motivated by divine love. His tender nature finds its expression and satisfaction in loving and being loved.

Even though we cannot see God with our eyes, he is a person. God does not hide from us but lives in a light that no material creature can approach.

God shows himself to each of us according to each creature's ability to understand the qualities of truth, beauty, and goodness. We cannot see love but we can feel what love does for us and how it makes us happy. In the same way, we cannot see the Father but we can feel his presence in our lives and experience that happiness.

Truth, beauty, and goodness are real spiritual facts and are united in God who is love. God's heart is forever open to us. The Father "delights in his children." Each of us can feel his nearness and love for us because the Father sends a small piece, a fragment, of himself to live inside of us—to spiritually help and guide each of us to him.

This fragment of God is called a Thought Adjuster and he is pre-personality which means your free will dominates. Never does God violate our free will. God the Father indwells the mind of man in the hope of guiding each person back to him in Paradise.

God the Paradise Father has planned an eternal destiny for us. We may choose to accept eternal life. But God not only planned our eternal destiny he *is* our eternal destination. In the Father's ascension plan, we progress and move forward, step-by-step, all the way to Paradise, eventually to be with him.

God is superb character—character in perfection. He is kind, loving, and forgiving. We never need to try to influence God because our sincere needs always guarantee the fullness of his love. He knows our needs even before we do.

The Father is fair and just. He is never angry or punishing. It is through our own choices that we sometimes hurt ourselves, but that should not be confused with punishment. It is true that God is amazingly powerful. He is the Creator. God created and controls the awesome energies and universe forces. Yet, we, his children, love the Father—not because of his awesome power—but because of his perfect and loving nature.

The Father knows and loves each of his children and we can know and love him in return. However, the Father does not make us love him. He allows us to choose. God's love is freely available to every child who accepts his love. Neither does the Paradise Father demand that we worship him or serve him. We must recognize, love, and worship him according to what is in our hearts.

God has given us free will. We are free to choose. The Father refuses to make us submit to his will. Therefore, "the affectionate dedication of the human will to the doing of the Father's will is man's choicest gift to God." (UB 1:1.2) There is nothing else of true value that man can give to God.

It is God's will that you share your inner life—trust the guidance that has been lovingly provided for you. It is also Father's will that you recognize you are a beloved child of his. That makes all other human beings your brothers and sisters. Value yourself as a son or daughter of the magnificent Father! Value each person you meet because they belong to the "brotherhood." We are all part of God's family and the Father does not want to lose a single child. However, no one is forced to accept the honor of being his child.

Everyone who knows even a small part of God wants to be like the Father. That is why the messengers of Paradise have forever carried God's loving message. The message is, "Be you perfect, even as I am perfect."

You cannot hope to attain God's eternal and divine perfection. Nevertheless, you can strive for perfection in your sphere or realm of existence. And, if you choose God's plan of eternal life, in the distant future, you will become a perfected being.

If you choose to be led by the spiritual force within you, then you cannot fail. You can reach the high destiny established by our loving, perfect Father. Your growing love for the Paradise Father and your desire to be like him is truly the biggest adventure of your life!

# 3. God, the Eternal Son

| GOD THE ETERNAL SON |
|---|
| Second Source and Center |
| Absolute pattern of personality |
| Co-creator, then Administrator |
| Revealer—Infinite in wisdom, truth, spiritual expression and interpretation. |
| Word |
| Expresses affection as a mother |
| Serves mankind |
| Attracts all spiritual reality Spirit-Gravity Circuit |
| Bestowal Plan incarnation (bestowal) of the descending Sons of God |
| The Eternal Son's Spirit Surrounds Us – His Spirit bathes all creation and draws us to God |
| The Eternal Son leads us to the Father |

God has no beginning but this is very difficult for mortals to understand. Most of us need to imagine a starting point and an order of events. At this imaginary beginning, from God "sprang" the Eternal Son. God is thus a Father, the First Great Source and Center. And, God is also the Eternal Son, the Second Great Source and Center, because the Eternal Son came only from God-himself.

This "process" of the Eternal Son from God the Father is a mystery to us. But God did not duplicate himself. The Eternal Son is the original and "only-begotten" Son of God. The Eternal Son "sprang" from the Father and **is one** with the Father.

The Eternal Son is the Father's concept of divine reality. The Eternal Son is God the Father personally revealed. The Son is *absolute personality*. God the First Source and Center is *father personality*. The Father is the source and giver of personality. The Original Son is the divine pattern of personality. He is the eternal pattern of personality.

The Father is first a creator, then a controller. The Eternal Son is first a co-creator and then a divine administrator. The Son administers the spiritual government. God the Father and God the Eternal Son are each unique and original. Both are perfect and both are changeless. Each expresses himself differently throughout creation. Each functions in different cosmic domains.

The Son is not only a creator like the Father, but he is also the Eternal Son of that same Father. The Father loves us as a perfect father. The Eternal Son looks upon all creatures both as a father and as a brother. He shares the sonship experience of all other sons of the Paradise Father.

When the Father expresses himself to his creatures, he does so through his Eternal Son. The Eternal Son is the living and divine Word.

The Eternal Son is by nature devoted to the revelation of the God of love to the universes. The Father is the source of the Son's love. The Son cannot love more than the Father, but he can express a quality of love known as divine mercy. The love of the Eternal Son is like the merciful affection of a mother. There is no difference in the amount of love, only in the way that their love is expressed.

The Father bestowed upon the Original Son the power and privilege of joining him in the divine act of producing additional Sons (Paradise Sons). This, the Father and the Eternal Son have done, and continue to do. It is the Paradise Sons who leave Paradise. They descend—to create or assist the imperfect creatures of time and space.

Lower creatures do not see the administration of the Eternal Son. But, the Eternal Son is personally present in each Paradise Son.

- God the Father's plan is progressive attainment. Some call it evolutionary ascension. But almost everyone knows it as the eternal life plan.

- The Eternal Son's plan is called the bestowal plan. He oversees the bestowal, or gift of the Paradise Sons upon the evolutionary worlds. There, the Paradise Sons are incarnated, to make real the love of the Father and the mercy of the Son.

To incarnate means to take on the form of a lower being. A Paradise Son incarnated as Jesus of Nazareth on our world. On that bestowal, he incarnated from his perfect spirit form to that of flesh and blood. Some bestowals do not involve incarnation. Sometimes the Paradise Sons are bestowed, but the lower orders do not see them or their ministry work.

Jesus was a Paradise Son carrying out his bestowal career. Urantia has confused God the Eternal Son with Jesus. Jesus was our universe Paradise Creator Son incarnated. But God creates all the Paradise Sons perfectly; they perfectly represent God. This may be the reason for the confusion.

The Eternal Son is the inspiration for all the Paradise Sons. All the Paradise Sons willingly take part in the Eternal Son's bestowal plan. These perfect Sons bestow themselves upon various creatures, *as* the creatures themselves.

The Eternal Son cannot improve upon the Father. But, the character and personality of the Father is amplified by the Son and through the Paradise Sons. It is a Paradise Son who reveals God the Father to men and angels.

- Personality is the gift of the Father. He is the center of personality gravity. He has gravity powers that draw all personalities to Paradise.

- The Eternal Son is the upholder of spirit realities. He is the center of spiritual gravity. The Eternal Son has powers that draw all true spirit values to Paradise.

Spiritual values travel at once through the Eternal Son's spirit-gravity. Prayers of value go to the divine being concerned. Prayers instantly transfer from the human mind to Deity. Material requests or selfish prayers fall dead. Such prayers do not contain spiritual value; they are unable to enter the Son's spirit-gravity circuits. The actual words of a prayer are not important. It is the heartfelt thoughts that determine the spiritual value. All love expressed for God is instantly received.

If we choose eternal life, our souls are actually pulled towards Paradise. This is by the Eternal Son's spirit-gravity circuit. We respond less to physical gravity and more to spirit gravity as we progress.

# 4. God, the Infinite Spirit

| GOD THE INFINITE SPIRIT |
| --- |
| |
| Third Source and Center |
| Absolute mind |
| Executive of the Father and the Son |
| Unifier—Infinite capacity to coordinate universe energies, spirits and minds. |
| Deed (Action) |
| Is love and affection applied |
| Inspires mankind to find God |
| Has drawing power on all minds. Mind-Gravity Circuit |
| Mercy Ministry Plan: Effective implementation of attainment & bestowal plans |
| The Infinite Spirit Connects Creation – His Spirit dominates and controls the universal mind circuits |
| The Infinite Spirit leads us to the Eternal Son |

God the Infinite Spirit, like the Father and the Son, has no beginning. The Infinite Spirit has always lived. He is called the Third Great Source and Center.

Again, we must imagine a sequence in our efforts to understand. When God the Father and God the Son shared the first exact thought-plan, God the Infinite Spirit "sprang" into being. This Third Great Source and Center acted. One billion perfect worlds flashed into being—the Havona (hah-vohn'-ah) worlds.

Havona is also known as the central universe. The Infinite Spirit created this perfect universe. It was in response to the united wills of the Father and the Son. But, the creation of the central universe, like God, has no beginning.

The Infinite Spirit is unique, original, and changeless; just like the Father and the Son. The Father expresses himself through the personality of the Eternal Son, the Word of God. The Father and the Son act together through the Infinite Spirit. The Infinite Spirit is the God of Action. As the God of Action, he is the ancestor of motion, change, and relationship.

Most people find it very difficult to understand how the three persons of God can be the same One God. How can the original Father, Son, and Spirit be One God at the same time?

There is a crude example in the physical world to help us understand. Consider that water is a liquid. Ice is a solid. Steam is a gas. All three have different characteristics. Yet, all three are the same chemically. All three are $H_2O$.

- The Father is infinite in love, spiritual thought, and purpose. The Father is the *upholder*.

- The Son is infinite in wisdom and truth. He is spiritual expression and meaning. The Eternal Son is the *revealer*.

- Paradise is the material side of infinity. It is force and energy potential. It keeps everything in balance. Paradise is the *stabilizer*. (See Chapter 7.)

- The Infinite Spirit has the unique ability of synthesis. Synthesis is the uniting of different parts into a whole. The Infinite Spirit is able to blend and unite all energies, spirits, and minds. The Infinite Spirit is the *unifier*.

God the Spirit shares the Father's perfection and love. But, the Infinite Spirit especially functions as the mercy minister. He is love applied. He is the combined love of the Father and Son. God the Father loves men. God the Eternal Son serves men. God the Infinite Spirit inspires us to find God. He is a divine minister.

The Infinite Spirit is present, not only as himself, but also as the Father, as the Son, and as the Father-Son. God the Spirit is the first of the Paradise Deities that we will recognize. We must go through him to the Son, then to the Father. It is only by the Spirit's patient ministry that we can discover the Son.

The Third Source and Center is the Absolute Mind. God the Spirit is the source of intelligence throughout all Creation. He is the intellectual center. He is the administrator of the realms of mind. The Infinite Spirit ministers to all minds on all worlds.

To delegate means to give another the authority to represent you. You might give someone tasks and they would be responsible for acting on your behalf. You would give them the power to act and make decisions for you. The Father delegates to his Son. The Son delegates to the Infinite Spirit. God the Spirit functions as the united (conjoint) executive of the Father and the Son. The Infinite Spirit appoints his representatives to carry out his wishes; he delegates as well.

Mind on the evolutionary worlds is a gift. This gift comes from the Seven Master Spirits. The Seven Master Spirits are a high order of personalities. They are created by the Infinite Spirit. The Infinite Spirit delegates to the Seven Master Spirits. Thus, it is the Seven Master Spirits that gift cosmic mind. Infinite mind, the mind of God, can ignore time. But, cosmic mind is conditioned by time. (See Chapter 8.)

The Infinite Spirit is the Absolute Intelligence—Mind. But, mind is not the divine Infinite Spirit. Sometimes on our world, the Third Source and Center is confused with the cosmic mind. God the Infinite Spirit is the universal intelligence. He is personally conscious of every mind. He knows every intellect. He keeps perfect and personal contact with all creatures of mind. All activities of mind are a part of the personal consciousness of God the Spirit.

- The Father pulls all personality to himself.
- The Son draws all spiritual reality.
- The Spirit attracts all minds.

The Infinite Spirit has a drawing power on all minds. He controls the universal mind circuit. All true intellectual values, divine thoughts, and perfect ideas, are drawn into the Infinite Spirit's circuit of mind.

The Infinite Spirit is a unique and distinct divine being. His functions and attributes go beyond mind. When energy and spirit interact, he dominates all reactions. He "exerts a mighty influence over energy and matter." (UB 9:1.4) God the Spirit has a power called antigravity. Antigravity is a force that makes gravity neutral. Antigravity is also a force that allows very high speeds. However, it applies only to physical gravity. It is not an action of mind. It is the exercise of equal force presence. (from UB 9:3.3)

The Third Source and Center has other powers also. He can neutralize energy. His powers slow down energy to the point that the energy becomes material. His methods are unknown to us. The Infinite Spirit is not energy. He is not the source of energy. And, he is not the destiny of energy. The Infinite Spirit is the *manipulator of energy.*

The manipulation and control of physical things awes us. However, the Infinite Spirit has other superb traits. They include patience, mercy, and love which are revealed in his spiritual ministry.

God the Infinite Spirit has many beings that represent him. Some are ministering spirits. Some are messengers. Others are teachers and advisors. Certain Paradise Sons of the Father and the Son incarnate. The Infinite Spirit and his Spirits do not come down to incarnate in the flesh. However, they do down-step themselves until some appear as angels. Angels are just beyond our visual range.

The Supreme Spirits are high beings. One order of the Supreme Spirits is the Reflective Spirits. The Reflective Spirits work throughout creation. Reflectivity is a unique power. It makes it possible to see, hear, and sense everything as it happens. The mental, material, and spiritual is revealed at the same time. This knowledge can be directed and sent anywhere in the superuniverses. Reflectivity allows the universe rulers to know about remote events instantly, as they happen.

The Father has an attainment plan. The Son has a bestowal plan. The Infinite Spirit has his plan of ministry. His service *supports* both the Father's plan and the Son's plan. All of the spiritual personalities of the Infinite Spirit participate in his plan of mercy ministry.

The Paradise Father, the Eternal Son, and the Infinite Spirit create personalities who go out into time and space. There, these perfect Sons and Daughters create evolutionary worlds and creatures.

Together, the Father and the Son create Paradise Sons. For every Paradise Creator Michael Son that the Father and Son create, the Infinite Spirit creates a companion. She is called a Creative Daughter Spirit. She is known as the Mother Spirit of a local universe in time and space. The term Holy Spirit is actually the spirit circuits of the Creative Daughters. The Holy Spirit is an original circuit that operates on behalf of a Creative Daughter. Her circuit is confined to the spiritual realm of her local universe. Her powers come directly from the Infinite Spirit.

There are many spiritual influences. One is the combined ministry of the Infinite Spirit and a local Universe Mother Spirit. All of the personalities of the Infinite Spirit are dedicated. They all minister the Father's love and the Son's mercy.

There are many names for the Infinite Spirit. The Universal Organizer is one name that gives a clear description. Just know that in your daily life you are in the care of spirit personalities created by the Infinite Spirit. "These spirit beings constitute the living ladder whereby mortal man climbs from chaos to glory." (UB 9:8.25)

# 5. Recap of God Concepts

| GOD THE PARADISE FATHER | GOD THE ETERNAL SON | GOD THE INFINITE SPIRIT |
|---|---|---|
| First Source and Center | Second Source and Center | Third Source and Center |
| Absolute I AM, reality, free will | Absolute pattern of personality | Absolute mind / intelligence |
| Creator, then Controller | Co-creator, then Administrator | Executive of the Father and the Son |
| Upholder—Infinite in love, will, spiritual thought and purpose. | Revealer—Infinite in wisdom, truth, spiritual expression and interpretation. | Unifier—Infinite capacity to coordinate universe energies, spirits and minds. |
| Thought | Word | Deed (Action) |
| Expresses Love as a father | Expresses affection as a mother | Is love and affection applied |
| Loves mankind | Serves mankind | Inspires mankind to find God |
| Draws all personality to himself Personality-Gravity Circuit | Attracts all spiritual reality Spirit-Gravity Circuit | Has drawing power on all minds Mind-Gravity Circuit |
| Attainment Plan: Evolutionary ascension— progressive attainment (eternal life) | Bestowal Plan: Incarnation (bestowal) of the descending Sons of God | Mercy Ministry Plan: Effective implementation of the attainment and bestowal Plans |
| Father's Spirit Lives In Us. He sends a small piece, fragment of himself, to live inside of us | The Eternal Son's Spirit Surrounds Us – His Spirit bathes all creation and draws us to God | The Infinite Spirit Connects Creation – His Spirit dominates and controls the universal mind circuits |
| The Father IS our eternal destination | The Eternal Son leads us to the Father | The Infinite Spirit leads us to the Eternal Son |

The Father and the Son, together, create the order of Creator Michael Sons.

The Infinite Spirit alone creates a companion for the Creator Michael Son called a Creative Daughter Spirit.

A Creator Michael Son and a Creative Daughter Spirit leave Paradise to represent God in time and space. They create the evolutionary local universes.

The Son and the Infinite Spirit, together, create the Magisterial Sons, another order of descending Paradise Sons that represent God to mankind.

# 6. The Paradise Trinity

"Deity is the source of all that which is divine." (UB 0:1.15) God the Paradise Father, the Eternal Son, and the Infinite Spirit are the three original persons of Deity. The Father, Son, and Spirit act personally and collectively. There are mathematically seven possible expressions of God the sevenfold:

1. The Father
2. The Son
3. The Spirit
4. The Father-Son
5. The Father-Spirit
6. The Son-Spirit
7. The Father-Son-Spirit

When they *function* together as united Deity, they are called the Paradise Trinity. Each is a separate Deity and at the same time, they function in and as the Trinity—as the One and only God.

To help you understand the Paradise Trinity imagine yourself and two friends as a team. Your team really has no personality or life of its own. But, through its three members and your personalities, the team can function as a working unit. Your team takes on a certain united character. Of course, the three perfect persons of the Paradise Trinity operate in perfect harmony and unity. Together they are as one.

Each of the persons of God has attributes. The Trinity is seen as having *functions*. Examples are:
- justice administration
- coordinated action
- cosmic over-control

As with all living associations, the Trinity is more than just function. A group's potential is always greater than the attributes of its individual members.

The First Source and Center (God the Father) functions outside Havona, the central universe, as follows:

1. As creator, through the Creator Sons
2. As controller, through the gravity center of Paradise
3. As spirit, through the Eternal Son
4. As mind, through the Infinite Spirit
5. As a father, he maintains parental contact with every creature through his personality circuit
6. As a person, he acts directly throughout creation by his exclusive fragments (Thought Adjusters)
7. As total Deity, he functions only in and as the Paradise Trinity

The Son functions as one with the Father except in the bestowal of the God fragments (Thought Adjusters). The Son is not involved with the mind activities of material creatures. He is also not concerned with the energy activities of the material worlds.

The Infinite Spirit, on the other hand, is amazingly diverse. He performs in the spheres of mind, matter, and spirit. God the Spirit is not directly involved with physical gravity; it is a feature of Paradise. The Infinite Spirit's service does not involve spiritual gravity; that is an attribute of the

Eternal Son. The Father's personality circuit is the Father's alone. But, in all other activities, the Infinite Spirit takes part.

The Trinity mystery is three distinct persons of Deity functioning as one and in one. Most of us will understand this mystery differently. However, whether you fully understand this mystery of God or not, know that we are all members of their universal family. Each of the three persons of the Trinity loves us with a divine love that is utterly beyond our comprehension.

# 7. The Master Universe

Creation is so vast it is almost unimaginable. This chapter gives you the 'big picture' and you do not need to remember the details. All details related to spiritual growth are in later chapters.

God the Father, God the Son, God the Spirit, and their divine associates are in fact present on the Isle of Paradise. The perfect Isle of Paradise, also called the Isle of Light and Life, is the geographic center of creation. It is the dwelling place of God. It is enormous and it is stationary. It is the only place in creation that never moves. It is the center of gravity. Paradise is the source of physical gravity. It is the perfect pattern of material reality. The Isle of Paradise is extra spiritual and it is the perfect material place. From Paradise, God's flood-streams of life, energy, and personality flow to all creation.

Havona revolves around the Isle of Paradise and is eternal. Eternal means never beginning and never ending. Havona is also known as the central universe and consists of one billion perfect worlds. The Isle of Paradise is at the heart of the central universe of Havona. Although it has no origin in time, the central universe does exist in space and time.

Circling Havona are seven superuniverses, designated as the grand universe. The superuniverses are created in time and space. Together they turn and spin around the central universe. Everything in the grand universe is evolutionary. Evolution means there is growth and development. Evolution is a technique of creation. At present, the seven superuniverses are incomplete. The central universe is a creation of perfection. It does not evolve. But, the trillions of worlds in time and space evolve. The evolutionary worlds are imperfect. Perfection is the goal.

Each superuniverse has 100,000 local universes. Each local universe will have ten million inhabited worlds. All these worlds are evolutionary. The grand universe is comprised of the seven superuniverses and the eternal spheres of Havona. The master universe is comprised of the grand universe and the four outer space zones. Paradise is not really a part of any universe. Beyond the superuniverses are outer space levels. Because God is infinite, creation will never stop.

Worlds in the local universes belong to systems. Systems combine to make constellations. Beyond the local universe, worlds are classed as to minor and major sectors. To give you an idea of how big creation is, each of the local universes will have ten million inhabited worlds! There will be seven trillion inhabited planets in the grand universe!

| Planets | Systems | Constellations | Local Universes | Minor Sectors | Major Sectors | Super-Universe |
|---------|---------|----------------|-----------------|---------------|---------------|----------------|
| 1,000 | = 1 | | | | | |
| 100,000 | = 100 | = 1 | | | | |
| 10 Million | = 10,000 | = 100 | = 1 | | | |
| 1 Billion | = 1 Million | = 10,000 | = 100 | = 1 | | |
| 100 Billion | = 100 Million | = 1 Million | = 10,000 | = 100 | = 1 | |
| 1 Trillion | = 1 Billion | = 10 Million | = 100,000 | = 1,000 | = 10 | = 1 |

Everyone seems to try to picture how a local universe or the superuniverses look in creation. The numbers can be confusing without a chart. The chart on the previous page is an example of just one superuniverse, although there are seven.

Artist John Byron did a stunning depiction of the master universe based on information in *The Urantia Book*. If you are reading a paperback edition then you will see a black and white picture below that does not do it justice. Therefore, please see the back cover with this picture in vibrant color.

Art by John Byron          Printed with permission from
                                          Jesusonian Foundation

The central universe is the direct creation of God. Local universes are each created and ruled by a different Creator Michael Son with his partner, the Creative Daughter Spirit. Then the local universes are organized into sectors. Sectors make up each superuniverse.

There are outer space levels beyond the grand universe. There is first a quiet space zone free from stardust. Past the quiet zone is a continuous belt of cosmic activity known as the first outer space level. There, we would find huge circuits of force. Also, energies are changing into material forms. Still greater activities are taking place in the second outer space level. A total of four outer space levels are destined to evolve.

The Infinite Spirit will create throughout infinity; always will the Infinite Spirit create. Potentially there is no limit to the master universe. However, as it now exists, the master universe is bordered by open space.

God has kept little control over the worlds of time and space He has given this supervision and care to his many orders of subordinate beings. The evolving worlds are well cared for and loved by many who represent God to man.

# 8. The Seven Master Spirits and Cosmic Mind

God the Father speaks only through his Son. The Father and the Son jointly act only through the Infinite Spirit. Outside of the central universe, God the Spirit speaks only by the voices of the Seven Master Spirits.

God the Spirit created the Seven Master Spirits. The Father and the Son did share in their origin, but those details are a mystery. The Seven Master Spirits hail from Paradise. Only Seven Master Spirits were created. They are the primary personalities of the Infinite Spirit.

All Seven Master Spirits represent God the Spirit. To the worlds in time and space, God's nature is portrayed in seven various ways. There are just seven possible combinations of the three persons of Deity.

1. The Paradise Father
2. The Eternal Son
3. The Infinite Spirit
4. The Father and the Son
5. The Father and the Spirit
6. The Son and the Spirit
7. The Father, Son, and Spirit

In spirit character and nature, the Seven Master Spirits are as one. But, in areas of identity, they are individual spirit beings. They have many functions. Their special domain is the care of one of the seven superuniverses. Even though this is true, each area of the grand universe receives their united counsel and wisdom. The personal touch and influence to our superuniverse comes from the seventh Master Spirit. He discloses the marvelous balance and blending of the divine natures of the Father, Son, and Spirit.

The Seven Master Spirits have many areas of activities. They are quite diverse. Some of the activities and influence of the Seven Master Spirits are as follows:
- Life initiation procedures of the Life Carriers
- Activation of the adjutant mind-spirits bestowed by the local Universe Mother Spirits. The adjutant mind-spirits are called the spirit of intuition, understanding, courage, knowledge, counsel, worship, and the spirit of wisdom. The adjutant mind-spirits are not personalities; they are more like circuits. (See UB 36:5 for interesting details and Chapter 14 of this book.)
- Fluctuations in energy such as linear-gravity of organized matter
- Bestowal of the ministry spirit of a local Universe Mother Spirit. This is known on Urantia as the Holy Spirit.
- Bestowal of the spirit of a local universe Michael Son. This is known on Urantia as the Comforter or the Spirit of Truth. (See Chapter 42.)

The Master Spirits, with the Infinite Spirit and the Supreme Being, (See Chapter 11), are actively engaged in reflectivity. The lines of spirit can be traced back to the Eternal Son. Physical energy can be tracked to Paradise. Mind leads back to the Infinite Spirit. The union of mind, material, and spirit enables the universe rulers to know about remote conditions as they happen.

The Master Spirits define every creature in their superuniverse. From their Master Spirit, each creature, man or angel, will forever have a "badge of natal identification." (UB 16:5.2) The Master Spirits also have a part in man's Paradise ascension. Progress in ascension leads man to the central universe. There, a pilgrim will instantly recognize the Master Spirit of his or her superuniverse.

The potential of intelligence in the grand universe is cosmic mind. The Master Spirits fully represent the Infinite Spirit and are the source of cosmic mind. (UB 9:4.3)

Mind is not a natural part of energy. Energy is material. But energy is receptive to mind; it responds to mind. Energy can have mind superimposed upon it. In other words, mind can be applied or added to energy. Pure spirit, on the other hand is always intelligent. Spirit is naturally conscious. (from UB 9:4.5)

- Energy is thing (material)
- Mind is meaning.
- Spirit is value. It is divine purpose.

The relationship between energy and spirit is created by the mind. The values of spirit are transformed by the mind into meanings. Our power of free will can apply the meanings of mind to both our physical and spiritual lives. The Paradise ascent involves growth in spirit, mind, and energy. The Father's gift of personality unifies these parts of our being.

The fact of cosmic mind explains the kinship of various types of human minds. Kindred spirits are attracted to each other. Then again, kindred minds are also attracted to one another. Just as material energy responds to gravity, the endowment of cosmic mind responds to reality. The cosmic mind responds to three levels of universe reality and they are:

1. *Causation.* (the relationship between cause and effect) This includes the physical senses. It includes the scientific realms of logic. Awareness of the difference between the factual and nonfactual is involved. Also, reflective conclusions fall into this category. Causation is the scientific form of cosmic discernment.

2. *Duty.* Duty is the reality of morals in the realm of philosophy. It includes reason and the awareness of right and wrong. Duty is the judicial form of cosmic discernment.

3. *Worship.* This includes the reality of religious experience. Worship includes the realization of divine fellowship. It includes awareness of spirit values. The assurance of eternal life is an aspect of cosmic mind. And worship includes "the ascent from the status of servants of God to the joy and liberty of the sons of God." (UB 16:6.8) Worship is the highest insight of cosmic mind. It is the worshipful form of cosmic discernment.

The above cosmic responses (scientific, moral, and spiritual) are innate in the cosmic mind. All free will creatures are given cosmic mind. The experience of living develops the three cosmic insights. They are the essence of self-conscious reflective thinking.

The gift of mind makes it possible for man to function as a rational and self-conscious being in the areas of science, philosophy, and religion. Matter/energy is recognized by the logic of the senses. Mind-reason knows its moral duty. Spirit-faith is the religion of spiritual experience. When they are unified, they produce a strong character. Moreover, it is the three cosmic intuitions that give validity to man's experience with things, meanings, and values.

"It is the purpose of education to develop and sharpen these innate endowments of the human mind; of civilization to express them; of life experience to realize them; of religion to ennoble them; and of personality to unify them." (UB 16:6.11)

Mind is of divine origin and has a divine destiny. But, "mortal minds are not yet of divine dignity." (UB 9:5.6) All too often, we mar our minds with insincerity. We subject our minds "to animal fear and distort them by useless anxiety." (UB 9:5.7) However, mind as we know it is not to become an object of great esteem.

And, it is not so much what mind understands as what mind *desires* to understand that insures survival. It is not so much what mind is like, as what mind is *striving* to be like that constitutes spirit identification. It is not so much that man is conscious of God, as that man yearns for God. And, that yearning results in ascension—progress. "What you are today is not so important as what you are becoming day by day and in eternity." (UB 111:1.5)

# 9. The Ancients of Days

The Paradise Trinity created seven orders of beings. All seven orders were created for specific service. There are just twenty-one Ancients of Days and they were created at the same time. The Ancients of Days are super-perfect and identical. The Ancients of Days are individuals but they do not differ from one another, as do the Seven Master Spirits.

The Ancients of Days represent the beginning of the personality records. That is why they are called *Ancients* of Days. When you reach Paradise and search the written records, you will find that the first entry in the personality section is the account of the creation of the twenty-one Ancients of Days.

The Seven Master Spirits determine the nature of their superuniverses. The Ancients of Days dictate the administration of the superuniverses. These high beings always govern in groups of three. There are times in which they work alone or as two together, but in the higher areas of their administration all three must act together.

The Ancients of Days never leave their residential worlds. Reflectivity allows the universe rulers to know about remote conditions instantly. The home world of the Ancients of Days is the focal point of reflectivity. Never is it necessary for them to leave their world.

The Ancients of Days hand out the judgment of supreme fairness. This they do for the seven superuniverses. In the central universe, perfection prevents disharmony.

In the area of authority, the Ancients of Days are the most powerful. They are the mighty direct rulers of the time-space creations. Aside from the Deities and their Paradise associates, the Ancients of Days are the perfect and divinely endowed rulers. They are the supreme rulers of the superuniverses. But they have not earned the right to rule through experience. The Supreme Being is an experiential sovereign. He will replace the Ancients of Days in the future. The Ancients of Days will become deputies to the Supreme Being.

Three Ancients of Days serve each superuniverse. They are the joint chief executives of the super-government. A corps of Perfectors of Wisdom and Universal Censors assist each group of three Ancients of Days. There are one billion assistants in each of those corps. The Perfectors of Wisdom also have three billion Divine Counselors assisting them. Ascended mortals who have attained Paradise may also be assigned to the service of the Ancients of Days.

One Perfectors of Wisdom, seven Divine Counselors, and one Universal Censor form a tribunal. They are the highest mobile advisory body in the universes of time and space. Such a group of nine is known either as a fact-finding or as a truth-revealing tribunal. When it sits in judgment upon a problem and gives a decision, it is as if an Ancient of Days had judged the matter. In all the records of the verdicts by tribunals, never has one been reversed by the Ancients of Days.

Mortal man encounters God the Sevenfold in the following order:
1. The Creator Michael Son (and Creative Daughter Spirit)
2. The Ancients of Days
3. The Seven Master Spirits
4. The Supreme Being
5. The Infinite Spirit
6. The Eternal Son
7. The Paradise Father

Urantian mortals on an ascension plan to Paradise become spirits when they leave their local universe of Nebadon. As young spirits, they begin the superuniverse system of training. This extends from the spheres of the minor sector of Ensa, the only group of minor sector training for Urantians. Next, we go through the ten major sectors. Then, ascenders go forward to the higher spheres of the superuniverse headquarters. All ascenders on the training worlds of the superuniverse are wards of the Ancients of Days.

The Creator Son of each local universe oversees its creation. These Sons devote themselves to the Paradise plan of mortal ascension. Because there is free will choice, no one must progress forward. Free will creatures may reject the ascension plan.

The Creator Sons also serve in the salvation of rebels and wrong thinkers. Such rebels can choose to reject all such loving efforts. Then, the Ancients of Days are required to authorize the end of life for such a choosing personality. Forces acting under the power of the Ancients of Days carry out the final decree of extinction.

The age of light and life is the final evolutionary attainment of a world of time and space. From the early times of primitive man, such an inhabited world has passed through the successive planetary ages. The seven stages of light and life are: (See UB 55:7-12.)

1. The first or planetary stage.
2. The second or system stage.
3. The third or constellation stage.
4. The fourth or local universe stage.
5. The fifth or minor sector stage.
6. The sixth or major sector stage. (The fifth & sixth are combined.)
7. The seventh or superuniverse stage.

Creatures progress and worlds advance. A local universe progresses as well. Over great time, it reaches spiritual harmony. Its circuits become impossible to tell apart from the superuniverse circuits. Such a local universe swings into the settled circuits of Light and Life. The Ancients of Days then determine the physical balance and spiritual loyalty of the local universe. If approved, the local universe receives membership into the superuniverse confederation. This is acceptance into the spiritual family of the super government.

# 10. Descending Sons of God

Mortals are ascending sons and daughters. We perfect by slowly evolving. Descending orders of sonship are beings created in perfection or near perfection. They go down, actually out, into time and space, even to the planets. Those Sons who come from the Deities of Paradise are the Paradise Sons of God. They are:

1. Creator Sons—the Michaels
2. Magisterial Sons—the Avonals
3. Trinity Teacher Sons—the Daynals

The Creator Sons are brought into being by God the Father and Son. The Creator Michael Sons are covered in Chapters 12 and 13. (The incarnation of our Creator Michael Son, as Jesus of Nazareth, is detailed in Chapters 36 through 42.)

The Magisterial Sons are the creation of the Eternal Son and Infinite Spirit. The Magisterial Sons are the planetary ministers and judges. They are magistrates to the time-space worlds. Their total number in the grand universe is about one billion. Each is a unique being.

Magisterial Sons are a self-governing order. Their own council on Paradise directs them. They work under the direction of a Creator Son when serving in a local universe. The Magisterial Sons have three roles on the inhabited worlds as follows:

- *Judicial.* Magisterial Sons close dispensations on the planets. A dispensation is a period marked by important growth or events. A new progressive era follows; a new dispensation begins. Magisterial Sons preside over the awakening of the sleeping souls who will go to the mansion worlds. They end suspended justice. They execute the age of probationary mercy. Then they reassign the celestial ministers to the tasks of the new dispensation. Ending a dispensation is a technical service. It does not involve incarnation (taking physical form).

- *Magisterial Missions.* When the levels of intellect and ethics have reached their limits, a magisterial mission is started. For the first magisterial mission, the Son comes as a fully visible adult male. Twelve Melchizedeks (mel-kizz'-uh-decks) always go with him. If the Magisterial Son can be seen, then the Melchizedeks will also appear as adult males. During later missions, the Son and Melchizedeks may or may not be visible. Urantia has never had a Magisterial Son bestowal. Our planet had the honor of becoming the mortal home world of our Creator Son, Michael of Nebadon.

- *Bestowal Missions.* When the spiritual status of a world nears its limit of natural attainment, a Magisterial Son is bestowed. A bestowal is the gift of a Paradise Son to an evolutionary world. Usually the Son is born of a human mother. The bestowal mission establishes the planetary status. The Paradise Son releases the Spirit of Truth, (Chapter 42). The Son also affects the universal coming of the Father's fragments, the Thought Adjusters. (See Chapter 1.) On our world, all these things took place when our Paradise Creator Michael Son incarnated as Jesus of Nazareth.

The Trinity Teacher Sons are the offspring of the Father, Son, and Spirit. Their numbers are always increasing. There are over twenty-one billion Teacher Sons at this time. These Sons are not creators, judges, or rulers. The Trinity Teacher Sons are concerned with moral and spiritual growth. These educators are devoted to the spiritual awakening and moral guidance of all the realms.

In Havona, the Trinity Teacher Sons reflect the nature of God the Father. In the superuniverse, they portray the nature of the Eternal Son. When in the local universes they reflect the character of God the Spirit. "In all universes they are the embodiment of service and the discretion of wisdom." (UB 20:7.4)

The Trinity Teacher Sons are devoted to the progress of both mortals and angels. They oversee all exams. They conduct all tests. They qualify personalities for service.

Trinity Teacher Sons serve on worlds ready for a spiritual age—a thousand years of cosmic growth. The Sons do not incarnate or become visible. Urantia has not yet been ripe for such a spiritual age.

The remaining four orders of descending sonship are the local universe Sons of God. They are:
4. Melchizedek (mel-kizz'-uh-deck) Sons
5. Vorondadek (voh-ron'-da-deck) Sons - Most Highs and Constellation Fathers
6. Lanonandek (la-non'-an-deck) Sons - System Sovereigns and Planetary Princes
7. The Life Carriers

Melchizedeks are the first order of divine Sons able to directly minister to mortals. All forms of intelligent life find these Sons to be kind friends, caring teachers, and wise counselors.

The Melchizedek Sons are a self-governing order. They are the pattern and teachers of self-government. They are like the eldest son in a large family. Their work is to teach, train, and counsel. Melchizedeks serve as observers and advisors. They have the full confidence of all intelligent life. There are over ten million of these Sons in Nebadon.

Chapter 14 presents more information on the local universe Sons of God.

# 11. The Supreme Being

Evolving minds are able to form rational thoughts. This is because all minds are able to form a universe frame in which to think. Conceptual frames serve as scaffolding. In time, the scaffolding gives way to cosmic understanding. "The understandings of truth, beauty and goodness, morality, ethics, duty, love, divinity, origin, existence, purpose, destiny, time, space, even Deity, are only relatively true; God is much, much more than a Father, but the Father is man's highest concept of God;" (UB 115:1.2)

On the evolutionary worlds, spirit struggles to coordinate spirit with mind within the universe thought-frame. This union of spirit and mind is expressed in and as the Supreme Being. The actual evolution of spirit dominance is through growth. That growth is based on the free will acts of the Creators and creatures.

In the physical life, a human is, in part, responsive to the dictates of personal mind. This mind may become dominated by the leadings of spirit. Such evolutionary growth adds to the unity of cosmic realities. The result is the production of a new child of the Supreme.

Effort is made by the personalities of time and space. The perfect ending of this effort is the act of the Supreme Being. The evolution of the parts is a reflection of the determined growth of the whole. All personally strive in the achievement and all personally participate in the destiny.

The Supreme Being stems from the Paradise Trinity. The perfect unity of the Trinity is expressed in the finite universes in the Supreme. He represents advancing evolution. He embodies spiritual growth.

God the Supreme is a spirit person. He is truth, beauty, and goodness. He is the Deity of evolutionary growth. This growth comes from both the actual and the potential. God the Father, Son, and Spirit are changeless. God the Supreme is the God of growth and change.

The Supreme Being is the bridge between the infinite and the finite. He completes finite reality. He bridges the complete and the incomplete. The Supreme transforms potentials to actuals. If not for the Supreme Being, the imperfect could not grow perfect. All growth is through the Supreme, the God of experience.

The Infinite Spirit expresses the perfect mind of God to all creatures. The Supreme Being expresses the evolving minds of all creatures to God.

The Supreme is the oversoul of the grand universe. He is the consciousness of the finite. He is the embodiment of Creator-creature experience. When we do the will of God, the Supreme becomes one step more actual. The Supreme Being is becoming the highest finite expression of the total will of God.

Man's evolution does resemble the growth of the Supreme in some ways. Man grows from the material to the spiritual. This is by the strength, power, and consistency of man's own decisions. Humans also grow as the Thought Adjuster penetrates and reaches down from the spiritual level to the soul level. Once the soul is born, it begins to grow in and of itself. The immortal soul evolves its own eternal destiny. This is by the partnership created by the spiritual Thought Adjuster and the decisions of the human mind.

God the Supreme "is not only Creator-evolved and Trinity-derived; he is also self-evolved and self-derived." (UB 117:3.7) He is a free will personality. The Supreme is making real his deity status. The human soul is likewise a free will, co-creative partner in its own eternal destiny. The Supreme's divine evolution is largely based on the wise actions of every being in existence.

When a human chooses eternal life, he is co-creating destiny. In the life of that ascending mortal, the finite God finds increased self-realization. But, if a creature rejects eternal life, that part of the Supreme, which was dependent on that creature's choice, experiences delay. As for the personality of the non-survivor, it becomes part of the Supreme. Everything of survival value which consists of truth, beauty, and goodness (the soul), is absorbed into the oversoul of creation, becoming a part of the evolving experience of the Supreme Being. (From UB 2:3.4)

Paradise is only possible for mortals because we are of the Supreme. We are members in the cycle of growth that is the Supreme Being. When we find the Supreme on our journey, it will feel as if we have returned home. He is our parent of experience. Mortals experience life as spiritually growing children. The Supreme grows in the experience of divine parenthood. He is both creature-like as well as creator-like.

"If you truly desire to find God, you cannot help having born in your minds the consciousness of the Supreme. As God is your divine Father, so is the Supreme your divine Mother, in whom you are nurtured throughout your lives as universe creatures." (UB 117:6.2)

Man does not ascend without effort. The Supreme Being does not evolve without purposeful and intelligent action. Creatures do not attain perfection by mere passivity. Self-conscious personalities have a cosmic responsibility. The Supreme is, in part, dependent upon the choosing of mortal will. We should choose well; our choices have cosmic effects.

The relation of man to the Supreme is the foundation for cosmic morality. Cosmic morality is an acceptance of *duty*. This morality goes beyond the sense of right and wrong. It is a morality based on the self-conscious appreciation of "experiential obligation to experiential Deity. Mortal man and all other finite creatures are created out of the living potential of energy, mind, and spirit existent in the Supreme. It is out of the very reality of the Supreme that the Adjuster, with the consent of the human will, weaves the patterns of the eternal nature of an ascending son of God." (UB 117:4.8)

The universe has descending God-revealing Creators. Also, the universe is full of ascending God-seeking creatures. We move up and down the living ladders together. It is through the Supreme that both descenders and ascenders achieve mutual understanding. It is the experience of eternal and universal brotherhood.

Sonship is the great relationship with God the Father. Being the Father's child is your position, your place, your status with the Father. It is by birthright. However, with God the Supreme, achievement is required before status. One must do something, not just be something. "He [The Supreme] is the sweetness of true success and the joy of everlasting achievement." (UB 117:1.1)

# 12. The Local Universe

God the Father and Son create original Paradise Sons. It is the new personality *ideal* of the Father united with the Eternal Son's new spiritual *idea* that brings forth the new and original Son. That perfect union produces a new Creator Son. The Creator Son flashes into being. He is an only begotten Son. He is a new, powerful, and perfect Paradise Son. Each Paradise Creator Son is of the Order of Michael. Each is unique in nature and character. No two of the estimated 700,000 Michael Sons are alike.

The Creator Michael Sons are the makers and rulers of the local universes. They are the designers, creators, builders, and managers of their domains. All must complete their long and unique experience of Paradise observation. All must complete their Havona training. Each devotes himself to the study of his older brothers' various creations in the superuniverse of planned action. After all this training, a Michael Son is permitted to choose the space site of his future local universe.

There are limits to the powerful prerogatives of a Creator Son. Among these are:
- A Creator Son must have the active support of the Infinite Spirit. The Infinite Spirit dominates energy/matter. New forms and changes of energy/matter must be approved.
- Mind is the gift of the Infinite Spirit.
- A Creator Son must have the consent of the Eternal Son. The Eternal Son controls creature designs and types. Any new type of beings or new designs must be approved.
- Personality is designed and bestowed by the Father.
- Spiritual design is controlled by the Trinity.

The creation of a local universe is complex. The unique physical creations are planned by the Paradise Architects. The Master Force Organizers direct pre-universe space and forces. Evolving energy must respond to linear gravity. Then, the power directors work with the evolved energies. They work alone in the pre-material stages. The power directors provide the physical groundwork. This includes suns and material spheres. A Creator Son cannot begin his work until the power directors have marshaled the space energies.

The Father and the Son produce the Creator Sons. God the Infinite Spirit makes an effective helper for each Son. The Creative Daughter Spirits are of the Infinite Spirit. A Paradise Creator Son and a Paradise Creative Daughter, together, descend from Paradise into time and space. There, in partnership, the two give rise to a local universe.

Upon their arrival, work is begun on the architectural world that will be the headquarters of their local universe. For ages, a local creation evolves. Suns become stable. Planets form and swing into their orbits. The work of creating the architectural worlds continues. These worlds will serve as constellation headquarters and system capitals.

Nebadon (neb'-ah-don) is the name of our local universe. Michael of Nebadon is our perfect and divine Creator Son. He is our Universe Father. His first act of physical creation was Nebadon's headquarters. The primary sphere is called Salvington (sal'-ving-ton). Circling it are 490 satellite worlds. It took about one billion years of our time from the first moves of the power centers to the arrival of the living staff on the completed spheres of Salvington.

Next, 100 headquarters worlds were built for the future constellations. Ten thousand headquarters spheres were built for the future local systems. These architectural worlds are designed for both physical and spirit beings, as well as for morontia (moh-ron'-chah) life.

Morontia life is the transition stage of being. It is the long phase between the material life and the spirit life.

Then our Universe Son and Daughter Spirit created their local universe children. (See Chapter 14.) These children are "a vast and wonderful array of diverse creatures." (UB 32:2.7) With this event, the Creative Daughter Spirit becomes changed in nature. She takes on the personal qualities of the Mother Spirit of a local universe.

Next, the government is provided. The supreme councils of the universe are the highest. Next in order are the fathers of the constellations. The sovereigns of the local systems follow. Finally, the worlds that become homes of the varied mortals are each presided over by a Planetary Prince.

When a Michael Son is absent from his universe, its government is directed by the first-born native being, Gabriel. Gabriel is the chief executive. He belongs to the order of Bright and Morning Stars. The advice and counsel of the Union of Days (Immanuel), is priceless in Michael's absence. Also, the Mother Spirit of a local universe always remains at headquarters.

Urantia belongs to the local system of Satania (sah-tan'-ee-ah). On average a local system has, or will have, one thousand inhabited worlds. Satania now has 619 mortal worlds. They are to be found in over 500 different physical solar systems. However, physical solar systems do not define the systems of a local universe.

Jerusem (jer-oo'-sem) is the headquarters of Satania. It is over 200 thousand light-years to the physical center of our superuniverse, Orvonton (or-von'-ton). Uversa (you-vur'-sah), the headquarters of our superuniverse, is far, far away in the dense Milky Way.

| Division | Name | Headquarters | Celestial Type Ruler | Name | Notes |
|---|---|---|---|---|---|
| Our Planet | Urantia | Dalamatia (Was on the Persian Gulf) | Planetary Prince Lanonandeks | Caligastia — (now) Machiventa Melchizedek | Rebelled & Replaced Machiventa was appointed by Michael |
| Our System | Satania | Jerusem | System Sovereigns Lanonandeks | Lucifer — (now) Lanaforge | Rebelled & Replaced |
| Our Constellation | Norlatiadek | Edentia | Most Highs-Constellation Fathers Vorondadeks | | Unnamed |
| Our Local Universe | Nebadon | Salvington | Creator Michael Son & Creative Daughter | Christ Michael or Michael of Nebadon & Mother Spirit | Mother Spirit is unnamed |

The table above shows how our planet fits into our local universe. The celestial beings are further described in coming chapters.

The superuniverses all evolve and progress. No universe is settled in Light and Life until its physical potential has been exhausted. The spiritual status of all its inhabited worlds must also be settled. Perfection is a progressive attainment. Except for the perfect beings of Deity origin, all free will creatures must evolve. Each begins in lowly estate and climbs slowly upward, in reality inward. All who choose eternal life will ascend. We work our way through our local universe system, constellation, and headquarters. Next is the path through the superuniverse. Then we advance through the central universe. Finally, the ascender arrives at the Isle of Paradise to be in the Father's presence.

# 13. Sovereignty of Creator Sons

The term sovereign can best be explained by the example of the United States. Each of our states has representation and equal rights. One state is no more important or powerful than another. All states have willingly given their sovereignty to the federal government. The result is interstate peace. The spiritual government throughout all of Creation is supremely sovereign. No planet, system, or constellation, no local universe, sector or superuniverse is more important than another is. No world or group is more powerful than another is. All give their sovereignty and loyalty to God. God is supreme.

A Creator Son is given physical possession of the local universe he creates. The Paradise Trinity and concerned superuniverse Master Spirit give their consent. Creator Sons truly have free will. A Creator Son could claim full sovereignty over his personal creation at any time. However, the Creator Sons take an oath not to claim sovereignty. Instead, they agree to earn that sovereignty. *Never* has a Creator Son broken his oath.

God has an attainment plan for mortals. Mortals ascend to Paradise. Likewise, God has an attainment plan for his Creator Sons. It is a bestowal-earned sovereignty plan. Each Creator Michael Son descends from Paradise. The Michael Sons create their local universes. Then, the Sons are bestowed, gifted, in the likeness of seven creature orders. He begins with higher creatures and descends to his final bestowal as a mortal creature born of woman.

The technique of bestowal is incarnation. An incarnated Creator Son appears in the likeness of his creatures on the level concerned. However, he not only appears like them, *he is* such a creature. While incarnated the Son shows the highest level of perfection of creature life. He demonstrates this to Paradise Deity. All intelligences learn from the Son's experience. To the entire universe, he reveals one phase of Deity will. Through his experiences, the Son achieves a new and higher relationship with the Supreme Being.

A Michael Son starts as a first-stage ruler. His incarnations gives him experience. That experience elevates him to the supreme stage of self-earned sovereignty.

Before his bestowals, a Creator Son rules supremely when there are no rebellions. But his limited rulership would not be clear if sovereignty were never challenged. If a rebellion should break out before a Son finishes his bestowals, the Paradise personalities take a very active role.

Rebellion after a Son's final bestowal is unlikely. He is a proven sovereign ruler. His rule is unchallengeable. Yet, should a rebellion occur, the Son could act in his own right.

A Creator Son rules on behalf of the Father. Before he completes his bestowals, he rules with self-imposed limitations. After each bestowal, a Creator Son goes to the "right hand of the Father." He gains the Father's acceptance of the bestowal. Then, the Son receives instruction as to his next episode of universe service.

After he has finished his bestowal service, he has valuable experience. With that experience, he is fully competent and worthy to rule his universe. He administers to his worlds in his own right. He is the King of Kings and Lord of Lords. The Creator Son has become a Master Son. A Master Son is a settled, supreme, sovereign ruler.

Master Michael of Nebadon completed his seventh and final bestowal as Jesus of Nazareth. He has since ruled in full power and glory as supreme sovereign of all Nebadon.

# 14. Local Universe Personalities

Each local universe has dual supervision. It is the beginning of the father-mother concept. The Universe Father is the Creator Michael Son. The universe mother is the Creative Daughter Spirit.

Every local universe is blessed with the presence of central universe and Paradise beings. At the head of the Paradise group in Nebadon is the ambassador of the Paradise Trinity. He is Immanuel of Salvington. Immanuel is a Union of Days, a high Trinity Son. He functions as advisor to our Creator Son. But, Immanuel gives counsel only upon request. He is a being of superb dignity. Immanuel has never viewed or treated Michael as a lower being. He regards Michael as his equal in authority, position, and character. And, Michael regards Immanuel as his elder brother.

Each local universe has only one being of the order of the Bright and Morning Stars. This first-born creation serves as chief executive to the Creator Michael Son. Gabriel, our Bright and Morning Star, is wonderfully like his parents but he is not a creator. Gabriel oversees universe policy. He is in charge of regular matters.

The Creator Son and Creative Daughter also bring forth the order of the Brilliant Evening Stars. Brilliant Evening Stars serve in many ways but mainly as officers of Gabriel. These super angels function as Gabriel's delegates. They are stationed at the headquarters of each constellation and system.

Archangels are the highest type of spirits being created in large numbers. Nebadon now has about 800 thousand Archangels. They are dedicated to the work of creature survival. Gabriel does administrative work; thus, he does not supervise archangels.

The Father Melchizedek (mel-kizz'-uh-deck) is the offspring of the Creator Son and Creative Daughter. Father Melchizedek is Gabriel's first assistant. He assumes the chief executive duties when Gabriel is gone. Father Melchizedek is concerned with procedures. He also heads special and emergency affairs.

The Creator Son and Creative Daughter, together with the Father Melchizedek, created the order of Melchizedek Sons. There are over ten million Melchizedeks in Nebadon. They cannot reproduce.

Melchizedeks are the first order of divine Sons to be able to directly minister to mortals. They are at the mid-point of descent. Their work is versatile. Often, they volunteer.

The Melchizedeks are almost perfect in wisdom. Although rare, they have been known to err slightly in judgment. Melchizedeks serve as mobile courts. They review and counsel on serious differences in the universe.

There are 490 Melchizedek worlds in our local universe. These worlds are thought of as the Melchizedek University. Our universe is young and we ranked low in the area of spiritual achievement. Our ethical progress was poor. We have had troubles in the area of administration. All this turned us into a vast clinic for other near-by creations. Student visitors and observers from other realms come here to learn. Our Melchizedek colleges are crowded with beings wanting to learn from our state of affairs! Nebadon's order of Melchizedeks is famous throughout our superuniverse because of all these factors.

The Creator Son and Creative Daughter brought into existence the Vorondadek (voh-rahn'-dah-deck) Sons. There are just one million of these sons. They do not reproduce.

Vorondadek Sons serve as heads of the constellation governments. They are known as Constellation Fathers. The ruling Constellation Father is called the Most High. He has two associates, a senior and a junior. These three positions are filled on each constellation. There are 100 constellations. Constellation Fathers rotate service.

The one hundred ruling Most Highs make up the supreme advice-giving cabinet of the Creator Son. They are mainly concerned with the welfare of the constellations. The unity of the supervision of the whole local universe is also their function.

Most of the work of the Constellation Fathers is lawmaking government. These fathers teach ascending mortals everything we need to know about universe legislation in time and space. Throughout the superuniverse, the Nebadon Vorondadek schools are unmatched.

Our creator parents brought into being the Lanonandek (lah-non'-an-deck) Sons. There are exactly twelve million of these Sons. Lanonandek Sons cannot have offspring. They are a lower divine order. They were required to pass through training on the Melchizedek worlds before serving. Based on testing, abilities, and character traits, they were forever assigned to one of three groups. These groups are as follows:

- Primary Lanonandeks serve as rotating System Sovereigns and assistants. Two or three serve together at the capitals of each system. One is appointed as the System Sovereign. Others are assigned as his assistants. Positions rotate. They are sovereign in the local affairs of the inhabited worlds of their system. They are the executive division of the universe. There are over 700,000 in this group.

- Secondary Lanonandeks are assigned as Planetary Princes. They are the continuous rulers of the planets. This is the largest group with over ten million Sons. Planetary Princes are at the head of the spiritual government of an inhabited world. They have a parental attitude towards their assigned worlds. The System Sovereigns are their supervisors.

- The third group of Lanonandeks has a little over one million Sons. They carry out the miscellaneous duties of a system. They sometimes function as custodians. At other times, they are observers. And, at times, they are messengers.

Lanonandeks are able to get closer to the lower intelligent beings. They also stand in greater danger of rebelling. Most are noble, faithful, and loyal. But, because of their sovereign status, they can fall into error. Some of these Sons have departed from the accepted techniques of universe government. Disaster followed such Sons. Yet, in executive ability, only Gabriel and his associates excel them.

The Life Carriers are a distinct order of universe Sons. They are the offspring of the Creator Son, the Creative Daughter, and one of the three Ancients of Days ruling their superuniverse. These Ancients of Days, who alone can decree the death of an intelligent being, participate in the creation of the Life Carriers.

There are one hundred million Life Carriers. Gabriel, Father Melchizedek, and the first-born Life Carrier direct them. The Melchizedeks tested and then split the Life Carriers into three grand groups. These groups are the senior Life Carriers, assistants, and custodians. The

Melchizedeks work closely with the Life Carriers. When Life Carriers go to establish life on a planet, the Melchizedeks go with them.

The Life Carriers are entrusted with designing and carrying creature life to the planets. They are the carriers and guardians of life. When they are assigned to plant life, a corps of Life Carriers goes to the planet. A corps of Life Carriers is one hundred senior carriers, one hundred assistants, and one thousand custodians.

The vital spark—the mystery of life—is bestowed *through* the Life Carriers, not by them. They make the "plasm" (DNA) but it is lifeless. The Universe Mother Spirit supplies the essential factor. From the Creative Daughter of the Infinite Spirit comes that energy spark which enlivens the body and denotes mind.

The Life Carriers agitate and organize otherwise lifeless matter. They start the required revolutions of matter. The Life Carriers transmit the spark of life on behalf of the Mother Spirit.

The Life Carrier Corps is given one-half million years on a world to establish life. At the end of this period, they stop all implantation efforts. After that, they may not ever add anything new.

Life Carriers are not permitted to experiment or interfere with free will. They are not allowed to dominate or influence moral creatures.

When a Planetary Prince arrives, the Life Carriers prepare to leave. Usually two senior Life Carriers and twelve custodians volunteer to stay on the planet. This small group serves as advisors. Urantia has two senior Life Carriers and twelve associates stationed here.

After the Creator Son and Mother Spirit finished their united cycle of creation, their solitary work began.

The Creator Son made the beautiful Material Sons of God. They are the Adams and Eves created for each local system. They are a reproducing order of sonship. Their offspring function as citizens of a system capital. But, some of the children are allowed to serve as Planetary Adams.

On a planetary mission, the Material Son and Daughter begin the Adamic race. Their mission is designed to blend with the mortals of that planet over a long period of time. Our Material Sons, our Adam and Eve, had a mission of "world-wide ministry of biologic upliftment, intellectual advancement, and moral rehabilitation." (from UB 73:7.4)

The Mother Spirit works alone to create many of the spirit beings found in the local universe.

An "adjutant" is a senior officer's assistant. There are seven adjutant mind-spirits in each local universe. They are the children of the Universe Mother Spirit. These adjutants represent the mind ministry of the Infinite Spirit. His ministry extends to the lower orders of life through the operations of a Mother Spirit.

The seven adjutant mind-spirits always go with the Life Carriers to a new planet. But, these mind-spirits are not entities or personalities. They are more like circuits. They are in fact a level of consciousness of the Mother Spirit.

The seven adjutant mind-spirits minister to the lower levels of mind. They are described in the order of attainment.

- *The spirit of intuition.* This is the primitive reflex instincts. This adjutant functions in the lower orders of animal life. This mind-spirit also makes contact with the non-teachable levels of human mind.

- *The spirit of understanding.* This is the coordination of ideas. It is the coordination of acquired knowledge. It is the phenomenon of quick reasoning. It is the gift of rapid judgment and prompt decision.

- *The spirit of courage.* This is the basis of character attainment. It is the intellectual root of moral stamina. Also, it is spiritual bravery. Facts inspired by truth become the intelligent urge to evolve and grow.

- *The spirit of knowledge.* This is the mother of adventure and discovery. It is the scientific spirit.

- *The spirit of counsel.* This is the social urge to cooperate. It is the ability of free will creatures to harmonize with their fellows.

- *The spirit of worship.* This is the religious urge. The functioning of the spirit of worship sets apart mortal mind from the lower animals. "Worship is the badge of spiritual ascension candidacy." (UB 36:5.11)

- *The spirit of wisdom.* This is the urge of moral creatures to progress and advance. "Wisdom is the goal of a purely mental and moral existence." (UB 36:5.12) This adjutant mind-spirit coordinates the work of all the other adjutants. This adjutant fosters primitive religions. Such religions are concerned with ethics and morals, the sense of human *duty.* Religion is thus built on conscience. The result stabilizes relatively ethical civilizations.

---

**Suggested Reading**

If you are familiar with the Hindu chakra system, an excellent book is *Spirits of Promise* by Gerdean O'Dell and N. Angus Bowen (published by Harp of God, May 2010). Gerdean presents a theory comparing the seven Adjutant Mind-Spirits with the seven primary chakras that is quite interesting.

---

Creature mind is the sole domain of the adjutant mind-spirits until mind can worship God. Mind is a divine bestowal. However, mind is not immortal without spirit insight. The immortal mind is able to worship and it craves survival. When the spirit of wisdom starts to function in a creature's mind, great things happen, although unconsciously.

- Function of all seven adjutants denotes that the mortal has connected with the circuits of the Holy Spirit.

- On Urantia, it also is the first functioning of the Spirit of Truth.

- Quite likely, the mortal has received their spiritual Thought Adjuster.

Angels are ministering spirits and messengers. We have seraphim, cherubim (chair'-uh-bim) and sanobim (san'-oh-bim). They make up the angelic corps of a local universe. They are the offspring of the Universe Mother Spirit.

Seraphim are spiritually superior to mortals. However, they share all our emotions except fear. They truly love humans. They appreciate our music, art, and real humor. They sympathize with our moral and spiritual struggles. Angels are not physical males and females. They are termed as positive and negative. They are children of the Universe Mother Spirit. They are referred to by feminine pronouns. Angels do not have physical bodies or wings and we will look very much like them on the mansion worlds.

Midway or halfway between mortals and angels are the midway creatures. There are two types of Midwayers.

- Primary Midwayers come from the modified mortal staff of the Planetary Prince. The primary Midwayers are the more spiritual group. There were fifty thousand of the primary Midwayers. However, over forty thousand of them joined the Lucifer rebellion. Primary Midwayers record the history of a planet. Their history exhibits are displayed at the system capitals.

- Adamson was the first child born to Adam and Eve on Urantia. Adamson went to the land of Nod and married Ratta. They gave birth to sixteen unique children. From those sixteen children 1,984 secondary Midwayers were born. Of those created, 873 rebelled. That left us with 1,111 loyal secondary Midwayers. Midwayers have diverse service on the planetary worlds. They live on a planet until the age of Light and Life. Neither group of Midwayers bears children.

Still, there are many other beings, revealed and unrevealed. We are the last and lowest created. We are the evolutionary creatures, also called mortals. Mortals are derived from the Life Carrier implantations. We are modified by the Adamic life infusion. Although lowest, we have a destiny of eternal achievement. We have a universe career wide open to the glory, grandeur, and heights of attainment!

# 15. Recap of Local Universe Personalities

| Creator Michael Son | Creative Daughter Spirit |
|---|---|
| Universe Father | Universe Mother |
| Created by God the Father and God the Eternal Son. | Created by God the Infinite Spirit. |
| **Universe Father and Mother Create Together** | |
| *Gabriel* – only 1 of his order called a Bright and Morning Star. He is the Chief executive to Michael. Responsible for universe policy and regular matters. | |
| *Brilliant Evening Stars* ("super angels") are the liaison officers of Gabriel. They represent Gabriel in each constellation and system. | |
| *Father Melchizedek* is Gabriel's assistant. In Gabriel's absence, he assumes his responsibilities. Responsible for practical procedures, and special or emergency commissions. | |
| *Melchizedek Sons* are advisory commissioners and a self-governing order. They are the pattern and teachers of self-government. Their work is to teach, train, counsel, and observe. | |
| *Vorondadek Sons* are heads of the constellation governments. They are the Constellation Fathers and the Most Highs. Universe legislation is their focus. They are the supreme advisory cabinet of the Creator Son. Their schools on universe legislation are unexcelled even on Uversa. | |
| *Lanonandek Sons* are the rulers of planets and rotating sovereigns of the systems. They are the Planetary Princes and System Sovereigns. (Derived from modified staffs of Planetary Princes are the Primary Midwayers. They are the planet's historians.) | |
| *Life Carrier Sons* design, carry, and plant life on new worlds then remain to foster its development. (An Ancients of Days collaborates in their creation.) Mortals evolved from the higher mammals derived from life implantations in the ancient sheltered seas and bays to later be modified by Adamic infusion. | |
| **Michael alone Creates** | **Mother Spirit alone Creates** |
| *Material Sons of God* are the Adams and Eves of systems. They are physical and spiritual uplifters of the planets. (Derived from the offspring of Adam and Eve are the Secondary Midwayers. They perform diverse planetary service.) | *Angelic Orders* (seraphim, cherubim, sanobim) are ministering spirits and messenger hosts. |

# 16. Eternal Life—The Beginning

Mortals who are resurrected and later choose not to continue (providing they really understand what they are choosing), will cease to exist. No one is forced to accept eternal life. It is the goal of your soul, you, to be united with your faithful Adjuster. This is a permanent, eternal decision. This process is called fusion. Fusion is the mystery of making God and man one.

Physical death is not a mortal necessity. The citizens on advanced worlds in the final era of Light and Life do not usually die. They are translated directly from the life in the flesh to the morontia existence. This fusion during physical life instantly consumes the material body. Those who might see such a spectacle would only see the translating mortal disappear in "chariots of fire." On such worlds, loved ones gather to witness the ascension of their loved one who leaves in spiritual flames. Utter joy has replaced weeping and sorrow.

Prior to fusion, the superuniverse authorities announce that the mortal has made a final choice for the eternal career. This is clearance for the fused personality to eventually leave the local universe. He or she will proceed to the headquarters of the superuniverse. From the superuniverse, the pilgrim of time will depart for Havona and the Deity adventure. But that is in the *distant future*.

There can be no future danger to the eternal career of a fused personality. Fusion with a fragment of the Paradise Father is divine validation. It means eventual Paradise attainment. Adjuster-fused mortals are the only class of human beings who go through the Havona circuits and find God on Paradise.

Developing a hearty soul during your life in the flesh will serve you through all of eternity. Your journey begins when you choose.

Choice and spiritual attainment, the ability to know God and the urge to be like him, are the characteristics of the soul. The soul of man cannot exist apart from moral thinking and spiritual activity. But, the soul of man is distinct from the Thought Adjuster. The Adjuster arrives at the same time the first moral activity of the human mind starts, and that is the occasion of the birth of the soul.

As a mortal, you begin your eternal life adventure when:
- You commit to doing God's will.
- You choose to follow the spirit guides within and around you.
- You strive to be God-knowing and Godlike with your whole heart.
- You truly desire eternal life.

The doing of the will of God is a willingness to *share the inner life* with God—to share your life with the Father's gift of the Thought Adjuster. Sharing is Godlike. Mortal children who follow the leading of their Thought Adjusters will, in time, know the will of God. Living the will of God is your eternal passport.

"The keys of the kingdom of heaven are: sincerity, more sincerity, and more sincerity. All men have these keys." (UB 39:4.14) We advance by decisions, decisions, and more decisions. The highest moral choice is to choose to do the will of God. If man thus chooses, he *is* great, though he be the humblest and least of mortals on Urantia.

During life in the flesh, the evolving soul is able to strengthen the super material decisions of the mind. The soul is super material. By itself, it does not function on the material level of human

45

experience. Neither can this sub-spiritual soul, without the Adjuster, function above the soul level. The soul cannot make final decisions until death divorces it from the material mind except when that mind gives such permission freely and willingly.

The personality's decisions are in the mind circuits during the physical life. As growth proceeds, this self, with its powers of choice, slowly becomes identified with the budding soul. After death and resurrection, the personality is fully identified with the soul self. The soul during physical life is thus the embryo of the future.

The striving to be Godlike is a nonstop effort before and after death. Life after death is, in essence, the same as the mortal life. Everything you do in this life that is good and adds to the enhancement of your future life helps to develop your soul. Real religion does not support moral or spiritual laziness. It does not encourage the vain hope of having Godlike perfection bestowed upon one because of physical death.

You can have seven distinct life phases:

1. *Planetary Mortals.* The first level of existence is the material or physical life. Mortals are all of animal origin. All mortals are evolutionary beings. Mortals have ascending potential. If you compare this life to other phases, this is a short period of time.

2. *Sleeping Survivors.* Mortals who spiritually advanced in their earth lives have guardian angels. The angels are called guardians of destiny. After death, these mortals are personalized on the third day, on the mansion worlds. Surviving souls that have not attained guardians of destiny cannot go to the mansion worlds right away. Such souls rest in unconscious sleep. A dispensation by a Son of God calls the rolls of the age; these sleeping survivors are then resurrected on the mansion worlds in huge groups.

   When Christ Michael did the roll call, the sleeping survivors were from the days of Adam to the days of the Master's resurrection. The passing of time is unimportant to sleeping survivors. They are unconscious. After resurrection, those who slept 5,000 years react just the same as those who slept five days.

3. *Mansion World Students.* All surviving mortals who are resurrected on the mansion worlds are at this stage. The mansion worlds are called detention worlds. Although correction is not to be confused with punishment. Mansion world students make individual progress. However, they advance in universe study as a group.

4. *Morontia Progressors.* After graduating from the mansion worlds, mortals are called morontia (moh-ron'-chah) progressors. Morontia is the long period between the physical and spirit life. It is just as real as a physical body or spirit form. However, it is not material or spiritual. At this level, mortals progress through the local universe. They are wards of the local universe. This stage is the long-term progress of intellect, spirit, and personality form. Before leaving the local universe, they receive confirmation. The Creator Son and Mother Spirit confirm that the mortal status is forever settled. Such mortals are then young spirits.

5. *Superuniverse Wards.* This stage does not function until the spirit career begins. Ascenders are now wards of the Ancients of Days. There are three types of these ascenders—those progressing through the minor sector, major sector, or the superuniverse headquarters. (From UB 30:4.22)

6. *Havona Pilgrims.* When you arrive on Paradise, you are a perfected spirit. The journey from the superuniverse to Havona is made alone. There is no more class or group

instruction. Evolutionary world training in administration is over. Now begins your individual and personal education. Instruction is intellectual, spiritual, and based on experience.

7. *Paradise Arrivals*. With residential status, you begin the course in divinity. Residence signifies that you have found God. You will be entered into the Mortal Corps of the Finality. (See Chapter 20.) It is a glorious stage. Nevertheless, it is speculated that in the coming ages, God has further plans for his mortal finaliters.

We are aware of one kind of death but there are actually three as concerns personality survival:

- Physical death is when the body and mind stop working. The Adjuster leaves the vanishing mind just as entry was made years before—without notice or fanfare.

- Intellectual or mind death occurs when human will-action has been destroyed. The mind can no longer make free will choices or act on those choices. Under such conditions, the Thought Adjuster is released. If prior to mind death the human chose eternal life, then their soul will survive.

- Spiritual or soul death occurs when someone *knowingly* rejects survival. They are spiritually beyond help because they have permanently embraced sin. They refuse all further help. After all concerned spirit beings have agreed, the rulers of the superuniverse order the release of the indwelling Thought Adjuster. The body and mind continue to function until physical death. But, in reality, this is permanent, final death.

The soul is completely unconscious during the sleep of death. The sleep of death is that period between physical death and resurrection. During the sleep of death your creature memory patterns, (your spirit mind), is in the possession of your detached Adjuster. Your identity, (your morontia soul), is in the safekeeping of the seraphic destiny guardians. If you do not yet have guardian angels assigned to you, the group custodians perform that service. The reuniting of the morontia soul and mind is the resurrection of a sleeping survivor.

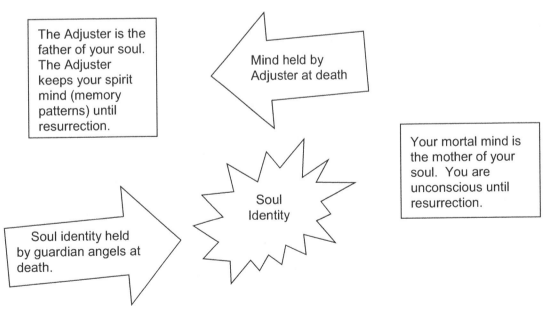

The Adjuster is the father of your soul. The Adjuster keeps your spirit mind (memory patterns) until resurrection.

Mind held by Adjuster at death

Your mortal mind is the mother of your soul. You are unconscious until resurrection.

Soul Identity

Soul identity held by guardian angels at death.

# 17. Eternal Life—The Mansion Worlds

Jerusem is the headquarters of the system of Satania, to which Urantia belongs. Jerusem is physically at the center. It is encircled by seven major transition worlds. They are called satellite worlds. Each of those seven transition worlds has seven sub-satellite worlds that circle them. There are 57 worlds including Jerusem, at our system headquarters. There are, or will be, one thousand inhabited worlds that are served in each system.

SYSTEM: SATANIA—619 inhabited planets (will have 1,000)
HEADQUARTERS: JERUSEM—7 major satellite worlds (transition worlds) each with 7 sub-satellite worlds

| Transition World | Notes of Interest | Training Focus |
|---|---|---|
| Finaliters World | Probationary nursery | Parenting skills, family life |
| Mansion #1 | Temple of New Life | Correction and cure of character defects |
| Mansion #2 | First sea of glass | Removal of intellectual conflict & mental disharmony |
| Mansion #3 | | Universe relationships, cosmic meanings |
| Mansion #4 | | Morontia culture & social life, local universe language |
| Mansion #5 | | Cosmic consciousness, superuniverse language |
| Mansion #6 | | Universe administration |
| Mansion #7 | | Preparation for Jerusem citizenship |
| Morontia World | | |
| Angelic World | | |
| Superangel World | | |
| World of The Sons | | |
| World of The Spirits | | |
| World of The Father | | |
| | | |
| JERUSEM Adams & Eves live here | 100 times larger than Urantia. Amphitheater seats 5 billion | Representative government, group activities. Melchizedeks have 30+ education centers. Ascenders start at the college of self-evaluation and end with the school of Jerusem citizenship. |

Jerusem is almost one hundred times the size of Urantia, but its gravity is a bit less. Jerusem's major satellites are each about ten times as large as Urantia. The seven sub-satellites are about the size of Urantia.

The seven mansion worlds are the seven sub-satellites of transition world number one. Uversa representatives have headquarters on each mansion world. In addition, celestial artisans maintain headquarters on each of the mansion worlds. Many groups have activities throughout the system headquarter worlds. You will eventually get to know all these orders of beings. The table helps to show the layout of our system headquarters.

The Temple of New Life is on mansion world number one. It has awakening chambers for as many as one million souls at the same time. Throughout all eternity, you will remember seeing the resurrection mornings. However, nothing can compare to the actual experience of survival and resurrection!

After your awareness and joy of experiencing survival, you are sure to notice your new morontia form. Morontia life forms are different. The morontia soul no longer needs the material flesh and blood body. Your personality form will progressively reflect your true beauty and inner self.

You no longer have a male or female body since your time of reproduction is over. However, you do retain masculine and feminine characteristics. You continue to eat and drink but there is no waste by-product. You eat morontia food, a kingdom of living energy unknown to our world. Although you are no longer flesh and blood, you are only slightly above the physical level. You are very far from the spirit level.

Space communication will be perfected. Your "anywhere reception" is made possible by carrying the "harp of God." This device makes up for your immature sensory ability. You cannot yet detect space communications.

We think of having five senses—seeing, hearing, smelling, tasting, and touch. However, we are told we actually have twelve. (Perhaps they consider a sense of time or a sense of direction as part of the twelve.) Havona natives respond to forty-nine sensation stimuli. Morontia senses are seventy! These are most likely acquired as we progress.

Following your awakening in the resurrection halls, you will be assigned a new home and given ten days (30 Urantia days) of free time. You will want to look in the registry for friends and loved ones that died before you, and visit them. You will also explore your beautiful surroundings and learn about the training program that will soon begin.

On earth, kindergarten teachers start with children of all different backgrounds, experiences, skill levels, and maturity. The only place to begin teaching is at each individual's level. Teachers on mansion world number one must have a similar situation. We are told, "You begin over there right where you leave off down here." (UB 47:3.7)

Training is called deficiency ministry. It is the correction and cure of character defects. It also corrects for a lack of experience. Family life and parenting defects, human intolerance and discrimination, are either corrected or are projected for future correction on Jerusem.

Mortals that evolved sufficiently on earth enjoy their ten days of free time on the first mansion world. Then they enter the translation sleep and advance to the second mansion world. Again, they are given ten free days. This continues until they arrive at their assigned world.

The probationary nursery is located on the first of the major transition worlds. The mansion worlds revolve around this major satellite. Children who died before making a choice concerning their Paradise career are cared for in the nursery.

From infants to about age sixteen, these children are personalized after death. They are always personalized as of their physical age at the time of death. They are in physical, material form except that they cannot reproduce. These children are allowed to grow up and choose the heavenly path just as they would have if death had not interfered.

Children under age five will receive Thought Adjusters when they grow up and make their first moral choice. After the nursery, children with Adjusters are assigned to families of the Material Sons. If a child decides against the Paradise path, then when death again overtakes them, it is final. There is no resurrection from such a second death. There is no adjudication of such cases. They simply become as if they had not been.

Rarely do children under the age of sixteen make a final choice. But, whenever their final choice is made, they are translated to the first mansion world. Translate means to change form. Rather than a second death, they fuse with their Adjuster and take the morontia form. Their final choice begins their Paradise ascent.

It is also mandatory that you have parenting experience. It is fundamental to understanding the relationship of the Paradise Father and his universe children. Generally, if you raised children during your life in the flesh you will have gained the necessary experience. This service of parental ministry is essential for men as well as women. All must experience parenthood. Service will be in the homes of the Material Sons on Jerusem or, in part, in the probationary nursery.

Mansion world students who have one or more children in the nursery and who lack in parental experience may apply for a Melchizedek permit. They receive a temporary transfer from ascension duties on the mansion worlds. They function as associate parents to their own and other children in the nursery. This service of parental ministry will be credited on Jerusem as the fulfillment of one-half of their training. The other half will come from serving the families of the Material Sons and Daughters.

Regardless of parental experience, mansion world parents with growing children in the nursery are allowed to collaborate. They plan, with the morontia custodians of such children, their instruction and training. These parents are allowed to visit as often as four times a year. It is one of the most touching scenes of the ascension career to see mansion world parents embrace their material offspring on one of their visits.

The first mansion world corrects biological shortages. Defects pertaining to sex life, family relations, and parental roles are tackled. If not fully resolved, they will be corrected on Jerusem.

When ready to advance to the next world you enter the transit sleep. You go to sleep with the seraphic transport. These angels provide transportation. You wake up in the next resurrection hall. It is almost the same, as when you woke up on the first mansion world except your Adjuster does not leave you as you advance through the mansion worlds. With each advancement, you wake up with a newly developed and adjusted morontia body.

On mansion world number two morontia groupings take form. Working groups, social groups, and communities begin to function better. Human intolerance and discriminations, such as caste systems, are disappearing. There are mortal survivors from all the system's inhabited worlds and many different celestial orders. Like the celestials, we are becoming friendlier and more fraternal.

When you arrive, you receive permission to visit the second major satellite world. It is headquarters for the morontia supervisors. Transition world number two also has the training schools for the various morontia orders. The second mansion world provides for the removal of intellectual conflict and mental disharmony. Mota (moh'-tah), unknown to us now, is a method for finding truth, beauty and goodness. These lessons use man's highest philosophic ideas alongside morontia mota. Mota teaching begins on the first mansion world but is more earnestly studied on the second.

A huge circular crystal about 30 miles deep is found on most architectural worlds; this sea of glass serves in many ways. It has beauty value. It serves as a landing field for transport seraphim who provide transportation for non-material beings. The crystal sea of glass has superuniverse reflectivity factors. It also modifies the currents of space for incoming physical energy streams. You will experience your first sea of glass on the second mansion world.

On the third mansion world, great personal and social achievement is made. Training becomes positive rather than corrective. Upon arrival, you are permitted to visit the third transition sphere. On this major satellite world is the headquarters of the angelic orders. It is also the home of their system training schools.

You continue to study mota. Human logic and philosophy are coordinated with mota. Urantia Paper 48, Section 7, explains the parallel method used. In one column are given the concepts of mota meanings. In the opposite column is the closest human philosophy. Actual mota is not revealed but 28 illustrations of human philosophy are given. For example, Number 11 is, "The weak indulge in resolutions, but the strong act. Life is but a day's work—do it well. The act is ours; the consequences God's." (UB 48:7.13) Real progress is made in the understanding of cosmic meanings. Intelligent understanding of universe relationships is now gained.

The real morontia career is underway on the fourth mansion world. Upon arrival, permission is given to visit the fourth transition world. This major satellite world is headquarters to the superangels. They include the Brilliant Evening Stars. The superangels also have their training schools on transition world number four.

True progress is made in the areas of morontia culture and social life. A new demanding, yet delightful, social order is introduced. It is based on the mutual appreciation and unselfish love of the shared Paradise destiny. Worshipful and divine perfection is the shared goal. There is an awareness of the God-knowing, God-seeking, and God-finding desire of the ascender.

There is increased appreciation of the broadcasts. On advanced worlds, mortals scan the latest broadcasts with the same interest we view our daily news. Actually, they hear the broadcasts. But, because Urantia was part of the rebellion, we are not familiar with the universe broadcasts.

The sea of glass has reflectivity properties. Uversa friends add the reflectivity technique to the Paradise broadcast. Everything heard then becomes visible. Reflectivity is the newsgathering and the decreed broadcast method of all creation. It is in constant operation, while the various broadcast services are periodic. Before leaving mansonia the fourth, you will have mastered the local universe language.

On mansonia number five, it is beginning to dawn upon the ascending mortals that a magnificent destiny waits for all who complete the Paradise ascension. It has been difficult but joyful. Study is becoming voluntary. Unselfish service seems natural. Worship is spontaneous. A real morontia character is budding. A real morontia creature is evolving.

Permission to visit the fifth transition world is given. This is the Sons' headquarters world. Here ascenders become personally familiar with the various groups of divine sonship.

A birth of cosmic consciousness takes place. You are becoming universe minded. Here you get a foretaste of Jerusem life. Instructors begin to prepare you for the constellation study worlds.

You mastered the local universe language before arriving. Now you devote time to perfecting the language of Uversa. All ascending mortals are bilingual from the system headquarters up to Havona.

On the sixth mansion world, instruction begins in the technique of universe administration. Organization of society is of a high order. The shadow of animal origin lessens. "Coming up through great tribulation serves to make glorified mortals very kind and understanding, very sympathetic and tolerant." (UB 47:8.7) Now you master the language of Uversa. Preparation begins for your constellation stay. It will continue on mansion world number seven.

Permission to visit the sixth transition world is given. The high spirits of the superuniverse are here. Many of these celestial beings are not yet visible. The first lessons in the spirit career are given. The spirit career follows the graduation from the morontia training of the local universe.

Fusion with your Thought Adjuster may have occurred previously but often does not happen until your time on the fifth or sixth mansion world. Fusion is true entrance into the eternal career of service. After you and your Adjuster are finally and eternally fused, then in fact, you have become an ascending son of God.

The Father has bestowed himself upon us. He has placed his own spirit within us. Therefore, he demands ultimate perfection of us. "Be you perfect, even as I am perfect." Fusion assures the success of the eternal career. Fusion joins you and God, as one, forever. It means eventual Paradise attainment and belonging to the order of the Corps of the Finality.

The perfect fusion of your mind and personality with the divine Adjuster is marked by a simple ceremony. In the presence of your friends, the messengers of confirmation say, "This is a beloved son in whom I am well pleased."

After confirmation of Adjuster fusion, you are introduced to your friends for the first time by your new name. Also, you are granted forty days of spiritual retirement. You are relieved of routine activities. During this time, you choose one of the optional routes to Havona. You also choose from the different techniques of Paradise attainment.

Coming from such lowly origins our progress is remarkable. However, we are still more or less semi-material and far from being spirits. In spite of your progress, you are still more or less material. You are far from being a true spirit. You are still a little lower than the angels are. Nevertheless, you are becoming a marvelous creature.

Preparation for Jerusem citizenship is the task and crowning achievement on the seventh mansion world. Hundreds of times throughout the mansion world ascension, you would have visited Jerusem but always as a guest. You have progressed as an individual but you will leave for Jerusem as part of a group. Often however, ascenders are permitted to wait on the seventh mansion world for a loved one to catch up to them.

Transition world number seven is the world of the Paradise Father. Permission is given to visit. You will find the Father's temple but you cannot see him. Here, you begin more spiritual worship of the unseen Father.

On this, the last of the mansion worlds, you are purged of the last remnants of the "mark of the beast." Urantia is an isolated and retarded world. Any differences between the more advanced, enlightened worlds and us are obliterated. You have gone from world to world as an individual. Now you and your fellows, together, will say an eternal good-bye to the mansion world career.

When the time comes to leave for Jerusem, everyone meets on the sea of glass to bid your graduation class farewell. The times of adjustment sleep and resurrection awakening are over when you leave the mansion worlds. From now until becoming a first-stage spirit, all progressive transformations are done without loss of consciousness.

The arrival of your class is welcomed by all Jerusem, which the prophets called heaven. The grandeur of Jerusem is beyond our human imagination. Jerusem perfectly harmonizes and accommodates all three phases of existence—the material, the morontial, and the spiritual. This beautiful architectural sphere, 100 times larger than Urantia, is light and temperature controlled. There are thousands upon thousands of small sparkling lakes. There is an abundance of physical plants and morontia life. All is beautifully balanced without struggle for existence.

Jerusem also has a transportation center compatible with the streams of energy. Transport birds fly at about one hundred miles an hour. Air machines fly five hundred miles per hour. Mount Seraph, about 15,000 feet high, is the point of departure from Jerusem. All transport seraphim take off from this location. They depart every three seconds. Transports arrive on the sea of glass.

The manufacturing and laboratory areas will astonish even the most experienced chemists and inventors. This is an area of perfect mechanical techniques and physical achievement.

The sea of glass has a huge amphitheater seating five billion beings. Listening to incoming universe reports is a favorite pastime. Everything heard is also visible in the amphitheater.

Many orders of beings are headquartered on Jerusem. However, the center of attraction is the domain of the Adams and Eves. These Material Sons are the highest type of sex-reproducing beings to be found on the training worlds of the universes. They really are material. These permanent inhabitants of Jerusem, with their children, live in vast estates. They are involved in the local administration of the capital sphere.

Physical beings are limited to certain planets. Being physical, the Material Sons cannot attend the Melchizedek University of Salvington. However, the Melchizedeks maintain instructors on the capitals of each system. They teach the younger Material Sons and ascending mortals. A Melchizedek education is the acme of perfection.

The Melchizedek Sons conduct over thirty different educational centers on Jerusem. Training begins with the college of self-evaluation. It ends with the school of Jerusem citizenship.

All the Sons join in an effort to qualify ascenders. Ascenders must be able to assume the responsibility of representative government. "The entire universe is organized and administered on the *representative* plan. Representative government is the divine ideal of self-government among non-perfect beings." (UB 45:7.3)

There are three orders of citizenship—the Material Sons, seraphim, and ascending mortals. All representatives must have received recognition from the Melchizedek schools of administration. Votes are cast based on the registered personal possession of mota—morontia wisdom. Votes cast at an election by any one personality has a value ranging from one up to one thousand. Jerusem citizens are classed by mota achievement.

Training will focus on group activities and your unselfish willingness to put the group before yourself. It is also mandatory that you have fulfilled your parenting experience. This is essential to understanding the Paradise Father's relationship with his universe children.

Attainment of each ascension goal is a fact. However, in the larger picture such goals are simply milestones on the long path to Paradise. But no evolutionary creature is ever denied the full satisfaction of goal attainment.

# 18. Eternal Life—Beyond the Mansion Worlds

From the system headquarters, we advance to the constellation worlds. One hundred systems are administered to by the constellation headquarters. Norlatiadek (nor-lash'-ee-ah-dek) is the name of our constellation.

The largest sphere is Edentia (e-den'-chah). It is located in the center. It is the seat of the administration of the Constellation Fathers, the Most Highs. Edentia is situated in a cluster of 70 major worlds. Each has ten satellites revolving around them. In total, there are 771 architectural worlds in a constellation headquarters.

Edentia is about 100 times larger than Urantia. The 70 major satellites are about ten times larger than our world. Each of their ten smaller satellites is about the size of Urantia. Like Jerusem, Edentia has no storms. Neither do they have winters or summers. The water of architectural worlds is the same as the evolutionary planets.

Like Jerusem, Edentia has tens of thousands of sparkling lakes. It has an amphitheater, sea of glass, and resurrection hall. The primary difference is that about half of Edentia is one vast natural park. It is described as the garden of God. On many planets these Gardens of Eden are so named in honor of Edentia. (from UB 43:1.7)

Edentia's garden/natural park is both enormous and exquisite. Plants and animals are material, morontia, and forms of life unknown to us. Material plants have the typical green coloration. Morontia plant life has a violet or orchid hue. Animals are unlike anything we would recognize now. All animal life is intelligent but non-speaking. All are gentle and friendly. There is nothing in all of Edentia to make any personality afraid.

Centered in the garden is the worship shrine of the Most Highs. Every tenth day of relaxation they lead all of Edentia in contemplation of God the Supreme.

Time spent on the 70 training worlds of transition is the most settled period in a mortal ascender's career up to the status of finaliter. It is typical morontia life. We are re-keyed as we progress through the seventy worlds. But we are conscious and keep our same morontia bodies.

The Melchizedeks have two special colleges on Edentia. One is the emergency school that studies the problems resulting from the Lucifer rebellion. The other is the bestowal school focused on problems from the fact that Christ Michael made his final bestowal on Urantia.

On the constellation worlds, we achieve the real socialization of our morontia characters. Training focuses on two areas. We will master group ethics and learn the secret of inter-relationships. The method used is unlike anything on Urantia.

We will be matched with ten associates that are similar in intellect but different in every other way. This group is then associated in companies of one hundred of the smaller groups. Next, we will be federated into a corps of one thousand.

We also will be grouped with others that are unlike us intellectually. Again, the groups are merged. After achieving working harmony, we will live in intimate contact with both similar and dissimilar beings.

We will live happily and work effectively. It is a period of bliss for morontia progressors. After graduating from world number seventy, we will live on Edentia. On Edentia, we hear for the first time the "assemblies of Paradise." The Faithful of Days are Trinity-origin Personalities. They share the story of their extensive careers.

Ascending mortals on Edentia get assignments serving on the 70 worlds. We also serve on Edentia. Programs are concerned with group, racial, national, and planetary welfare. The Most Highs do not advance individuals on the inhabited worlds. They rule in the kingdoms of men.

On the system headquarters, we went from near animal to morontia creatures. On the constellation headquarters, we are midway between our former and future estates. On the Salvington worlds, we will evolve to the status of true spirits.

---

### Suggested Reading

Urantia Paper 44, "The Celestial Artisans" is fascinating. The celestial artisans' chief realm of activity is in the constellations. Mortal ascenders may apply to the artisan corps. Enlistment is for, at least, 1,000 local universe years. That is 8,200 years in Urantia time.

---

From Edentia we join ascending mortals from all the Nebadon constellations. Together, we will attend the relevant training worlds. The goal is the attainment of Salvington citizenship. Salvington is the headquarters of our local universe, Nebadon. Salvington is at the center. Seventy primary spheres encircle Salvington. Each has six satellite worlds revolving around it. The 490 spheres are divided into ten groups. Each group has seven primary and 42 satellite worlds.

We will start at the world called Melchizedek. Most training takes place on the associated satellite worlds. However, we will live on the primary spheres. The sphere of Melchizedek is probably the most interesting place in Nebadon. Even after reaching Paradise, we will never forget our first day on this unique world. Here we learn the disciplines of the Salvington educational system. Time will be spent in review and preparation.

| Group | Worlds of the: | Primary | Satellite | Activity |
|---|---|---|---|---|
| 1 | Melchizedeks | 1 | | Home of Melchizedeks |
| | | | 1 | Review of initial planetary life of mortals |
| | | | 2 | Review of mansion world experiences |
| | | | 3 | Review of experiences on Jerusem |
| | | | 4 | Review of constellation experiences |
| | | | 5 | Review of Edentia experiences |
| | | | 6 | Correlation of above - preparatory to entering college |
| | | 2 | | Physical life schools & laboratories of living energies |
| | | 3 | | Morontia life |
| | | 4 | | Initial spirit life |
| | | 5 | | Mid-spirit life |
| | | 6 | | Advancing spirit life |
| | | 7 | | Supreme self-realization |
| 2 | Vorondadeks | 8-14 | | Universe legislation (by Constellation Fathers) |
| 3 | Lanonandeks | 15-21 | | Local systems administration (by System Sovereigns) |
| 4 | Life Carriers | 22-28 | | Life—planning, designing, evolution, associations |
| 5 | Finaliters | 29-35 | | (restricted—special schools) |

The table shows that the six satellite worlds of the first primary sphere are for Urantia ascenders. Those from other inhabited worlds review their own planetary life history. Those from other systems or constellations study accordingly. All this is to prepare us to enter the primary schools of the universe. Some of the other groups are also listed on the table to give you an idea of what is studied.

The schools of universe administration are on the Melchizedek home world. The original Father Melchizedek heads the highest universe administration course, at the College of High Ethics. Also, there are many other schools. Their subjects are energy, matter, organization, communication, ethics, and comparative creature existence.

However, the Melchizedeks are not the only instructors. At the College of Spiritual Endowment, even the Paradise Sons of God cooperate with the Melchizedek and seraphic teachers in training ascenders. A Paradise Trinity Teacher Son conducts the high College of Wisdom.

The second group of 49 worlds is the area of the Constellation Fathers, the Most Highs. Here, we secure the height of our education in universe legislation. Even the schools on Uversa do not surpass Nebadon's schools on local universe legislation.

The Lanonandeks comprise the third group in the Salvington circuit. Experienced System Sovereigns teach system administration. Before, we were observers. Now, we actually participate in the administration of ten thousand local systems. In all these schools of applied knowledge we really do the things we are being taught.

The Melchizedeks oversee the Life Carriers' worlds. These worlds are the fourth group. Training includes the study of life associated with mind. Also, we are taught "mind and spirit in living things." On their home world we learn of the types of life design, life patterns, pattern control (trait determiners), and different life plans.

The fifth group is restricted. Personalities of the super and central universes are here to execute assignments in Nebadon. The remaining five groups do not pertain to Father-fused mortals.

After attaining Salvington, we will be attached to a universe service corps. We serve in a variety of universe activities. At each level of achievement, we reach back and down to extend a helping hand to those who follow us in the upward climb. Therefore, we are assigned to celestial personalities as helpers, students, observers, and teachers.

Thus far, we have been morontia progressors—taught, trained, nurtured, and guided by the personalities of Nebadon. As citizens of Salvington, we are prepared for our superuniverse adventure. We will become wards of The Ancients of Days as we pass from the final morontia stage. Real spirit identities are acquired just before we leave Salvington.

Michael of Nebadon is our Creator Son. He and our local Universe Mother Spirit confirm our spirit status. This confirmation forever settles our status as ascending mortals. Never has a superuniverse ward gone astray.

As young spirits in the superuniverse our training continues. The local universes are divided into systems and constellations. The superuniverses are divided into minor and major sectors. Uminor the third is the headquarters of our minor sector. It is surrounded by seven worlds. There we learn the higher physical studies of the ascendant life.

Our education continues through the study worlds of the ten major sectors. Umajor the fifth is the headquarters of our major sector. Seventy spheres surround it. These worlds provide advanced intellectual training of the superuniverse. The more perfected we become, the more difficult it is to relay any comparable earthly descriptions. However, all ten headquarters of the major sectors are most likely similar.

Uversa (you-vur'-sah) is the headquarters of our superuniverse, Orvonton (or'-von'-ton). It is surrounded by seven primary worlds. Each primary world has seventy satellites. The higher universities for advanced spiritual training are on the satellite worlds. There are thousands upon thousands of institutions devoted to universe training and spirit culture.

Ascending mortals receive the same general education. However, our training does vary. Special groups and classes are taken through special courses of instruction. Some ascenders are put through specific courses of training.

We are then re-educated and re-examined in preparation for our Havona adventure. "The reason for all this experience is not now fully apparent, but no doubt such training is wise and necessary in view of their possible future destiny as members of the Corps of the Finality." (UB 30:4.24)

# 19. Eternal Life—Paradise

Departing graduates are dispatched for Havona direct from the shores of Uversa. The long journey is always made alone. Upon arrival, you will thank your transport seraphim for the long and safe trip. You will be introduced to your sponsors. Next, you register your arrival. You will send a loving and thankful message to Michael of Nebadon. He is our Universe Father who made the sonship career possible. Following these formalities, you receive a long period of free time.

From now on there are no more class or group instructions. You have finished the technical and administrative training of the worlds of time and space. Your personal education begins. This will be your individual spiritual training. Your personal instruction is intellectual, spiritual, and based on experience.

Havona, the central universe, is not a time creation. This never-beginning, never-ending universe consists of one billion perfect spheres. Each Havona world is perfect. However, no two worlds are the same. The central universe spins around the stationary Isle of Paradise as one vast plane.

The central universe worlds are "arranged" in concentric circuits. Seven Havona circuits surround three circuits of Paradise. Each circuit differs and all are perfect. Each Havona circuit is a representation of the Infinite Spirit. These representatives are called the Seven Spirits of the Circuits. They manage the conduct of celestial affairs in each circuit. Physically, all these circuits are the same system. Their "separation" is in respect to function and administration.

All the worlds of Havona are of a material nature. They are just as real as Urantia. There are exactly one thousand basic chemical elements. Havona natives respond to forty-nine different sensations. In other words, the natives of the central universe have forty-nine senses. The morontia senses are seventy, and the higher spiritual orders range from seventy to two hundred and ten. None of the physical beings of the central universe would be visible to Urantians. Neither would any of the physical stimuli cause a reaction in our sense organs. If a Urantia mortal could be transported to Havona, he would be deaf, blind, and lacking in any sense reactions while there.

Time does not exist on Paradise. However, time is relevant to both celestial and terrestrial beings. Each Havona world has its own local time based on its circuit. The length of a year is the same for all the worlds in one circuit because a circuit swings around Paradise uniformly. The length of a year is longest at the outermost circuit. It is shortest at the innermost circuit. There is also a Paradise-Havona standard day. The standard day is based on the length of time it takes for the first, or inner, Havona circuit to complete one revolution around the Isle of Paradise. It takes almost one thousand years for these worlds to complete their circuit. "A day is as a thousand years with God." One Paradise-Havona *day* is just about seven minutes less than one thousand years of our Urantia calendar year. This Paradise-Havona day is the standard time measurement for the seven superuniverses. However, each superuniverse also uses its own time standards.

The Eternal Son's spiritual gravity is very active throughout the central universe. All spiritual personalities are drawn inward towards the home of God. This Godward urge is intense. The ambition to attain God is stronger in the central universe. This is because beings who have attained Havona are more fully spiritualized. They are more responsive to the spirit-gravity pull of the Eternal Son.

Also, the Infinite Spirit draws all intellectual values toward Paradise. The mind gravity of the Infinite Spirit functions with the spirit gravity of the Eternal Son. Together, they constitute the urge of the ascendant souls. That urge is to find God, to attain Deity, to achieve Paradise, and to *know* the Father.

Havona is spiritually and physically perfect. Everything physical or spiritual is (perfectly) predictable. Mind and personality are not predictable. But, throughout eternity, Havona natives have never been guilty of disobeying the will of Deity. Never have these perfect beings sinned.

Neither has sin appeared in any creature who has entered Havona as a pilgrim. There has never been one instance of misconduct—not by any creature—created in, or admitted to, the central Havona universe. So perfect and so divine are the methods of selection in the universes of time that never has an error occurred. No mistakes have *ever* been made. No ascendant soul has ever been prematurely admitted to the central universe.

There is no government of Havona. None is required. There are no regular courts. Neither are there legislative assemblies. Havona needs only administrative direction. Havona is the ideal of *self*-government.

Administration is chiefly planetary. The Trinity-origin Eternal of Days on each world directs it. Eternals of Days are perfect administrators. They teach with supreme skill and direct their planetary children with perfection of wisdom.

The billion spheres are the training worlds of the high personalities native to Paradise and Havona. They also serve as the final proving grounds for ascending mortal creatures. In harmony with the Paradise Father's plan of creature ascension, the pilgrims land on the worlds of the outer seventh circuit. Then more training and experience follows. Ascenders advance inward, planet-by-planet and circuit-by-circuit.

There are an enormous number of ascenders who have climbed to glory from the dark worlds of space. In Havona, they are ministered to, taught, and trained. Each world will offer a definite task to be achieved. Life is rich and full, complete and satisfying. But, such activities and even the Havona thought processes are completely different from anything we can imagine now.

You will advance inward from the seventh to the first circuit.
7. When you first attain the central universe, you are received and housed on the pilot world of the seventh Havona circuit. As you progress spiritually, you will attain identity comprehension of our superuniverse Master Spirit. Then you are transferred to the sixth circuit.
6. After you have attained a realization of God the Supreme, you are taken to the fifth circuit.
5. After attaining the Infinite Spirit, you are transferred to the fourth circuit.
4. Following the attainment of the Eternal Son, you are removed to the third circuit.
3. When you have recognized the Paradise Father, you go to the second circuit of worlds.
2. You will become more familiar with the Paradise hosts.
1. Arrival on the first circuit of Havona means you are accepted into the service of Paradise. From this inner circuit the ascending pilgrims pass inward to Paradise. There you will be admitted to the Corps of the Finality.

Not until you visit the last of the Havona worlds, "will the tonic of adventure and the stimulus of curiosity disappear." (UB 14:5.7) Then will the adventure of time be replaced by the forward impulse of eternity.

Monotony points to immaturity and inactivity. It is immaturity of creative imagination. It is the inactivity of the spiritually endowed intellect. But, by the time you reach Havona, you have "already attained emotional, intellectual, and social, if not spiritual, maturity." (UB 14:5.8) Monotony does not exist in the Havona career.

You will find undreamed-of changes facing you as you advance from circuit to circuit. Your astonishment will be beyond words. Each of the billion study worlds is a university of surprises. Continuing amazement and unending wonder are the experiences of those who pass through the Havona circuits.

"Love of adventure, curiosity, and dread of monotony—these traits inherent in evolving human nature—were not put there just to aggravate and annoy you during your short sojourn on earth, but rather to suggest to you that death is only the beginning of an endless career of adventure, an everlasting life of anticipation, an eternal voyage of discovery." (UB 14:5.10)

# 20. The Corps of Mortal Finaliters

There are seven Corps of the Finality (see UB 31:10.1) But the only known destination for Adjuster-fused mortals is the Corps of Mortal Finality. There are also non-mortals that belong to the Corps of Mortal Finality. What every member has in common is a fragment of the Paradise Father. The corps is grouped into one thousand finaliters called a company. Of that number, 999 are permanent, having taken an oath. The vacant position is filled temporarily. A company of mortal finaliters is comprised from the following groups.

1. *Havona Natives.* Havona natives must achieve certain experience working with evolutionary beings. Those experiences will create the ability to receive a Thought Adjuster. Millions upon millions of Havona natives are on a volunteer waiting list. These perfect beings are of great assistance. They provide the viewpoint of one born in perfection. Thus, the corps embraces both perfect and perfected beings with experience. Other corps are open to Havona natives. Yet, the possibility of being admitted to the Corps of Mortal Finaliters is considered a thrilling adventure. However, only one Havona native in one thousand is admitted to a mortal corps. (see UB 31:01)

2. *Gravity Messengers.* Gravity Messengers are all assigned to the primary Corps of Mortal Finaliters. No other group or corps has such messengers. The Gravity Messengers are able to transcend time and space. They are able to use all energies, circuits, and even gravity. Mortal finaliters cannot defy time and space. However, they have Gravity Messengers subject to their command who can. Unlimited numbers of Gravity Messengers may be attached to a finaliter company. But, only the chief of his fellows is mustered into the Corps of Mortal Finaliters. The chief has a permanent staff of 999 fellow messengers. He may also use the unlimited number of messengers in reserve when needed. In a company of 1,000 mortal finaliters, only the chief Gravity Messenger is a member. The others serve on assignment. Gravity Messengers are modified and personalized Adjusters. Each is a direct personalization of a fragment of the Paradise Father. A mortal is a personality that fuses with a fragment of God the Father. The Corps of Mortal Finaliters thus embraces both beings—personalized and fused Adjusters.

3. *Glorified Midway Creatures.* After a world is settled in Light and Life, the Midwayers are released from permanent citizenship status. They start their Paradise ascent in company with the mortals. The secondary Midwayers are all Adjuster-fused. They are all mustered into the mortal corps. (see UB 31:6)

4. *Glorified Material Sons.* After a world is settled in Light and Life, the Adam and Eve of that world may choose to humanize. Then they would follow the same course of mortal ascension to Paradise. All such Adams and Eves are mustered into the Corps of Mortal Finaliters. Any Adam or Eve that defaults in their planetary mission is compelled to follow the mortal ascension plan. (see UB 31:5)

5. *Adopted Seraphim.* Mortal guardian angels are often allowed to go through the ascension career with their human wards. Many of these seraphim, after fusion, join their subjects to take the mortal finaliter oath. (see UB 31:4)

6. *Glorified Mortals.* Ascendant mortals make up the largest part of the Corps of Finality. Together with the seraphim, they usually total 990 members in each company. While numbers vary, mortals far outnumber the angels. The remaining ten positions are filled by non-mortal and non-seraphic personalities. Currently, members reside on Paradise. They temporarily serve in the Corps of Light and Life. (see UB 31:3)

7. *Unrevealed Personalities*. Note there is a consistent pattern of sevens—the sevenfold pattern. We are advised that this group exists but no further details are revealed.

Finaliters serve throughout the superuniverses. One or more companies are constantly in service on Urantia. Mortal finaliters also administer the worlds settled in Light and Life. There is nowhere in the universes that they are not assigned.

Mortal finaliters are grouped in companies. But, the finality oath is administered individually. It is an oath of eternal importance. The oath of allegiance is only to the Paradise Trinity.

Urantian mortals attain:
1. *The Paradise Creator Son (and Creative Daughter)*. These are the Creator Parents.
2. *The Ancients of Days*. This is in the superuniverse.
3. *The Master Spirits*. This is in the central universe.
4. *The Supreme Being*. We attain the personality of the Supreme in the central universe.
5. *The Infinite Spirit*. The first Paradise attainment.
6. *The Eternal Son*. The second Paradise attainment.
7. *The Paradise Father*. The third Paradise attainment.

Ascending mortals are spirits of the first order in the minor sectors of the superuniverse. They advance to second-stage spirits in the major sectors. While progressing through Havona, they become third- and fourth-stage spirits. They become fifth-stage spirits when they find the Paradise Father. Upon taking the oath, that forever makes them a member of the Corps of the Mortal Finality, they become a sixth-stage spirit.

This is not complete. The pattern is sevenfold. There must be a seventh-stage spirit status. They have attained the present limit of spirit progression. They have not attained *finality of spirit status*. They have achieved the present limit of creature perfection. They have not achieved *finality of creature service*. They have experienced the fullness of Deity worship but not *finality of experiential Deity attainment*.

During this present age, we share in the unique experience of God the Supreme's evolution. Sometime in the eternal future, the evolution of the Supreme will become complete. It will be a fact of history. The opportunity to participate in this experience will have passed. New universes will not have this experience.

Already in the outer space levels, there are at least 70,000 gigantic clusters of matter. Each is greater than any one of the present seven superuniverses. At some point, they will be organized. At some point, they will be administered to and served.

Mortal Finaliters are perfected spirits. They have gone from the lowest material worlds to the spiritual heights of Paradise. Through experience, they know every step of the ascender's existence. They have been trained to the limits of their capacity. They know every detail of every divine principle. They are capable of just and efficient, as well as merciful and patient, administration.

It is logical to speculate that the seventh Corps of Finality is destined for future service in the universes forming in outer space. The Mortal Corps of Finaliters is the primary corps. What role we will have is not yet revealed. But, throughout the grand universe, we, the animal-origin children of time, are viewed as having a glorious destiny available to us.

# 21. Sonship with God

This chapter draws upon teachings from twenty-four different Papers in *The Urantia Book*. Most passages are not direct quotes. Many references are included for those who wish to further their study of the Urantia teachings.

Many orders of universe beings are created in dual phases. Among mortals, this difference is described as male and female. Among angels, the difference is described as positive and negative or aggressive and retiring. Material Sons are both the Adams and Eves. Eve is of the order of Material Sons.

The word sonship is not intended to be sexist. However, there is no appropriate English word that describes both sonship and "daughter-ship" with God. Sonship also means daughter-ship in these teachings. Males and females are equal in God's eyes. (see UB 150:1.3)

Never, even in the Corps of the Mortal Finaliters, will a mortal change so much as to wipe out the trends we call male and female. These variations will always continue to interest, stimulate, encourage, and assist one another. The pilgrims who were once men and women will aid each other in the Paradise ascent. They will always depend on cooperation to solve universe problems and overcome cosmic difficulties. (see UB 84:6.6)

The Supreme Being is also called the Universal Mother and Mother Supreme. (see UB 117:6) The Eternal Son is sometimes called the Original Mother Son. (see UB 7:6.7) And, the Infinite Spirit is called the Paradise Mother Spirit. (see UB 8:2.2) However, the masculine pronoun is always used—he, his, him. But God, the First Source and Center, is most often referred to as God the Father. It may seem confusing because we tend to think in terms of male and female rather than in the context of divine natures and relationships.

"God is the Father; man is his son." (UB 188:5.1) The love of a father for his son becomes the central truth in the relationship of Creator and creature. God is not a king who seeks justice or punishment of the evil-doing subject. God is really a Father.

If you are the 'subject' of a kingdom, then you are made to hear the law of the Universe Ruler. But, when you discover yourself, through faith, as a son, you do not see yourself as a law-subject creature of an all-powerful king. Instead, you know yourself to be a privileged son of a loving and divine Father. When God's will is your *law*, you are a noble slave subject. But when you believe in sonship, Father's will, becomes your will. Then you are elevated to the high position of a free child of God—a liberated son. (see UB 141:2.2)

A mortal child transfers his ideas of authority and power, from his parents, to God. His entire religious experience is shaped by this. It matters whether love or fear dominated his relationships. Slaves, for example, experienced great difficulty in transferring their master-fear into concepts of God-love. (see UB 92:7.11)

Many earthly parents are not conscious of the impact they have upon their children. Many do not realize that they set the stage for their child's relationship with God.

A young child is fully dependent on his parents and home life. From his parents and home life, he learns *all* his early concepts—intellectual, social, moral, and even spiritual. The family represents to the young child everything he can first know of either human or divine relationships. The child derives his first ideas of the universe from the mother's care. From his earthly father he gets his first ideas of the heavenly Father. The child's later life is made happy or unhappy, easy or difficult, based on his early mental and emotional life. He is shaped by these social and spiritual relationships of the home. A human being's *entire afterlife* is hugely influenced by what happens during the first few years of existence. (see UB 177:2.5)

But it is a reach for the children of time to conceive of the Father in eternity. A child can best relate himself to reality by first mastering the child-parent relationships. He will enlarge this concept. It will include the family as a whole. The growing mind will adjust to the concept of family relations—then to relationships of the community, the race, and the world. In time, he will understand relationships—of the universe, the superuniverse, even the universe of universes. (see UB 8:1.11)

Unfortunately, we live on a very dysfunctional world, as Part Two will explain. Some people cannot compare God to an earthly father. In such cases, it may be best to think of God as your divine Parent. (see UB 174:1.3) Whatever your highest concept may be, just know that God is even greater. And, the name you give to God is not important. God (the First Source and Center) has never revealed himself by name, only by his nature.

God deals with man, his child, based on the child's motivation—his purpose and intent. God does not base his relationship on our actual virtue or worthiness. (see UB 103:4.5) More and more we will love our Maker. We will give to God an affection like that given by a child to a *worthy* earthly parent. As a father, a real father, a true father, loves his children, so the Paradise Father loves his created sons and daughters. (see UB 2:5.9)

Some physical life memories die with the material brain. Memories without spiritual meaning or value do not last. They served as onetime scaffolding. They will no longer have a purpose. "But, personality and the relationships between personalities are never scaffolding." Mortal memories of relationships have cosmic value and *will* persist. (see UB 112:5.22) Therefore, it is important to understand our relationship to God and with God.

Mortals stand as the lowest order of intelligent and personal creation. We humans are divinely loved, and every one of us may choose to accept the certain destiny of eternal life. It is a fact that even such lowly material creatures as us are the sons and daughters of God. We are children "of grace and mercy, mortal beings belonging to the divine family." We are entitled to regard ourselves as being the sons of God. This is because a fragment of the Paradise Father indwells us. This makes us *directly* related to the divine Father of all the children of God. (see UB 40:6.8)

Every son of God shares the Fatherhood of God. And, the Father loves *each* of his sons. "That affection is not less than true, holy, divine, unlimited, eternal, and unique." It is a love given individually, personally, and exclusively. Such a love dominates all other facts. Sonship is the greatest relationship of the creature to the Creator. (UB 40:10.13)

God has descended as the Adjuster to become man's partner. The fragment of God, which indwells the mind of man, is the absolute assurance that man can find the Paradise Father in partnership with this divine Adjuster. Your Adjuster came forth from God to find you and sonship you even in your days of the flesh. (see UB 107:0.3)

To see God by faith means you gain true spiritual insight. "And, spiritual insight enhances Adjuster guidance." This, in the end, expands God-consciousness. (UB 140:5.13)

The great challenge to modern man is to achieve better communication with the divine Adjuster that dwells within the human mind. Man's greatest adventure in the flesh is in the well-balanced and sane effort to move the borders of self-consciousness out through the realms of soul-consciousness. Then, it is to make a wholehearted effort to reach the borderland of spirit-consciousness. Spirit-consciousness is contact with the divine presence. Such an experience is God-consciousness. It is the religious experience of knowing God. Such spirit-consciousness is the reality of sonship with God. Otherwise, sonship is the experience of faith. (see UB 196:3.34)

But, remember that sonship is a *gift*. No child has to *earn* the status of son or daughter. "The earth child comes into being by the will of its parents. Even so, the child of God comes into grace and the new life of the spirit by the will of the Father in heaven." Therefore, sonship must be *received* as by a little child. You earn righteousness—character development—but you receive sonship by grace and through faith. (UB 144:4.3)

A relationship cannot exist without some kind of communication. Prayer, even with its element of self-interest, is a means of communication—sharing your life with God. Through prayer, you may increase your God-consciousness. God-consciousness is awareness of the divine presence within you.

"Prayer is the sincere and longing look of the child to his spirit Father." It is the process of exchanging the human will for the divine will. Prayer is a part of the divine plan for changing 'what is' into 'what should be'. (UB 144:4.9) When we pray for help over the concerns in our life, many times the answer to our prayers is our own changed attitudes toward life. (UB 118:10.23)

When mortals first learned that prayers could not bully God, prayers then became petitions seeking favors. The truest prayer is a communion, closeness between man and his Maker. (UB 91:2.3)

The sincerity of any prayer assures it will be heard. However, the spiritual wisdom contained in a petition is important. It determines the time, manner, and degree of the answer. A wise father does not *literally* answer the foolish petitions of his ignorant and inexperienced children. Nevertheless, the children may derive much pleasure (and real soul satisfaction) from the making of such absurd requests. (see UB 146:2.6)

"Egoistic prayers involve confessions and petitions." Often, they "consist of requests for material favors." Prayer is a bit more ethical when it deals with forgiveness and seeks wisdom for improved self-control. (UB 91:4.3) Also, prayer is not a method of escape from conflict. It is "a stimulus to growth in the very face of conflict." "Pray only for values, not things." Pray "for growth, not for gratification." (UB 91:8.13)

Prayer is not a process of getting your way. It is a program of taking God's way. Praying teaches us how to recognize and do the Father's will. It is really true that, when your will is aligned with God's, you can ask anything thought of by that will-union, and it will be granted. (UB 180:2.4)

Words are irrelevant to prayer. Words are merely the intellectual channel used. "God answers the soul's attitude, not the words." (UB 91:8.12) When prayer seeks nothing for the one who prays or anything for his fellows, then such attitudes of the soul rise to the levels of true worship. (see UB 91:4.3)

To some individuals, prayer is the calm expression of gratitude. To others it is an expression of praise or devotion. Personal and spontaneous prayer is often the soul's expression toward the spirit. And, "prayer should be the communion of sonship and the expression of fellowship." Prayer, when prompted by the spirit, leads to cooperative progress. The ideal prayer is a form of spiritual communion leading to intelligent worship. "True praying is the sincere attitude of reaching heavenward..." (UB 144:2.2)

**Suggested Reading**

Urantia Book Paper 91, The Evolution of Prayer, is a short but enlightening Paper. Sections 4. Ethical Praying, 8. Praying as a Personal Experience, and 9. Conditions of Effective Prayer are especially helpful.

At the human level, prayers are most often a method of talking to God. In any relationship, it is equally important to listen. Meditation can be a form of listening. Meditation is a matter of quieting (relaxing) your body and mind. Healthy meditation, also called Stillness, requires nothing more than sitting quietly to allow God to work in a static-free mind. It is refreshing. It never leaves you feeling tired.

The contact of the mortal mind with its indwelling Adjuster is often favored by devoted meditation. However, loving service—unselfish ministry to one's fellows—more commonly aids it. (see UB 91:7.1) In today's hectic world, many people simply do not make the time to sit quietly to meditate. But loving service can have a similar effect.

The combination of meditation and relaxation opens your heart and mind. Meditation makes the contact of mind with spirit, even if you are not aware of it. Your ability to relax will determine your spiritual receptivity. It is not always easy to sit still and to relax. But, when such an effort is successful, it is an exchange. It is an exchange of weakness for strength, fear for courage, the mind of self for the will of God. And, that is worship. (see UB 160:3.1) "The reflective powers of the mind are deepened and broadened by worship. Prayer may enrich the life, but worship illuminates destiny." (UB 102:4.5)

The great difference between prayer and worship is that prayer has an element of self-interest, but worship is for its own sake. There is no element of self-interest in true worship. We simply worship God for what we understand him to be. Worship asks nothing and expects nothing. We do not worship the Father because of anything we may get out of it. We give devotion and we worship because we recognize the Father's loving nature and personality. (see UB 5:3.3)

The worship experience consists in the attempt of the Adjuster to communicate to the Father. He expresses the longings and desires of the human soul. Those hopes are the joint creation of the God-seeking mortal mind and the God-revealing immortal Adjuster. Therefore, worship is the material mind's cooperation, with the Adjuster's guidance, to communicate with God as a faith son. (see UB 5:3.8)

Worship is a personal communion with the very source of reality. Man seeks, unconsciously through worship, to *be* better and eventually the son attains the *best*. (see UB 196:3.19) Thus, it is fitting that in our prayers we ask to receive help to be our spiritual best, and to be a more loving and serving son or daughter. Consciously seeking to be your spiritual best will result in spiritual growth.

All growth is unconscious. Spiritual growth cannot be learned or lost, given or received. (see UB 100:1.7) We cannot will ourselves to grow on any level. Yet, we can develop attitudes and perspectives, as well as habits, which favor spiritual growth.

Although not a complete list, habits that favor growth and support your desire to be your spiritual best include: (see UB 100:1.8)

- Awareness that a fragment of God indwells you
- Living in partnership—in the conscious presence of God
- Awareness that your fellows are also indwelt by God
- Recognizing the value of your fellows—seeing others as God sees them
- Sharing your spiritual life with your fellows
- Problem-solving through prayer
- Reflective meditation on cosmic meanings and divine values
- Avoiding selfishness
- Loving service
- Refusal to presume on divine mercy
- Sincerity
- Sonship with God

"The Spirit never *drives,* only leads." Are you a willing learner? Do you want to attain spirit levels and reach divine heights? If you sincerely desire to reach the goals set before you, "then the divine Spirit will gently and lovingly lead you along the pathway of sonship and spiritual progress." (UB 34:6.11) The heavenly Father has lovingly provided for us. All we need to do is to accept, with grace, our rightful place in the Father's family.

# Summary of Part One

Congratulations! You have gotten through Part One, which is the most difficult. Part One began with the most important concept of the Thought Adjusters. It is the fragment of God within you that makes it possible for you to have an intimate relationship with God the Father. Your Thought Adjuster, combined with your free will choices, create your soul. And, it is your soul that can (and most likely will) live forever.

God the Father gifts us with the Thought Adjuster and spiritual personality. Our spiritual personality is gently pulled (as if attracted by a magnet) to the Father in Paradise. You now realize that it is a long, long journey to Paradise. The Father has an attainment plan for us, his ascending children. We, as evolutionary ascending beings, will someday attain perfection. We begin life as the lowest free will creatures but have a glorious destination full of adventure.

The Eternal Son attracts all spiritual realities like a magnet. He insures that all our true prayers and worship are received. The Eternal Son also has a plan. His plan is for descending beings. Descending personalities are those beings created in perfection or near perfection. Part Two will help you appreciate the contribution the Eternal Son makes in our lives.

The Infinite Spirit attracts all minds (and through him, we are gifted with mind). God the Infinite Spirit also has a plan. It is a ministry plan that supports both the ascension plan and the descending bestowal plan of the Father and the Eternal Son. It is the Infinite Spirit, through our Mother Spirit, that personally nurtures us. With your Adjuster and the personalities of the Infinite Spirit, you are divinely ministered to daily, even if you are not conscious of their assistance. How empowering to know how lovingly we are cared for!

We are taught that God the Father, Son, and Spirit are located in Paradise. Paradise is at the center of all Creation. However, God does not leave Paradise.

You may initially struggle with the teaching that God the Father and the Eternal Son produce Paradise Sons. The Infinite Spirit produces the Creative daughter Spirits, and this too may be hard to believe at first. But it is true that a Paradise Michael Son, with his partner, a Creative Daughter Spirit, left Paradise in order to create our local universe of Nebadon. Together, in time and space, they directly created our evolutionary universe and beings. Our planet, Urantia, is part of a system that is part of a constellation that is part of the local universe of Nebadon. Our direct, creative divine parents are Mother Spirit and Michael of Nebadon. They fully and perfectly represent God and this may account for part of our confusion.

As huge as Nebadon must seem, it is only a small part of Creation. Yet we are individually loved and nurtured. Every phase of creation is well organized and divinely ministered to according to needs. Every personality has purpose, potentials, and goals.

We have learned that the universe is teeming with life. We are all intertwined, destined to live loving lives of service to others. Most of the celestial personalities are encountered personally during our eternal life adventures. Eternal life is detailed, organized and surely seems exciting.

Even after attaining our destiny (God the Father), the adventure is not over. We will have earned a place in the Corps of Mortal Finality. By that time (as we understand time now) it is speculated that we will have an important role in the creation taking place in the outer space zones.

Part One closes with the chapter on sonship (daughter-ship) with God. Such a partnership is made possible by the gift of the Adjuster that indwells you. With the teachings of Part One, you are now prepared to understand the amazing history of our world and how it has shaped all of humanity. Part Two is much easier to understand. Happy reading!

# Part Two

## The Unfolding of Events
## That Shaped Our World

# 22. Development of Urantia
## *Celestial Activity*

*[Part Two of "Quivering on the Brink" is a timeline of activities on our world. Woven into this timeline are the known celestial activities that affected our world. These celestial activities are indented and italicized for clarification. –Mary Ebben Livingston]*

Urantia is of origin in our sun. Our sun comes from the Andronover nebula. Although large, Andronover is only a part of the local universe of Nebadon. The nebula was initiated about 875 billion years ago. The breakup and birth of our sun occurred about six billion years ago.

Three billion years ago, our solar system reached a level of stability. It is working much the same today as it was then. During that period, events were happening elsewhere in our local universe of Nebadon.

> *Almost one billion years ago, Michael embarked on his first bestowal mission. Michael gave a farewell broadcast to Nebadon. He said his elder brother, Immanuel, would take charge. Michael would be on an unexplained mission to do the will of the Paradise Deities. Only the Divine Minister, Immanuel, and Gabriel knew the nature and whereabouts of Nebadon's Creator Son. (from UB 119:1.2)*

> *Three days later, a broadcast from the Melchizedeks proclaimed the arrival of a strange Melchizedek. The arrival was not of their number but wholly like their order. The Ancients of Days had issued orders, agreed to by Immanuel. They requested that the new Melchizedek Son be received into their order. Further, he should be assigned to the emergency service of the Melchizedeks of Nebadon.*

> *Nothing showed in the Salvington records for one hundred Urantia years. The records then note the return and continuation of rulership by Michael. But, a record of the service of the unique Melchizedek Son is kept in a temple. The record includes 24 emergency missions performed by this Son. It certifies that this visitor, in the likeness of a Melchizedek, lived, worked, and faithfully performed all duties.*

> *The record ends by stating that he became the chief of Melchizedeks. He earned their love by his matchless wisdom, supreme love, and superb devotion to duty. "He loved us, understood us, and served with us, and forever we are his loyal and devoted fellow Melchizedeks." (UB 119:1.5)*

Our earth's crust began to stabilize about 850 million years ago.

> *About this time, trouble began with the protest of a System Sovereign called Lutentia. It involved a judgment passed by the Constellation Fathers and approved by the Faithful of Days. This System Sovereign was so unhappy with the verdict that he led a rebellion. It was against the Creator Son of Nebadon. When a new System Sovereign was requested, Michael left his headquarters sphere and gave authority to Immanuel.*

> *Three days later, a new and unknown member of the order of Lanonandek Sons reported. He had orders from the Ancients of Days and certified by Immanuel. The*

*orders requested that the new Son be assigned as acting System Sovereign to replace Lutentia.*

*No System Sovereign was ever more loved, honored, or respected. In justice and mercy, he set the troubled system in order. He ministered to all his subjects and even offered to share the system throne with Lutentia if only he would apologize to Immanuel.*

*Lutentia knew the strange System Sovereign was Michael. Still, Lutentia refused mercy. However, millions of his misguided followers accepted forgiveness. When the permanent System Sovereign arrived, all mourned the loss of the temporary Sovereign. All felt he was the noblest and kindest ruler ever known in Nebadon. They called him the Savior Sovereign.*

*At the good-bye party, Lutentia sent this message, "Just and righteous are you in all your ways. While I continue in rejection of the Paradise rule, I am compelled to confess that you are a just and merciful administrator." (UB 119:2.6)*

*Three days after this System Sovereign left, Michael assumed rule of Nebadon.*

Continents and oceans formed about 700 million years ago. This meant Urantia was nearing the right conditions for the support of life.

*About this time, the Life Carriers of another planet requested an acting Planetary Prince. This planet's Prince had defaulted when their System Sovereign went astray. This was the second such rebellion in all of Nebadon up to this time.*

*Michael placed authority in the hands of Immanuel. He then said good-bye to his partner, the Universe Mother Spirit. Michael vanished from the dispatching field of Salvington. He appeared unannounced three days later.*

*The mysterious Material Son was made the Planetary Prince of world 217. He worked alone for one whole generation on the isolated world of rebellion. He won the repentance of the defaulting Planetary Prince and his whole staff. He also restored the planet to the loyal service of the Paradise rule. Then a visible Material Son and Daughter arrived to the redeemed world. At that point, the emergency Planetary Prince took formal leave.*

*Three days later Michael was in his place on Salvington. Soon after, the superuniverse broadcasts carried a fourth announcement. It revealed the further progress of the sovereignty of Michael in Nebadon.*

It was 550 million years ago that the original life patterns were started on Urantia. This was done at the same time in three different water realms.

*Around this time, the universe broadcasts reported the unannounced arrival of an unknown seraphim. He had tested out as belonging to the supreme order of the angels. He was assigned to the corps of the teaching counselors. A teaching counselor is what we might call a private secretary. This counselor worked for 26 different master teachers on 22 different worlds. His last assignment was as helper to a Trinity Teacher Son. The Trinity Teacher Son was never sure as to the identity of his associate.*

*Throughout this era, all supreme seraphim were of special interest. Everyone knew that the beloved Sovereign was abroad in the universe; and he was disguised as a seraphim. Concerning angels, our Creator and Ruler is "in all points tried and tested in the likeness of seraphic personality." (UB 119:4.4)*

The change from vegetable to animal life happened 100 million years after the marine implants. This was about 450 million years ago. Sudden, but expected, changes would continue. Evolution was well planned.

Four hundred million years ago, vegetable and animal marine life was spread over the whole planet. These were single cell life forms. Then suddenly animals with many cells began to appear. They dominated the waters.

Over the next 90 million years, land elevations and sinkings occurred. This caused natural displacement of the waters. The land plants thus migrated farther and farther from the seashores.

*A little over three hundred million years ago, Michael passed universe affairs to Immanuel. Michael announced that he was going to Uversa. Uversa is the headquarters of our superuniverse. The Uversa broadcasts soon reported that an unannounced ascender had arrived. He was unnumbered. The pilgrim was of mortal origin from Nebadon. Gabriel of Nebadon accompanied the pilgrim. The report said that the ascender was a true spirit received into their fellowship.*

*The superb personality was called Eventod. He was the exact likeness of the spirit stage of an ascending mortal. He lived and performed his duties in common with his fellows. He proved worthy of the confidence and trust of his superiors. And, Eventod proved worthy of the respect and loyal admiration of his fellows.*

*Eventod advanced with a group of ascending mortals to Havona. There he met with the Ancients of Days and then immediately left Uversa with Gabriel. Soon Michael and Gabriel appeared on Salvington.*

*Michael was incarnating in the likeness of his various orders of universe beings. He started as the highest order of Melchizedeks. He would probably end with the lowest order, that of a mortal of flesh and blood. Speculation is made about the method of incarnation. It is amazing that a universe Creator can assume the personality, and live the life, of one of his own lower creatures. Nevertheless, it remains a mystery to everyone except the Sons who incarnate.*

Another 30 million years passed, (340 million years ago). The sudden appearance of the fish family occurred. That was followed by the sudden appearance of the fern family on land. As the fern family overran the land, the carbon dioxide levels dropped.

About 210 million years ago, land snails, scorpions, and frogs suddenly crawled out from the waters upon the land. Soon after, insects along with spiders, roaches, crickets, and locusts covered the land. Slowly marine life gave way to the second stage of evolution on land.

*About 150 million years ago, Michael made another announcement. He addressed the gathered residents of Salvington. Michael said that for his sixth bestowal he would assume the career of a morontia mortal of ascending status. He also stated his plans for his seventh and final bestowal. He would take the likeness of mortal flesh on some evolutionary world. Michael then left in full view of everyone. A seraphim and Gabriel went with him.*

*The morontia mortal, Michael, was known as Endantum. On all points, he was tested—just like his fellows from the material worlds of an entire constellation. Michael was the friend and caring helper of even the lowest form of created intelligence.*

*Salvington inhabitants knew when Michael would return. Millions of beings gathered in celebration. Many expressed appreciation for a Sovereign so very interested in his creatures. Michael replied, "I have simply been about my Father's business. I am only doing the pleasure of the Paradise Sons who love and crave to understand their creatures." (UB 119:6.5)*

Dinosaurs suddenly appeared. This was about 140 million years ago. Over a span of 25 million years, the dinosaur age peaked and faded. The dinosaurs had evolved into larger and larger creatures. They required enormous amounts of food. But dinosaurs lacked the intelligence to survive. Finally, when the land was so overcrowded by dinosaurs, they literally starved to death.

Suddenly, 90 million years ago, the trees appeared. Pines, redwoods and other trees replaced the fern forests. Twenty-five million years later, just as suddenly, the family of flowering plants mutated and spread over the world.

The evolutionary march continued. Fifty-five million years ago the first of the true birds suddenly appeared. From reptilian ancestors suddenly sprang the first of the early mammals. This was about 50 million years ago. They evolved to live on land, in treetops, in the air and under the water.

The more modern types of mammals began to make their appearance 30 million years ago. At that time, there suddenly appeared hoofed types such as the horse. Also, the early ancestors of the lemurs made their first appearance. By the close of this age, the ancestral forms of most living things were then alive. Changing climate and terrain continued the migration and adaptation of living things.

About one million years ago, there occurred three sudden mutations of the lemur type of mammal. (Today's lemurs are primates, a class of animals including monkeys, apes, and man. The lemurs of a million years ago resembled, but were not the same as today's lemurs.) They would become ancestors of the humans. North American lemur types of animals had migrated to Asia. Among their offspring, there suddenly appeared the dawn mammals.

Just seventy generations later, suddenly, a new and higher group appeared. These are called the mid-mammals. This was followed by the third sudden mutation. Finally, the Primates appeared.

The progressing Primates suddenly produced two human beings. They are the ancestors of mankind. Urantia was then registered as an inhabited planet.

# 23. The Establishment of the Human Races
## *Celestial Activity*

The ancestry of the human species came from early lemurs, as did the modern type of lemurs, gibbons, and apes. These early lemurs, now extinct, were ancestors to both species. We did not evolve from modern lemurs, gibbons, or apes. The direct ancestry of mankind took place in southwestern Asia. These early ancestors migrated to the Persian peninsula. The superior descendants of this early lemur type of mammal founded two great groups. One was the modern simian (monkey or ape) tribes. The other was the present-day human species. Man and ape are related only in that they sprang from the mid-mammals.

The two superior mid-mammals were twins, one male and one female. They were the direct animal ancestors of the first humans. These two primates stood erect and grew to a height of over five feet. They learned to communicate by signs and sounds, although they could not make the rest of their tribe understand them. Finally, when they were about 14 years-old, they fled from their tribe. They established a new species, the Primates, on the west coast of the Mesopotamian Peninsula.

From the dawn mammals, to the mid-mammals, until the two superior Primates, took about 21,000 years. Suddenly the first two humans were born. The birth of these twins occurred 993,475 years ago (from the year 2000). These two humans, a male and a female, had perfect human feet and thumbs. In appearance, they most closely resembled today's Eskimos.

New emotions developed such as respect and vanity. The emotions of worship, such as awe, reverence, gratitude, and humbleness, grew. Fear and lack of knowledge of natural events gave birth to primitive religion.

The twins learned to communicate verbally but could not teach much to their parents. One day, when about nine years old, they decided to live with and for each other, and to flee their tribe. Fear of displeasing their father and of being hunted down by their tribe postponed this decision, but they did make plans.

They were about 11 years-old when the plan to leave was realized. Just before leaving, there was a gibbon raid. Their mother was killed while protecting them. Their father arrived to defeat the gibbons, but the twins went through with their plan. They fled northward that very night. Their father was so heartbroken he refused to eat. He later wandered off into the forest where he was beaten to death by hostile gibbons.

*The Life Carriers watched this progress evolve. But before the planetary circuit could begin, the seven adjutant mind-spirits had to function. When the twins were 10 years-old, the spirit of worship made its first contact. When the final decision to flee was made, the spirit of wisdom began to function on Urantia. This was the establishment on Urantia of "mind of will dignity." Acknowledgment came from Salvington, Edentia, and Jerusem. The age-long supervision of the planet by the Life Carriers was ended.*

*The twins called themselves Sonta-an and Sonta-en. Sonta-an meant, "loved by mother." Sonta-en meant, "loved by father." Throughout Nebadon, they were known as Andon and Fonta. Andon means "the first Father-like creature to show human perfection hunger." Fonta means "the first Son-like creature to show human perfection hunger." But not until their time of Thought Adjuster fusion did they have the names Andon and Fonta bestowed upon them.*

Andon discovered the idea of fire from chips of flint on their northward journey. But not until the nights grew cold did they try to start a fire. For two months, they tried unsuccessfully to ignite pieces of wood. Then Fonta thought to use an old bird's nest as kindling. This discovery allowed them to defy the climate and forever made them independent of their animal relatives.

Andon and Fonta's first child was born about two years after leaving. They named him Sontad and wrapped him in protective coverings. Proper care for newborns set them apart from their animal ancestors. Nineteen children, almost 50 grandchildren, and six great grandchildren would be born in their lifetime. All of these Andonites (an'-don-ites) showed a clannish spirit, hunting together and living in semi-caves that interconnected.

It was at the age of 42 that falling rocks from an earthquake killed Andon, Fonta, five children, and 11 grandchildren. Sontad then assumed leadership of the clan with his wife, his eldest sister. For 20 generations this family of Andon and Fonta held together. However, food competition and social tension broke up the Andonites. And so, the descendants of Andon and Fonta moved westward. They established over 1,000 settlements in what is now France. For thousands of years they lived along the river Somme, camping near the edge of forests and streams. As the Ice Age descended south, their descendants had to live in caves for protection.

Over the next 10,000 years, Andonite culture and spiritual growth stopped. The hunger urge led to a form of animal worship by the Andonites. The early Hebrew animal sacrifices evolved. Later, the Christian doctrine of atonement for sin by the "shedding of blood" developed. Both of these practices came from the Andonites.

After 10,000 years, a leader named Onagar brought peace. He led the tribes in the worship of the "Breath Giver to men and animals." Onagar taught his new doctrines of one God and a life after death called the "Great Beyond." His people were the first to cook meat instead of eating raw flesh. But, this golden age of primitive man declined. It was at its lowest 900,000 years ago or roughly 100,000 years after the birth of Andon and Fonta.

Badonan was a great-great-grandson of Andon. About 850,000 years ago, his descendants wiped out their inferior neighbors. Those neighbors had mixed with the forest apelike creatures. They were more like animals than humans. The descendants of this improved Badonite stock were termed a new people—the Neanderthals.

The Neanderthals dominated the world for almost 500,000 years. They made tools of flint, were excellent fighters, and traveled far. They drifted, hunted, and fought, and overall made little progress. Their very primitive religion was based on horrible fears of natural forces such as clouds, mists, fogs, and especially the dark. When the moon shone, they managed their fear. But on moonless nights, they would panic and sacrifice their best tribes-people to persuade the moon to shine again. And, human sacrifice long persisted even though the purpose changed.

About 500,000 years ago, there were about one hundred superior Badonite families. These Neanderthals lived in the northwestern highlands of India. One of these families was the Sangik (san'-gick) family. They suddenly began to bear unusual children. Their children had very high intellects. But what was so different was that they turned various colors when exposed to sunlight. They became the ancestors of the six colored races of Urantia.

*On other evolutionary worlds, the events are different. There is a usual sequence. First, the red man evolves. Ages later, one by one, the remaining five colored races make their appearance. Then, the first will-creatures, the Andon and Fonta of the planet, appear. And then, the Planetary Prince and his staff arrive. Urantia however has proved to be very unusual. Our Andon and Fonta evolved first. Then, the six evolutionary races appeared at the same time and in one family. Then, the arrival of our Planetary Prince occurred half a million years after the appearance of human will.*

Of the 19 children in the Sangik family, five were red. The red peoples were remarkable and, in many ways, superior to Andon and Fonta. They were the most intelligent group. They established a tribal civilization and government, and they did not practice plural mating. They unfortunately became weakened from fighting among themselves. They also did not get along with their yellow brethren in Asia and were driven out.

About 85,000 years ago, the almost pure red race migrated to North America. A decline in intelligence and spiritual culture followed. They would have become extinct from tribal wars except for the appearance of a great spiritual leader, Onamonalonton. He brought peace and revived the worship of God, the "Great Spirit." Many of his descendants are among the Blackfoot Indians. But, again, tribal wars prevented the establishment of a great civilization. When the white man discovered North America, the red man would not serve and could not rule. When two races do not blend, one of them is doomed.

Of the Sangik family, two children were orange. The orange people were builders; they loved building anything and even built up huge mounds of stone just to see which tribe could build the biggest mound. Porshunta was their wisest leader. He lived about 300,000 years ago. The orange people lived along the Nile until killed off by the green people almost 100,000 years ago. The green and indigo people absorbed the survivors.

Four of the Sangik children were yellow. The yellow people had a brotherly spirit. They also developed farming-based homes and communities. They entered a period of great spiritual darkness until about 100,000 years ago. Then a brilliant leader named Singlangton proclaimed the worship of the "One Truth." The survival of the yellow man in modern China is due to their being one of the more peaceful nations of Urantia.

Two of the Sangik children were green. One of the less progressive groups was the green race. They had a cultural leader named Fantad early in their establishment, who led them in worship of "The One Source of Life." Their later migration from the highlands of India into three areas greatly weakened them. Those that went to Africa destroyed their almost equally inferior orange cousins. Both races had leaders with giant strain characteristics, many being eight and nine feet tall. Most of the giant strain green race were in Egypt and later blended with the indigo race.

Four of the Sangik children were blue. The blue people had the intelligence of the red man and the soul and sentiment of the yellow man. They were most responsive to the Planetary Prince's staff and were thrown into confusion and turmoil when the Lucifer rebellion occurred. Fortunately, about 500 years later a great teacher named Orlandof led many tribes back to the worship of the true God known as "Supreme Chief." Later they were upstepped again by the descendants of Adam and Eve who preferred the blue people to the other persisting colored races. The artifacts from the Old Stone Age are those of the blue race. Today's white races are descendants of the blue people, slightly mixed with the yellow and red people.

Two of the Sangik children were indigo. The black people, last to migrate, took over Africa. Except when taken as slaves from time to time, they remained. Because they were isolated like the red man, neither received the benefit of mixing with the descendants of Adam and Eve. Orvonon was a great spiritual leader and enlightener of the indigo peoples. He taught about the "God of Gods."

Thus was the founding of the human species nearly a million years ago and the birth of the evolutionary colored races about half a million years ago.

# 24. The First Epochal Revelation on Urantia

At the same time as the appearance of the six colored races, the Planetary Prince and his staff arrived. This was about five hundred thousand years ago. There were almost half a billion primitive humans scattered over Europe, Asia, and Africa back then. Headquarters for the Prince and his staff was set up at the center of world population in Mesopotamia.

Our Prince was named Caligastia (cal-ah-gas'-chah). He was a Lanonandek Son of the secondary order. Caligastia had served as a personal staff member of Lucifer, our System Sovereign. While working for Lucifer, he completed five assignments of honor and trust. No other Planetary Prince had richer experience. Caligastia was well prepared for this assignment. Urantia was thought to be fortunate. We were getting an experienced and brilliant mind.

Caligastia repeatedly sought a commission as a Planetary Prince. Several times he was not approved. He was finally assigned to Urantia. He had earned a record of loyalty and devotion that was enviable. However, he did have a restlessness about him. And, he had a tendency to disagree in minor matters about established order. Caligastia was secretly falling in love with himself. He was developing pride.

As usual, a corps of assistants and aides came with the Prince. Prince Caligastia had an assistant that was second in command. He was named Daligastia (dal-ah-gas'-chah). The headquarters was named Dalamatia (dal-ah-may'-shah) in honor of Daligastia.

Of the planetary staff, the members known as the Caligastia One Hundred were the most fascinating. Over 785 thousand ascendants in Jerusem applied for the mission. Caligastia chose one hundred for the Urantia mission. Each chosen member was from a different planet of origin. None was from Urantia.

The One Hundred arrived by seraphic transporters. The Life Carriers had an extracted portion of life plasm from fifty human males and fifty human females. The life plasma (DNA) represented the best strains of the Andon and Fonta descendants. The DNA was transferred into the bodies built for the Caligastia One Hundred. From the time of arrival, the creation of special bodies with the human DNA, until consciousness, took exactly ten days.

The One Hundred morontia ascenders were given human bodies for the mission. The process is called repersonalization. A great deal of our mythology comes from the repersonalization of the One Hundred. But legends became garbled over time. Even one hundred years ago, people did not know about DNA and so the term "life plasma" is used in the Urantia Papers. Imagine how mysterious it must have been half a million years ago for primitive man to explain what happened.

The corporeal (celestials in material bodies) staff of fifty men and fifty women were more or less human. They embodied the DNA of one of the human races—the Andonites. However, they ate a vegetarian diet while the evolutionary races were entirely meat eating. The Caligastia One Hundred did help change the diets of the races of Urantia.

The staff was of dual nature. Their bodies were in part human but they were also attuned to the life circuits of the system. The life currents of the system circulated through their material forms and prevented aging and death. The energy that came from the system circuits was derived from the fruit of the Tree of Life, sent from Edentia.

The fifty human men and fifty human women were all Andonites. When they donated their human plasm, or DNA, they were modified. Their bodies were adjusted to the life currents of the system. Thus, by eating the fruit from the Tree of Life they would live without aging along with the staff. The fruit from the Tree of Life however, was of no value to any of the other humans.

The Caligastia One Hundred were immortal, or undying. The normal plan for a mission like theirs required them to live on Urantia for thousands and thousands of years. Not until mankind advanced and a new age began would another Son of God arrive. Upon completion of their mission, they would each resume their journey to Paradise. Each of the One Hundred had volunteered, gone through the intense selection process, and had been trained for the mission.

The Caligastia One Hundred had been given material bodies. They were able to produce a new order of physical beings. But they were instructed not to do so except under certain conditions. They followed their instructions and did not have physical sex. However, they did explore every phase of mind and soul contact. During the thirty-third year, two of the staff discovered a soul relationship. They claimed it was non-sexual and non-physical. It resulted in the first primary midway creature. The staff and celestial beings could see the midway creature. But, the Midwayer was invisible to normal humans. Caligastia told his corporeal staff to produce more Midwayers. In the end, the original corps of fifty thousand primary Midwayers was created.

The Caligastia One Hundred were organized into the following ten councils: (UB 66:5)
1. The council on food and material welfare
2. The board of animal domestication and utilization
3. The advisors regarding the conquest of predatory animals
4. The faculty on dissemination and conservation of knowledge
5. The commission on industry and trade
6. The college of revealed religion
7. The guardians of health and life
8. The planetary council on art and science
9. The governors of advanced tribal relations
10. The supreme court of tribal coordination and racial cooperation

Each trusted commission was to advance their area slowly. And, they were very wise. They trained the best people of the nearby tribes. Upon request, they sent them back to their people as emissaries of social uplift. It is a mistake to rob mankind of their evolutionary growth. Even though primitive religion and morals take ages to obtain, it is progress. The Caligastia One Hundred knew the arts and culture of Jerusem. Nevertheless, such knowledge was nearly valueless on a barbaric planet. Superior beings must avoid upliftment of the backward races by over-teaching.

Slavery to tradition can produce a stable setting. However, it can also suppress the ideas and inventions of people. All of Urantia was deadlocked by tradition until the Caligastia One Hundred arrived. The One Hundred taught individual initiative within the social groups.

There was one great task to achieve. They wanted to transform man slowly from a hunter to a herder. Then the hope was that man would later evolve into a peace-loving, home-abiding farmer. The process of uplifting the social customs of the peoples of Urantia involved their relationship with superior minds with a higher culture. It was slow but effective. "Their motive was progression by evolution and not revolution by revelation." (UB 66:6.6)

And, for three hundred thousand years, they slowly worked.

# 25. Failure of the First Epochal Revelation
## *The Lucifer Rebellion*

Caligastia had been the Planetary Prince of Urantia for three hundred thousand years. He was assisted by Daligastia, many celestial hosts, the Caligastia One Hundred and their modified human associates.

Lucifer was the System Sovereign. Satan was his first assistant. Lucifer was planning to announce his "Declaration of Liberty." This was about two hundred thousand years ago. At that time, Satan made one of his inspection calls to Urantia. He informed Caligastia of Lucifer's plan. Prince Caligastia knew what he was doing and he agreed to side with Lucifer. He would betray Urantia upon the announcement of rebellion.

To understand the rebellion, it helps to know the difference between error, evil, sin, and iniquity. (see UB 67:1.5)

- Error is misunderstanding. It suggests a lack of mental sharpness.

- Evil is a lack of wisdom. Evil results in poor decisions, unbalanced thinking, judgments, and actions. Both error and evil are unintentional.

- Sin is a conscious choosing to oppose spiritual progress. It is *knowing* what God's way (God's will) is, but choosing to do otherwise. Sin is spiritual poverty.

- Iniquity is persistent sin. It is sin that has become a habit. It denotes a loss of control. The personality will disintegrate as it reaches cosmic insanity.

Those that chose to join the rebellion committed grievous sin. Some of Lucifer's followers would repent. However, many, like Lucifer, Satan, and Caligastia, would become iniquitous.

Soon after Satan's inspection, Caligastia had a long talk with Daligastia. The two called a meeting of the ten councils. It was announced that Caligastia would proclaim himself absolute sovereign of Urantia. All the groups were told to turn over their functions and powers to Daligastia until they reorganized.

Van was chairman of the supreme council of coordination. He convinced everyone not to participate in this act of rebellion. Van planned to appeal to Lucifer. He did not know Lucifer was behind the rebellion. The council leaders were shocked when the orders from Lucifer came back. The orders appointed Caligastia as sovereign ruler of Urantia. And, the orders demanded absolute loyalty to Caligastia.

Van then gave a seven-hour speech. In it, he formally charged Daligastia, Caligastia, and Lucifer of rebellion. They were standing in contempt of the universe of Nebadon. Also, Van appealed to the Most Highs of Edentia for support and confirmation.

Meantime, without warning, the system circuits were cut off. Urantia was isolated! Now Van was cut off from all outside counsel and advice. This was due to the magnificent being, Lucifer. He had issued his manifesto in Jerusem. Because of his manifesto, all incoming, outgoing, and interplanetary broadcasts stopped in the system of Satania.

*Stated in the Lucifer Declaration of Liberty was:*

*(1.) The reality of the Paradise Father: Lucifer charged that the Paradise Father was a myth. He claimed that the Paradise Sons invented the First Source and Center so that they could control the universes. He said God the Father did not exist and the finaliters were conspiring with the Paradise Sons. Basically, he said that God was a hoax—a big lie—and all who claimed to have seen the Father were liars.*

*(2.) The universal government of the Creator Son Michael: Lucifer agreed that Michael was his Creator-father. However, he claimed that Michael had no right to rule Nebadon in the name of an imaginary God. He declared that the planets should rule themselves. Further, Lucifer attacked the Ancients of Days because they did the executions. He said that eternal life was certain, except for the executions.*

*(3.) The attack on the mortal ascension plan: Lucifer attacked the whole plan of mortal ascension. He claimed that too much time and energy went into carefully training mortals. Besides, Lucifer claimed, mortals had a destiny that was a made-up story. He said that ascenders should enjoy the liberty of individual free will and not have to do all that training.*

*Satan then proclaimed Lucifer the "friend of men and angels" and the "god of liberty." Planetary Princes were promised supreme rule if they sided with Lucifer. They could join the local system's confederation. The new confederation was organized by Lucifer and directed by Satan.*

*Michael sought the advice of his Paradise brother, Immanuel. After their meeting, Michael announced he would follow the same policy he had used with the other two system rebellions in the past. He would maintain an attitude of non-interference.*

*Gabriel then took command of the loyal beings of Satania. This was on behalf of the Creator Son, Michael, whose authority had been challenged. Gabriel served on the Jerusem sphere dedicated to the Father. He displayed the emblem of the Trinity government of all creation. It is three azure blue concentric circles on a white background.*

*There was a terrible war in heaven. Not a physical war for this was much worse—eternal life was in jeopardy. Various personalities journeyed to hear Lucifer in the planetary amphitheater and then to hear Gabriel; they went back and forth until they arrived at a final decision. And, each being was free to choose.*

*It was over two years of system time before Lucifer's successor was appointed. Thirty-seven Planetary Princes committed their worlds to the Lucifer cause. Lucifer and his followers were dethroned. They lost all governing powers. However, they were permitted to go freely about the system, even to the planets. The last time Lucifer and Satan were present on our world was when they joined together to confront the Son of Man. Not until the completion of Michael's final bestowal was the Lucifer rebellion ended in Satania. Then, the first steps of the hearing of Lucifer's case began.*

Seven crucial years passed after the planetary circuits were severed. Van assembled the faithful. Out of fifty thousand Midwayers, only 9,881 remained loyal. These loyal Midwayers faithfully guarded their new settlement for Van. The settlement was east of Dalamatia and it had no walls for protection. The loyal group had possession of the priceless Tree of Life and it needed to be guarded.

Of the Caligastia One Hundred, only forty remained loyal, including Van. From the one hundred modified Andonites, fifty-six remained loyal. These ninety-six beings were allowed to eat from the fruit of the Tree of Life. Their altered human bodies would last indefinitely.

Prince Caligastia was a traitor. He led the disloyal rebels on Urantia. The sixty rebel members of the Caligastia One Hundred chose Nod as their leader. Realizing that without the Tree of Life they were doomed to extinction, Caligastia ordered them to start sexually reproducing. Their descendants were known as the Nodites (nod'-ites) and their dwelling place was called the land of Nod.

For seven long years, Van waited without word. His unshakable loyalty to the universe government was the result of the following:
- clear thinking
- wise reasoning
- logical judgment
- sincere motivation
- unselfish purpose
- disciplined character

Further, Van had an unquestioning dedication to the doing of the will of God.

The outstanding human hero of the rebellion was Amadon (am'-ah-don). Amadon was a male descendant of Andon and Fonta. He gave his DNA to the Prince's staff. Amadon was Van's human assistant. Amadon had no universe experience and a minimum of intelligence. Caligastia was brilliant, experienced, and highly intelligent. Yet, Amadon resisted all of the false teachings of Caligastia.

Finally, a council of twelve Melchizedeks arrived. The immortal beings who were loyal, except Van and Amadon, were taken to Jerusem. The loyal Andonite mortals (not DNA donors) became known as Amadonites (am'-ah-don-ites). They were led by Van and Amadon. The descendants of the Amadonites were a biologic upliftment. Moreover, these Amadonites furnished leadership for the world.

Van and Amadon were sustained by the Tree of Life They, along with the council of twelve Melchizedeks, remained on Urantia for over 150,000 years.

*These narratives (Urantia Papers) were presented in 1934. At that time, the first hearing in the case of Gabriel vs. Lucifer took place. Since Michael's final bestowal, Lucifer had been detained on a prison world of Jerusem. When the case opened, Satan joined him.*

*Also, at the time of Michael's bestowal, Caligastia was judged but left free on Urantia. Caligastia has no power over any human unless they really want to be cursed with his sinful presence. The faithful child of God has nothing to fear from Caligastia.*

*It has been about two thousand years of our time since Michael's bestowal. While it may seem as if the case against the rebels has dragged on, recall that one thousand years of our time is only one day of Paradise-Havona time. Thus, it has been slightly more than two days since Michael left Urantia and Lucifer's hearing began.*

Liberty must be understood in order to realize the impact of the Lucifer rebellion.

- Uncontrolled self-will and self-expression is pure selfishness.

- False liberty leads to the unjust power over others.

- No being has the right to deny any other being the right to love and be loved, the privilege of worshipping God and of serving his fellows.

- No being has the right to deny another being the prerogatives of will and the potentials of personality.

Lucifer and his followers put their selfish wills against the eternal purpose of God's will. In doing this, Lucifer and his supporters tried to deny mortals their free will choice and their experience of attaining the Father.

The rebels were allowed to roam the entire system to promote their doctrines of discontent. In spite of that, no Satania worlds were ever lost since the fall of the thirty-seven. Not even younger worlds peopled since the day of rebellion were lost. (see UB 53:7.15)

Caligastia "sold us out." We, along with the other rebellious planets, were placed in isolation more than 250,000 years ago. This was to protect the loyal worlds from contamination. We cannot begin to know what it must be like to have free, open planetary communication with the rest of creation. We can only speculate what it must be like to have the circuits open.

As a planet, we share the effects of the choices Prince Caligastia made. This is similar to experiencing the results of decisions made by the President of our country. We do not get credit or blame for the choices of others. We are personally responsible for our own choices. While our planet may be in isolation, we as individuals are just as loved, cared for, and ministered to as always.

# 26. Information on the Lucifer Rebellion

**The Lucifer Rebellion –**
**The third and last rebellion in the local universe of Nebadon**

| System of Satania information regarding the Lucifer rebellion | | | |
|---|---|---|---|
| Origin & Other Information | Total Number | Number remaining loyal to Michael | Number joining Lucifer rebellion |
| System Sovereign—Lucifer | 1 | | 1 – initiated system-wide rebellion in Satania |
| Planetary Princes | Potentially 1,000 Existed 619 | 582 worlds remained loyal in the system | 37 – Planetary Princes committed their worlds to rebellion |
| **World of Urantia information regarding the Lucifer rebellion** | | | |
| | | Remained Loyal | Joined Rebellion |
| Planetary Prince—Caligastia | | | Committed Urantia |
| Caligastia 100 | 10 councils | | |
| Van—Court of Coordination - Leader of loyal men, Midwayers, and angels | | 10 | 0 |
| Nod—Industry and Trade - Leader of rebels | | 0 | 10 |
| Ang—Food and Material Welfare | | 4 | 6 |
| Bon—Animal Husbandry | | 0 | 10 |
| Dan—Animal Conquest | | 0 | 10 |
| Fad—Education | | 6 | 4 |
| Hap—Revealed Religion | | 10 | 0 |
| Lut—Health | | 0 | 10 |
| Mek—Arts and Sciences | | 10 | 0 |
| Tut—Tribal Government | | 0 | 10 |
| 100 modified human associates (Amadon being the human hero) | | 56 | 44 |
| Primary Midwayers | 50,000 | 9,881 | 40,119 |
| Secondary Midwayers (after Adam and Eve) | 1,984 | 1,111 | 873 |

# 27. The Interim - Evolution Continues

Mortal will creatures are termed primitive men up to the arrival of the Planetary Prince. Then a new dispensation begins. On *normal* worlds, this is the era when government appears on earth. A high state of civilization develops during this time.

The primitive world has an evolved religion of fear and ignorance. The first revelations of higher truth and universe organization are presented to them. Religion makes progress slowly. Revelation is given in steps or stages. It then is marked by evolutionary growth. However, this is not the age of 'The Prince of Peace.'

Racial struggles and tribal wars continue. This leads to intense nationalism. National life begins to replace tribal groups. It is a slow advancement but very normal.

The great social achievement of this age is the emergence of family life. This includes the realization of sex equality. These two factors are preliminary to the fuller realization of the ideals of home life. Also, the age of agriculture, supportive of home life, makes its appearance. An achievement of this age is to promote the increase of the higher types of mortals and curb the lower. "But life on an inhabited world is so changed by rebellion that you can have little or no idea of such a regime on a normal planet." (UB 52:2.1)

Van and Amadon stayed for over one hundred and fifty thousand years after the Lucifer rebellion. The policies of the twelve Melchizedeks were faithfully carried out by Van. This is how the remnants of civilization were preserved.

Within a thousand years following the rebellion there were over three hundred advanced groups of Andonites. They were slightly mixed with the Sangik races and Nodites. These groups were scattered throughout the world.

- The Andonites were the first human race—the aborigines. "Amadonite" is a cultural and religious description. In view of race, the Amadonites were Andonites.
- The Sangik races were the six colored races from the same family.
- The Nodites were descendants of the rebel members of the Prince's staff—the rematerialized beings that received the human life plasm (DNA), but became mortal after the rebellion. They comprised the eighth race of Urantia. "Nodite" is both a cultural and racial term.

|   | RACE CALLED | BACKGROUND |
|---|---|---|
| 1 | Andonites | The Andonites were descendants of the first two humans, Andon and Fonta. They are the aborigines or original evolutionary humans. |
| 2 | Red Man | |
| 3 | Yellow Man | |
| 4 | Blue Man | The Sangik family (Andonites) gave birth to the colored races. |
| 5 | Indigo/Black | |
| 6 | Orange Man | |
| 7 | Green Man | |
| 8 | Nodites | Sixty of the staff and 44 of the DNA donors that were modified joined the rebellion. They lost their immortal status. Their leader was Nod, their descendants, Nodites |

After the destruction of Dalamatia, the Nodites divided into three groups. One group remained near the Persian Gulf. Another group migrated east of the Euphrates Valley. The third group went west to the Syrian shores of the Mediterranean Sea. The Nodites freely mixed with the Sangik races. Some of their descendants later joined Van and his loyal followers north of Mesopotamia near Lake Van. These Nodites and Amadonites (followers of Van and Amadon) were among the "mighty men of old"—they were the most advanced and cultured peoples on earth.

The chief task during this period is to foster natural evolution. This work with the human race continued slowly. Finally, Urantia was ready for the dispatch of a Material Son and Daughter.

---

### Suggested Reading

Papers 68 through 71 of *The Urantia Book* describe the evolution of civilization, culture, education, industry, nationalism, and government. These insightful papers give a detailed account of how and why mankind evolved to our recent stages. Approximately 40 pages, they are a wonderful background and contrast to Paper 72, "Government on a Neighboring Planet"

# 28. The Second Epochal Revelation
## *Celestial Activity*

The physical (biologic) stage of the Urantia peoples evolved normally. However, cultural decadence swiftly followed the Lucifer rebellion. Spiritual poverty was a concern. Van and his associates preached the coming of a Son of God. He would be a racial uplifter and a teacher of truth. He would also be a worthy successor of the traitorous Prince. However, the majority of people did not care or have any interest in this teaching.

Van and Amadon had gathered over three thousand willing workers. The volunteers were dedicated to preparing for the expected Son. This was eighty-three years before the arrival of Adam and Eve.

It took three years to select the site that would become the Garden of Eden. It was a long narrow peninsula, almost an island. The connecting area was only 27 miles wide. The peninsula projected westward from the eastern shores of the Mediterranean Sea. The next two years were spent moving the world's cultural headquarters, including the Tree of Life, to the new site.

The Garden was to be a park of floral beauty and grandeur. Animals were kept on the mainland and any meat for the workers was brought over. Never were animals slaughtered in the Garden. The plans for Eden provided land, homes, and other buildings for one million people. Administrative buildings were to the north. To the west would be the schools. To the south were built homes for the volunteer workers. And, "east of Eden" homes were built for the promised Son and his offspring. At the center of the Garden of Eden was the exquisite stone temple for worship of the Paradise Father, and Van planted the Tree of Life in the middle of the temple.

Even when only one-fourth complete, the Garden was impressive. It had thousands of miles of irrigation ditches. There were over twelve thousand miles of paved paths and roads. Over five thousand brick buildings existed. And, there were so many trees and plants they were beyond counting. The sanitary rules kept the water pure. Waste was buried until they later set up a sewage disposal system. Not until the nineteenth century did mankind again have such advanced health methods.

*All of the senior Material Sons and Daughters applied for the Adamic adventure on Urantia. The Adam and Eve chosen had worked in the testing labs of Jerusem for fifteen thousand years. They directed the division of applied energy to changes in living forms. Prior to this work, they had been teachers in the Jerusem citizenship schools.*

*The couple was examined and instructed. They were made aware of the duties of rulership on such a strife-torn world. They each took oaths of allegiance to the Most Highs of Edentia and to Michael of Salvington. In the beginning, they would be subject to the Melchizedeks on Urantia. The Melchizedeks would decide when to turn over rulership to Adam and Eve.*

*Adam and Eve had one hundred children. The children went with their parents to the headquarters of their order. There, Adam and Eve would go through a process that would dematerialize them. The seraphic transports cannot serve material beings and that is why this process is in place.*

*The children rejoiced that their parents would be the visible rulers of Urantia—planet 606 in the system of Satania. The children said good-bye and wished them divine speed. Adam and Eve then fell asleep in the personality lapse of consciousness. The seraphic transports then embraced them for the trip.*

At noon and unannounced, the seraphic transports settled slowly to the surface. They landed near the temple of the Paradise Father on Urantia. This was 37,914 years ago (from the year 2000). Ten days passed before the rematerialized Adam and Eve regained consciousness at the same time. They awoke in the temple and were greeted by Van and Amadon.

Adam and Eve were the founders of the violet race. They would not begin the program of racial upliftment until their own family reached one-half million pure offspring. The job ahead of them was a difficult one. Thousands of people would come to see them over the next few months. Still, Adam and Eve felt isolated and lonely. They missed the usual broadcasts and the normal planetary exchanges. On a normal world, they would have worked with the Planetary Prince and his staff. Instead, there was broadcast silence and a fallen Prince making their work difficult.

By the end of the first week, the excited people had decided that Adam and Eve were really gods worthy of worship. Adam explained the orders of divine sonship and that they were to worship no one but God. It became the custom to worship the Father in the temple the seventh day of the week; this was the origin of the Sabbath day.

After seven years, the Melchizedeks turned over world affairs to Adam. They then returned to Jerusem. Things went fairly well inside the Garden. However, when Adam and Eve tried to improve the outside world, they met opposition. The people outside of Eden were savages. They were barbarians and barely civilized human beings. Caligastia opposed Michael and the normal care that humans received. He had his own wicked plans and was a problem for everyone. Adam tried to warn against Caligastia but it was very difficult. Caligastia and his followers were invisible to the people. They did not really understand the warnings.

Adam and Eve had initiated and taught the people inside the Garden about many, many things:
- prayer and worship
- sex equality
- home life
- health and sanitation
- trade and commerce
- social and civil codes of behavior
- education

And, their school system was unsurpassed!

After 117 years, (four generations), their family numbered 1,647 pure-line Adamites. Progress seemed impossible outside of the Garden. The humans outside of Eden were in spiritual darkness. Their minds and morals were at a low level. Moreover, they spoke hundreds upon hundreds of different local languages. These people were wholly unprepared for unity. The idea of the brotherhood of man would have no meaning to them. (from UB 75:1.3)

It is doubtful that any other Adam and Eve of Nebadon faced such a difficult mission. Yet, success was a matter of settling down to the long, long test of endurance. But both grew impatient, especially Eve. It was through Eve's impatience and Adam's errors of judgment that they departed from the ordained plan. They quickly brought disaster upon themselves and hindered the progressive growth of all Urantia.

# 29. Default of the Second Epochal Revelation
## *Celestial Activity*

Eve had been instructed before the Urantia mission of the dangers ahead. She had been warned not to stray from the side of her mate. Caligastia visited Adam and Eve often but they, and their children, were not swayed by the ideas of compromise or short cuts. However, Caligastia did not give up. He decided to stop working on Adam and to lay a trap for Eve, the mother of the violet race. Caligastia would use certain Nodite members, namely Serapatia (sair-ah-pah-tay'-shah) and Cano.

Serapatia became leader of the alliance of Nodite tribes about the time Adam had finished his first one hundred years in the Garden. Serapatia was honest, sincere, and very impressed with Adam's work. He gave his full support to Adam's program. The majority of his people then followed, and Adam and Eve were greatly pleased with this progress.

Serapatia never knew Caligastia was using him for his sinful plans. Soon Serapatia was on the commission of tribal relations. He met with Adam and Eve—especially Eve—to discuss plans for improvement.

One day Serapatia had an idea while talking to Eve. The Nodites were the most progressive and cooperative race. If a leader was born to them that was part origin in the violet race, then they would have a powerful tie binding them to the Garden. He believed this would be the best thing for the world and that it would be real progress. Under such conditions, Serapatia would see progress in his own lifetime. These plans secretly grew for over five years. At last, Eve agreed to a secret meeting with a Nodite leader named Cano.

Cano was extremely handsome. He had a brilliant mind. He was supportive of both the Adamic and Serapatia plans. Further, he was the sincere spiritual leader of the near-by colony of friendly Nodites. Before Eve quite realized what was happening, and being influenced by the charming Cano, she agreed to go through with the Serapatia plan. Eve added her own impatient ideas and support to the more far-reaching divine plan. Eve consented and had sexual relations with Cano; she conceived a child.

Adam knew something was wrong as soon as he saw Eve. He soon heard the whole story from Eve of the Serapatia plan, which was then operating with the divine plan. Eve had agreed to join in the practice of good and evil.

"Good" was carrying out the divine plan according to their oaths of trust. "Evil" was the twisting of plans resulting in conflict and planetary confusion. Adam understood the whole situation the moment he heard what happened. He had only pity and sympathy for his erring mate. Eve was truly pathetic as the realization of default swept over her.

Adam could not bear the thought of serving alone on Urantia. Thus, the next day he looked for Laotta (lay-oat'-tah). She was the talented Nodite woman who was head of the Garden schools. Adam then purposely made the same foolish choice Eve had made. Adam, in his love for Eve, deliberately chose to share the same fate as his mate.

When the people in the Garden heard what had happened to Eve they went wild. They declared war on the near-by colony and killed every man, woman, and child. Cano, the father of the unborn child, Cain, which Eve carried, was also killed. Serapatia was so overcome by guilt and fear that he drowned himself in the river.

Adam wandered alone for thirty days, which was unbearably painful for Eve. Their children tried to comfort her but not knowing where Adam was, or what had happened to him, was terrifying for them all. Adam returned to make plans for their future although he was not sure of the nature of their offense.

It was seventy days from the default of Eve, when the Melchizedeks returned to take back rulership over the world affairs of Urantia. Adam then knew they had failed, but he did not know what would happen—how they would be judged. Still there were more problems.

News spread of the killing of the Nodites in the near-by colony. Other settlements were preparing to attack the Garden. Adam, Eve, their children and twelve hundred faithful followers left the Garden to find new homes.

Three days later, their caravan was stopped by seraphic transports from Jerusem. It was declared that Adam and Eve's children who were under the age of twenty would be taken to Edentia as wards of the Most Highs. Those over the age of twenty could choose to stay on Urantia with their parents or go with the younger children. Two thirds chose to go to Edentia as wards of the Most Highs. Adam and Eve, who had begun their mission with such high hopes, who had left the Garden in disgrace, would have to continue with the loss of more than three-fourths of their children.

While the caravan was stopped, Gabriel appeared. He announced that the Planetary Adam and Eve of Urantia had been judged. Adam and Eve were in default for violating their agreement of trust as rulers of Urantia. Because of their default, they became mortals.

Adam and Eve would live out their lives as a man and woman of Urantia. Adam and Eve were greatly relieved to have been judged in default rather than in contempt or rebellion of the universe government. Had they only had more patience, they would have been eventually successful.

*Soon after the default, it was announced that Michael had chosen Urantia for his final bestowal. All eyes watched the small but highly honored world of Urantia. Our planet was to be where Michael would take the most dangerous step in his career.*

# 30. The Second Garden

The land between the Euphrates and Tigris Rivers (today it is mostly Iraq) became home to the second garden. While on the journey, Laotta died giving birth to her daughter, Sansa. Eve, who was stronger, survived the birth of Cain and raised Sansa with her son.

Abel was the first child born to Adam and Eve in the second garden. He often reminded Cain that Adam was not his father and the boys grew to hate one another. One day when Abel was 18 years old, he infuriated the 20-year-old Cain so much with his taunts that Cain turned and killed Abel.

When Adam and Eve learned what had happened, they supported Cain's decision to leave the garden. Cain thus went to the land of Nod and married Remona, his distant cousin. The Serapatia plan for a uniting of the Adamites and Nodites was somewhat realized. Cain brought great peace in his lifetime between the surrounding tribes.

Adamson was the firstborn child of the first Garden. He had chosen to remain on Urantia with his parents after the default. However, his mate and their thirty-two children had decided to go to Edentia. Adamson and twenty-seven followers moved from the second garden to start a new settlement.

Adamson married Ratta, the last descendant of two of the fallen staff of the Planetary Prince. They gave origin not only to a great line of world leaders but also to the secondary midway creatures. Every fourth of their offspring was of a unique order. There were sixteen of these children and they were often invisible to mortals. They lived and died as mortals. However, the sixteen children gave birth to 1,984 secondary Midwayers who live on and on but do not reproduce.

Of the secondary Midwayers, 873 failed to align themselves with the rule of Michael. There were 1,111 loyal and trusted Midwayers. They will continue to serve until our planet enters the final stages of Light and Life.

The remaining children and descendants of Adamson and Ratta are called the Adamsonites. They maintained a high culture for nearly seven thousand years. They fostered great civilizations in Greece, Mesopotamia, Europe, and India.

Adam and Eve also had a son named Seth born in the second garden. Seth was born one hundred and twenty-nine years after Adam and Eve arrived on Urantia. He was dedicated to improving the spiritual status of the Adamites. Seth became the head of a new priesthood called the Sethites. Sethite priests worked in the areas of religion, health, and education. They led religious services, worked as physicians, were sanitary inspectors, and taught in the garden schools.

Seth's son, Enos, started the new worship services. Seth's grandson, Kenan, trained the missionaries that went near and far. The Sethite priesthood of the garden was outstanding. Their religious concepts of God and the universe were advanced. For their time, their health practices were excellent. Their teaching methods have never been matched. But it would be a mistake to confuse the Sethite priests of the garden with the later moneymaking, dishonorable priests of the later tribes and nations.

Adam and Eve missed their deported children and the first Garden. Nevertheless, this magnificent and noble couple faced their situation with grace. They greatly advanced the people in culture and mental growth. They laid the groundwork for art, science, literature, architecture, health, and religion. Their education methods were the best.

The Urantia races received only a small portion of Adamic heritage due to the default. Even so, the physical uplift was substantial. The DNA of the founder of the violet race, (the ninth race), mixed with the best strains of the Nodites, comprised the Andite race.

Adam and Eve had made serious errors in judgment. Nevertheless, they did not deliberately sin or rebel. They often thought, and were comforted by, the only personal message they received from Michael. In part, Michael had said that he had given careful thought to the circumstances of their default. He remembered the desire of their hearts to be loyal to the Father's will. Then Michael said that they would "be called from the embrace of mortal slumber" when he came to Urantia if they had already not been called. (UB 76:5.3)

Even though they were not clear about the full meaning of the message, they always taught that a Son of God would sometime come. They truly hoped that the world of their blunders, Urantia, would be the world selected by the Paradise bestowal Son. If that were the case, then Urantia would turn out to be the most fortunate and envied planet of all Nebadon.

Eve died of a weakened heart at the age of 511 and Adam died 19 years later. Three days after Adam's death, they and 1,316 others from the first Garden were resurrected. They had left Jerusem as Sons of God but they returned as sons of man—ascending mortals. They have been assigned as two of the twenty-four advisory councilors who now serve on Urantia.

# 31. The Interim - After the Second Garden

The second garden was in truth, artificial. This was because it did not evolve slowly or naturally. The culture of the violet race was dependent on Adam's presence. When Adam died, their civilization was doomed to fall to the levels of the surrounding peoples.

The second garden was the center of civilization for about thirty thousand years. It was located in Mesopotamia that is now mostly Iraq. However, it also includes parts of (NE) Syria, (SE) Turkey, and (SW) Iran. Various centers of culture existed from the times of Adam. For the main part, outside of these centers, Urantia suffered in savagery.

Around 19,000 B.C. the Adamites were a nation of about four and one half million people. The violet race kept their peaceful traditions. When they became overpopulated, they did not go to war to get more land. It was their practice to send excess citizens as teachers to other races.

Migrations and racial blending of the Adamites set the world stage for the Andite era. The Andites were the pure-line violet race mixed with the Nodites and evolutionary man. The Andites had one-eighth to one-sixth DNA from Adam. They were the best humans to appear on Urantia since the pure-line violet people. The Andite age lasted about nine thousand years, until around 6,000 B.C.

As the pre-white Andites united more and more with the Nodites, they grew militant. Peaceful migration grew to become actual conquests. These Andites would later be called the Aryan conquerors of India.

Smaller groups of Andites journeyed to India, China, Japan, northern Africa, and the Pacific Islands. But migration drained the biological reserves of their homelands. This ended up strengthening the surrounding peoples. Wherever the Andites went, they gave the people art, music, humor, and manufacturing. They were experts with animals and farming. Their presence usually improved the religious beliefs and moral practices as well.

One hundred and thirty-two Andites left Japan in a fleet of small boats. They reached South America and were the ancestry of the later rulers of the Incas. These Andite sailors also biologically altered the native groups of the Pacific Islands. Easter Island was long a religious and administrative center of one of the lost groups.

The Andites poured out of Mesopotamia from 8,000 to 6,000 B.C. They were forced out by the hill tribes to the east and the plainsmen of the west.

- Sixty-five percent spread over Europe. They blended with the newly appearing white races that were a mix of the blue men and earlier Andites.
- Ten percent, including many Sethite priests, moved to areas of Iran and Turkestan. Turkestan is now called Turkmenistan. Iran is west of Iraq where the second garden was located. Turkmenistan is north of Iraq to the east of the Caspian Sea.
- Ten percent went northeast to Sinkiang, which is a large region of China. They mixed with the earlier Andite yellow inhabitants.
- Another ten percent went across Saudi Arabia and entered Egypt.
- The last five percent of the Andites had avoided marriage with the surrounding tribes. They refused to leave their superior culture at the mouth of the Euphrates and Tigris rivers. They were a small minority and the last of the Andites in Mesopotamia. They became known as the Sumerians.

The age of the higher culture of the second garden ended as the inferior surrounding stocks infiltrated. In the end, the northern barbarians conquered the Andites in Mesopotamia.

The Andites passed from the pages of history. This was due to the migration of their superior people who merged with their inferior neighbors. Yet, remnants of the Garden culture persisted and can even be found today.

---

### Suggested Readings

Are you curious as to how we got "from there to here?" Urantia Paper 81, "Development of Modern Civilization" answers this question well.

Some of the best read and insightful papers are the marriage and family papers, Papers 82 through 84.

The religion papers (85 through 92) are very intriguing. All eight of these papers are presented in 60-82 pages depending on which edition of *The Urantia Book* you use. (Both publishers have identical words but the formats differ.) You may find that the things you knew from the heart take shape and fit better into your growing understanding.

Reading these papers (81-92) will give you an in-depth understanding of the history and events that brought us to modern times.

---

## Quick Overview of the Ten Races of Urantia

| | RACE CALLED | BACKGROUND |
|---|---|---|
| 1 | Andonites | The Andonites were descendants of the first two humans, Andon and Fonta. They are the aborigines or original evolutionary humans. |
| 2 | Red Man | |
| 3 | Yellow Man | |
| 4 | Blue Man | The Sangik family (Andonites) gave birth to the colored races. |
| 5 | Indigo/Black | |
| 6 | Orange Man | |
| 7 | Green Man | |
| 8 | Nodites | The Caligastia One Hundred served on the Prince's staff. They were ascendant beings given physical bodies with Andonite DNA. They had super bodies because they also ate from the Tree of Life and were immortal. Sixty of the staff and forty-four of the DNA donors that were modified joined the rebellion. They lost their immortal status. Their leader was Nod and their descendants were called Nodites. |
| 9 | Adamites Violet Race | Adamites were the pure-line descendants of Adam and Eve. |
| 10 | Andites | Andites were the mix of Adamites and Nodites. They became known as Sumerians. But, early Andites, with a lot of Nodite DNA, became militant. They were called the Aryan conquerors of India. Later, they also mixed with evolutionary man. The "white man" was a mix of Adamites, Nodites and the Blue Man. |

# 32. The Third Epochal Revelation

After the default of Adam and Eve, the human races continued to make intellectual progress. However, they slowly lost spiritual ground. Revealed truth was threatened with extinction. Worse, the concept of God had grown hazy by about 3000 B.C.

The Melchizedeks knew of Michael's planned bestowal but they did not know when it would happen. They asked that some provision be made to preserve the light of truth on Urantia. They were told that it was their responsibility. One of the twelve planetary counselors then volunteered. He is called Machiventa (mack-ah-ven'-ta) Melchizedek.

Machiventa would personalize on earth as a temporary man of the world. This had only been done six times in all the history of Nebadon. But, the Salvington authorities granted permission. Machiventa was incarnated near the city of Salem. Salem would become known as Jebus, and then later as Jerusalem. It was 1,973 years before the birth of Jesus.

No human witnessed the materialization of Machiventa as a full-grown man. He then simply entered the tent of a nearby shepherd. He must have shocked the man when he said, "I am Melchizedek, priest of El Elyon, the Most High, the one and only God." (UB 93:2.1)

Within a few years, Melchizedek had a following of pupils, disciples, and believers. He organized his schools at Salem to teach revealed truth. But to the majority of students, Edentia was heaven and the Most High was God.

Machiventa wore an emblem showing three concentric circles. The circles stood for three aspects of the Paradise Trinity—infinite, eternal, and universal. The students believed the emblem stood for the three kingdoms of men, angels, and God. Even the convert Abraham believed the symbol stood for the three Most Highs of Edentia who acted as one. Nevertheless, no effort was made to change these beliefs. Most students were not taught beyond the fact of the rulership of the Most Highs of Edentia.

Some, though, were taught the more advanced truth of the local universe. And still, to a few, Melchizedek taught even higher truths. To his brilliant disciple, Nordan the Kenite, and his students, he taught the truths of the superuniverse and of Havona. Melchizedek also taught the superuniverse truths to Katro and his family, whom he lived with for more than thirty years. And, these truths were passed on, even to the days of their famous descendant Moses. Melchizedek taught in line with each student's ability. All the same, they were always taught the doctrine of one God, a heavenly Creator, a divine Father. He prepared the people for the appearance of Michael, teaching that another Son of God would come but that he would be born of a woman.

Machiventa's teachings of the one God, the Father of all, were further stressed to Abraham. Abraham was taught that God would accept man on the simple terms of personal faith. And, when Michael appeared on earth, he confirmed all that Melchizedek had taught.

The worship ceremonies of Salem were simple and basic.
- Belief in El Elyon, the Most High God and only Paradise Father
- Acceptance that the Most High God gives favor to faith not to sacrifices or burnt offerings
- The promise to obey the seven commandments of Melchizedek
- To tell the good news to all men

But then, even this was too much and too advanced for most of the men of those days. For too long they had believed man was born under penalty to the gods. They believed that sacrifices and gifts were the only way to get forgiveness from God. It was beyond their understanding that salvation was a gift. However, Abraham did believe, at least halfheartedly.

Abraham attended the Salem school at three different times. He finally became a convert and one of Melchizedek's most brilliant students. It was not by chance but by choice, that Salem was selected for the appearance of Machiventa. There were many factors such as trade, travel, and civilization. But, contact with favorable families was quite important. Favorable families would likely have children that would become leaders. Terah, the father of Abraham, proved this to be true. In this respect, Abraham may be regarded as chosen.

Terah and his family learned of Melchizedek from a teacher in Ur. Ur was a Sumerian city-state in ancient Mesopotamia. It was located in what is now a modern city in Iraq. Once a coastal city near the mouth of the then Euphrates River on the Persian Gulf, Ur is now well inland.

After the death of Terah, Abraham and his brother, Nahor, were invited to come to hear the Salem truths. They were told that in their enlightened offspring the entire world would be blessed. Nahor decided not to go but Lot, Abraham's nephew, went with his uncle to Salem.

Abraham and Lot lived in the hills near Salem where they could set up a defense against the northern raiders. On a trip to Egypt for supplies, Abraham worked for a distant relative on the throne. Abraham was the commander of two military operations. He and his wife, Sarah, lived at court but gave up those honors to return to his more spiritual work in Salem. But Abraham was military-minded. It was with great difficulty that Melchizedek stopped Abraham from rounding up the nearby tribes with the sword—so that they might more quickly learn the Salem truths!

Melchizedek had set up peaceful relations. He allowed only a defense policy for Salem. When he would not approve Abraham's schemes for conquest, Abraham went to Hebron. There, Abraham launched a military capital. Hebron, Israel was located about twenty miles south of Salem.

Abraham was greatly feared by the surrounding petty kings. He played on their fears, waiting for a chance to attack. His excuse came when it was said that some of the rulers raided the property of his nephew, Lot, who lived in Sodom. After his attack and victory, Abraham became leader of a confederation of tribes. Eventually, the king of Sodom also joined the Hebron military alliance.

Abraham was well on his way to having a powerful state in Palestine. However, the thought that he had no son to succeed him began to worry him. He talked to Melchizedek who convinced him to give up his scheme of material conquest. Melchizedek encouraged him to rule in favor of the spiritual kingdom of heaven. Melchizedek explained that the backward tribes were killing themselves with their foolish practices. He said they would be so weakened that the greatly increased descendants of Abraham could easily overcome them.

Abraham believed Melchizedek and made a formal covenant. It stood for the agreement between divinity and humanity.
- God agrees to do *everything*.
- Man agrees to *believe* God's promise.
- Man agrees to follow God's instructions.

Man had believed that they were saved only by works—sacrifices and offerings. Now Melchizedek again brought the good news that salvation—favor with God—was to be had by *faith*.

Abraham's name at birth was Abram. After the birth of his own son, Isaac, Abram publicly changed his name and accepted the covenant. He took over the civil and military leadership of Salem. He improved the temple and provided new tents for the school. Abraham also improved the herds and dairy operation. Further, he contributed to the better handling of the Salem missionaries. Abraham was not overly religious. However, he was a shrewd and able businessman. Abraham was completely sincere and he believed in Machiventa Melchizedek.

Melchizedek trained missionaries. They went out from Salem, Mesopotamia, and Lake Van to remote regions of both Europe and Asia. Some even reached the British Isles, Iceland, and Japan. But, the tribes were backwards. Except in Palestine, the truth of one God never claimed a whole tribe or race. The new teachings were absorbed in the older beliefs, superstitions, and magical practices. But, new revelation is always tainted by the older evolutionary ideas.

# 33. Termination of the Third Epochal Revelation
## *Celestial Activity*

Soon after the destruction of Sodom and Gomorrah, Machiventa Melchizedek decided to end his bestowal on Urantia. There were many reasons for this decision. Mainly, it was that he was becoming more and more regarded as a demigod. The nearby tribes and even his associates were starting to reverence him with superstitious fear. Melchizedek had plainly told his followers that he must sometime leave just as he had come. But they were not prepared. One night he said good night and went to his tent. By morning, he was gone. His celestial fellows had taken him.

The Salem schools nearly disappeared. Abraham never fully got over the loss of Melchizedek. He left Salem and soon made converts. However, the beliefs became tainted by superstitions. Their practice of sacrificing first-born sons was nothing that Melchizedek taught.

Even so, Abraham became a great spiritual leader who was respected by all tribes and honored by all kings. Before his death, Abraham arranged with his brother, Nahor, a wife for his son Isaac. Abraham died confident in his faith in God, which he had learned from Melchizedek in the vanished schools of Salem.

Joseph, Abraham's great-grandson, was a firm believer of the Melchizedek traditions. He also believed in the later teachings of Abraham and Isaac. Nevertheless, it became harder for each generation to accept the teachings. Yet, the traditions of Salem were what Moses built upon when he led the Hebrews out of Egypt.

Within five hundred years, many thought the whole story of Melchizedek and his teachings was a myth. The full records of those days seemed impossible, even fantastic. The later Hebrew priests and scribes did not believe the accounts either. Their massive editing of the Old Testament led to many distortions. Talks between Abraham and God were really talks between Abraham and Melchizedek. Contacts with the "angel of the Lord" were really visits with Melchizedek. The ages of Abraham and his only wife, Sarah, were changed to make Isaac's birth miraculous.

The Jews, as slaves in Babylon, felt inferior as a nation. In order to overcome this, they swung to the other extreme. They claimed themselves the chosen people of God. They destroyed or changed their records. They raised Abraham and their other leaders high above all others; this included Melchizedek. In doing this, they lost sight of Melchizedek's teachings of the promised bestowal Son. Few of their descendants were willing or able to receive Michael when he came to earth as Jesus of Nazareth.

*Machiventa Melchizedek returned to assume his career as one of the twelve councilors of Urantia. For nineteen centuries, he worked with the many prophets. His goal was to keep the truths of Salem alive until Michael's bestowal.*

*After the triumph of Michael on Urantia, Machiventa was re-assigned. He served as one of the twenty-four directors of Urantia working on Jerusem. Recently he was raised to the position of personal ambassador of the Creator Son. He was given the title of Vicegerent (deputy) Planetary Prince of Urantia.*

# 34. The Spread of Melchizedek's Teachings

Many noble men and women spread the teachings of Melchizedek. They reached the entire Eastern Hemisphere. They were the most eager and aggressive missionaries of any religion on Urantia. The Salem missionaries preached the one God of Melchizedek, the Most High of heaven, and of salvation through faith. However, there were distortions of the original teachings. Superstitions, old rituals, and dogmas altered the teachings. Sacrificial ceremonies went on to undermine the teaching that by faith we are saved. Around six hundred years before Michael's bestowal, the problem had become severe. Melchizedek's mission might have been in danger of failing.

The teachings spread but in 600 B.C., Urantia had an outstanding century. It happened because Melchizedek, acting with other spirit agencies, was able to work with the humans of those times. Great religious, moral, and philosophic teachers marked the period. These teachers were all over the civilized world. And, through these teachers, the Melchizedek teachings were revived.

In China, Lao-tse was a man of great spiritual vision. He taught that Tao was the One First Cause of all creation. He understood the Trinity concept and God's eternal purpose. He presented the doctrine of returning good for evil. He also compared true faith to the attitude of a little child. The teachings of Lao-tse were later perverted into the beliefs of "seeing, doing, and thinking nothing." Yet, he never taught such error. Today, Taoism has very little in common with the concepts actually taught by Lao.

Also in China during that time were the teachings of Confucius. His writings were really the wise sayings of ancient philosophers but he put morals in the place of magic. Confucius was extreme though, regarding order and respect for ancestors. Today his writings are the basic moral fabric of culture for nearly a third of the world.

In India, the Vedic cult of many gods was coming under the direction of the Brahman teacher-priests. They merged the Salem teachings with the idea of a Father-Brahma as the source of all gods. However, they would never accept the teaching of salvation through simple faith. To combat the new teachings, the Brahman priests changed their Rig-Veda and later the Vedas. The Rig-Veda was one of the most ancient of sacred books. By doing this, they established their rituals of worship and sacrifice. Their religion became so tainted with superstition and ritual that it has the widest range of theology ever devised by man.

Self-focus and the perpetuation of self, led to a belief in an endless round of incarnations. This doctrine of reincarnation held that souls could return as man, beast, or weeds. This was followed by the invention of the doctrine of eternal escape. To escape from self, one must achieve absolute union with Brahman. Brahmanism was replaced by Buddhism, which later became the basis of Hinduism.

In time, there was a return to the Vedas and the Hindu theology. Hinduism is tolerant toward other religions. It claims Buddha and Christ are incarnations of Vishnu. The Hindus rejected the teachings *about* Jesus. They saw those teachings as a foreign "white man's religion." There is a great need today for the portrayal of the Jesusonian gospel—the teachings *of* Jesus. The framework and structure are present in India for the original gospel. The dogmas and doctrines are what make it a Western religion.

Gautama Siddhartha was born in Nepal, India. He put together the theories that later grew into the religion of Buddhism. His teachings removed all grounds for superstition, magic rituals, and fear of ghosts or demons. His teachings did away with the practice of salvation through physical pain, sacrifice, and priests. He taught the best godless philosophy ever invented by man. The disciples of Siddhartha called him "the enlightened one, the Buddha."

The great weakness of Buddhism is that it never led to a religion of unselfish social service. A low-caste civil ruler named Asoka, endorsed Buddhism. He was remarkable. Over a 25-year period, Asoka trained and sent out over seventeen thousand missionaries. This made Buddhism the dominate religion of one-half of the world. Buddhism lives today because it promotes calmness, self-control, and happiness.

In Europe, the Cynics maintained the purest form of the Salem teachings. Their beliefs were later worked into the newly forming Christian religion. The Jewish soldiers who fought in Europe also spread much of the Salem doctrine. Jewish theology, Greek philosophy and Christian ethics all stemmed from Melchizedek's teachings.

When the Salem missionaries reached Greece, they found the traditions of Adamson and the Andites. These teachings had become greatly tainted by the inferior slaves brought to Greece. The Salem teachings were then nearly destroyed by the Hellenic barbarians that arrived. Their beliefs were the basis of the Greek mythology that lasted a thousand years. The Salem teachers had influenced the Hellenic people; no priesthood ever arose in Greece. When mythology died out, the Greeks were without a national religion and no priesthood to foster one.

In the sixth century before Christ, the Greeks made outstanding progress. Greek morals, ethics, and philosophy advanced far beyond the God concept. However, the imbalance between intellectual and spiritual growth was as harmful to Greece as it proved to be in India. The Greeks did not realize that "true religion is the cure for soul hunger, spiritual disquiet and moral despair." (UB 98:2.2)

Too few of the Salem missionaries made it to Italy. Those that did were unable to overcome the spreading priesthood. The priesthood there had a new galaxy of gods and temples, which became the Roman state religion. This religion of the Latin tribes mostly consisted in forms, vows, and taboos. It was doomed to collapse because it was more patriotic than religious.

The mystery cults followed in both Greece and Rome. This was possible because they had no real religion and the common people craved salvation. The most devastating mystery cult was the Mother of God sect. It had its headquarters in those days on the exact spot of the present church of St. Peter's in Rome.

Ikhnaton was a young, remarkable king of Egypt. He swung his whole nation from the belief in many gods to the Melchizedek teaching of El Elyon, the One God. He outwardly worshipped the sun god. But he taught his followers a religion of a personal relationship between man and the Father of all. His concepts of Deity were far above the later Hebrew concepts. His ideas failed because they were not nationalist, which the people of those times demanded. The greatest weakness of his doctrine was that it was too advanced since only the educated of Egypt could understand it. Upon his death, the priests returned to power and destroyed most of his writings. But, twelve of the Old Testament Psalms were actually written by Ikhnaton, not by Hebrews.

In Iran during the sixth century before Christ, Zoroaster taught about the Seven Master Spirits. He had learned these teachings in Ur, Mesopotamia. His religion was one of action rather than rituals. He dared to battle with evil, inaction, and backwardness. The Jewish beliefs of heaven, hell, and devils derived from his teachings. Iranian priests revived the ancient worship of Mithras for a while. It coexisted for some time with Judaism and Christianity. Both Judaism and Christianity were influenced by the teachings of Zoroaster. Through them, Islam was also influenced by Zoroaster.

The Salem missionaries did not always flourish. Their teachings failed to take root in the Arabian Desert. Arabian families and clans worshipped their own gods. There were scattered beliefs throughout the desert. The only thing that brought the people together was the strange respect they had for the black Kaaba stone in a temple in Mecca. The Islamic religion was built upon this common point of interest. Their religion has two weaknesses. One lies in their use of military force to further their religion. The other lies in their degradation of women. Their strength is their clear presentation of Allah as the one and only Deity.

Machiventa Melchizedek incarnated as the priest of Salem. One of his goals was the eventual spread of the idea of one God. Another equally important purpose was to prepare the people for the bestowal of Michael, Son of that one Paradise God.

# 35. The Development of Judaism

Factually, the Hebrew religion is based on the covenant between Abraham and Melchizedek. The Jews and Arabs that came from the Arabian Peninsula settled in the Levant. The Levant included Lebanon, Syria, Jordan, and Israel. And, these people were called Kenites. In terms of evolution, the Hebrew religion adopted the creed of the Kenites in Palestine. The Kenites were influenced by:

- Moral teachings from Egypt
- Religious thought from Babylon
- Concepts of good and evil from Iran

Thus, it was through the Hebrews that all of these religious thoughts and ideas of morality were later passed to the Western world.

Semites were tribes who spoke a language in the same language family. The Babylonians, Canaanites, Hebrews, and Arabs were among the people called Semites. The Semites were among the most blended peoples of Urantia. They had hereditary factors from almost all of the world's races.

The early Semites believed that a spirit indwelt everything. They thought the spirits should be feared and worshipped. Yahweh was one of thousands of their nature gods. Yahweh was also associated with the Sinai volcano of Mount Horeb. Various versions of Deity endured. At different times, the Semites and immediate descendants of Abraham worshipped both Yahweh and El Elyon. After the days of Melchizedek and Abraham, certain tribes of Semites, because of their unusual religious beliefs, were called the children of Israel. Later they were called Hebrews, Jews, and the "chosen people."

Abraham's offspring formed the nucleus of the later Jewish people. However, they were not the ancestors of the Semites. Neither were they ancestors of the vast majority of people who formed the clans of Israel who chose to follow Moses as the children of Abraham.

As time passed, there was confusion of terminology. The Semites disliked speaking the name of their Deity. They used many names such as The Most High, The Ancients of Days, The Creator of Heaven and Earth, The Lord, Angel of the Lord, The Lord of Hosts, Lord God of Israel, The Spirit of God, The Almighty, The Holy One, and The Father in Heaven. The name Jehovah was not used until 1500 A.D. and was used as the completed concept of Yahweh.

Among the more educated of Egypt, there was a tinge of the El Elyon concept of Melchizedek's teachings. The Hebrew captive slaves practiced the old Yahweh ritual of magic and sacrifices. They hardly had a religion worthy of a name because they did not have a true concept of God. Following their escape from Egypt, this downcast, ignorant group of humans learned of a Supreme Creator. Moses was their great leader, teacher, and organizer.

Moses' mother was of the royal family of Egypt. His father was a Semite liaison officer between the government and the captives. It was their common belief in the Melchizedek teachings that brought about this unusual marriage. Moses cast his lot with the people of his father and negotiated peacefully for the freedom of his fellow Semites. The king agreed to let them return to the desert. They agreed to maintain friendly relations with the Pharaohs. They also agreed not to join any alliance against Egypt. The king broke his agreement. He claimed his spies had discovered disloyalty among the slaves. About a year later, the Egyptian military was fighting both Libyan and Greek invasions. Moses then led his followers out of Egypt in a spectacular night flight.

Moses had been taught the Melchizedek teachings from his parents. But his followers knew little about these teachings. By the time they reached Mount Sinai, Moses had made an enlarged concept of Deity. He wisely decided to proclaim his expanded concept as that of his people's olden tribal god, Yahweh. Moses felt cursed as he tried to teach his new and higher idea of Deity to the ignorant slaves. The ancient term Yahweh had always been represented by a golden calf.

After their third week's stay, Mount Sinai erupted. This allowed Moses to impress upon his people that their God was mighty, terrible, fearful, and all-powerful. Their limited understanding made it necessary to speak of God as being in man's image. Moses portrayed God as subject to anger, wrath, and severity. Yahweh was seen as being influenced by man's conduct. Yahweh, under the teachings of Moses, became the God of Israel. They, his followers, became the chosen people. Later, after the Jews in Babylon were freed, the God of Israel became the God of all nations.

The Hebrews had no written language at the time of the exodus, and it was more than a thousand years after Moses' death that the traditions were recorded; even then, very little of his great work is on record. It was sad how Moses tried to instill his sublime concepts of El Elyon, the Most High, to the ignorant Hebrews. He feared to present the mercy of God. Instead, he awed his people with the fear of God's power, justice, and revenge on the disobedient.

Before Moses died, he turned over the command of the Hebrews to Joshua. He desperately tried to hold the concept of a supreme Yahweh in their minds. However, by the time the Hebrews reached the fertile lands of Palestine, they were regressing. They almost lost sight of Moses' higher teachings. They almost lost their chance to be the group who conserved the Melchizedek teaching of one God until the time of Michael's bestowal. The long line of spiritual leaders from Moses to Malachi did what no others had done. They converted their deity concept into Yahweh as a Father. Yahweh may not have been the Father of the individual, but at least he was the Father of their race.

Samuel was the first of the Hebrew prophets. He came from a long line of Salem teachers. He was devoted to turning Israel back to the worship of the supreme Yahweh of Moses' time. He withstood almost total opposition. Samuel was only able to win the service of the more intelligent half of the Hebrews. The other half continued in the worship of their tribal gods and lowest concepts of Yahweh.

Samuel's greatest gift was the teaching that Yahweh was changeless and perfect. He taught that Yahweh was not subject to whims and was not like a repenting man. Yahweh became a changeless Creator and director of all creation. For the first time since Moses, they heard comforting promises for the humble and poor. These downtrodden people began to take hope. They began to believe that they could improve their spiritual status with the changeless Yahweh who kept his promises.

In the tenth century before Christ, the Hebrew nation divided into two political groups. They differed in their attitude toward land. One group believed in Yahweh and the other in the Baal cult, but it was not a religious dispute. It was about land. The southern, wandering Arabians looked at land as a gift from Yahweh that could not be sold or mortgaged. The northern, settled Canaanites freely bought, sold, and mortgaged their lands.

Baal meant "owner" and the Baal cult promoted the right to own and sell land. In addition, Baal was supposed to be the god of land fertility who sent rain and the favor of good crops. The Canaanites (Baal worshipers) owned houses, lands, and slaves and lived in the cities. Each Baal had a sacred place, priesthood, and a "holy woman." From the land issue, there were social, economic, moral, and religious disputes.

The prophet Elijah shifted the Yahweh-Baal issues from the land to the religious views. He made a moral issue out of the olden land practices and began a campaign against the Baalites. Baals were many and Yahweh was one; the one God won out over the many. Elijah restored the northern kingdom to the concept of God as it had been in Samuel's time. Elisha followed next and he kept those religious practices as well.

Amos was also a leader who followed Elijah. He further raised the concepts of God. He dared to denounce the immoral acts of the northern tribes in Palestine. Crimes, getting drunk and oppressing others was not acceptable. The Hebrews heard that Yahweh would not accept sin in their lives (the chosen people), any more than he would accept sin from any other people. He proclaimed Yahweh the "God of all nations." Amos saved the doctrine of the supreme Yahweh. He thus furthered the Melchizedek revelation.

After Amos was stoned to death, Hosea continued the moral warnings. He preached forgiveness through repentance, not by sacrifice. He proclaimed a gospel of loving-kindness and divine mercy.

A period followed with widespread moral consciousness. Threats of punishment against personal sins and national crimes were proclaimed. It was during this time that the first Isaiah appeared. He preached the eternal nature and infinite wisdom of God.

Micah and Obadiah built upon Isaiah's soul-satisfying gospel. They went on to denounce the priests and their system of sacrifice. They would have overthrown the whole bloody ceremony except for the stubborn, resistant priests.

Jeremiah fearlessly took the next bold step. He declared that Yahweh was not on the side of the Hebrews in their military battles. Rather, Yahweh was the God of all nations, all the earth, and all the people. Jeremiah raised the Deity level of Yahweh to world, even cosmic, dignity. Many found it difficult to conceive of Yahweh apart from the Hebrew nation. The priests and civil rulers threw Jeremiah in a dungeon for treason.

The national Yahweh fell as the Hebrew armies fell to the Babylonians. The Jewish priests resented losing. So, they altered their history by the invention of fables and miracles. They wanted to restore the Jews as the chosen people. Their intention was to bolster the dwindling courage of their fellows in captivity. They never claimed to be writing by inspiration nor did they claim to be writing a sacred book. Later, these writings and others were assembled into a book that claimed to be perfect. Except for Isaiah the second, the priests would have had more influence over their captive fellows.

Isaiah believed in the elder Isaiah's God. Their God was just, loving, righteous and full of mercy. He believed, as Jeremiah, that Yahweh was the God of all nations. This preacher never stopped proclaiming the God of love. He portrayed the majesty of the supreme Yahweh, God of love, ruler of the universe, and Father of all people. He was such an outstanding preacher that he made converts equally among the Jews and their captors. Once again, the Melchizedek gospel shined forth to bless mankind. The writings of the second Isaiah may be found in the Bible, (Isaiah 40-45). They are the most sublime and true writings of the spiritual concept of God that man had until the arrival of Michael.

The teachings of the two Isaiahs should have prepared the way for the acceptance of the promised Messiah. But, the priests were devoted to their false ideas of nationalism. So, the Isaiahs were not fully successful. As a nation, the Jews lost their political identity over time. The sincere Hebrew religion lasted because Yahweh was clear-cut, vivid, personal, and moral. The

Jews loved justice, wisdom, truth, and righteousness. However, they lacked creative philosophic discovery in the realms of truth.

Thus, this is the long and successful story of the incarnation of Machiventa Melchizedek. His teachings were the Third Epochal Revelation on Urantia. The Paradise God concept was alive in the hearts of men and women. Urantia was ready for the Son of that same God.

Michael was born a creator. He was educated as an administrator. He trained as an executive. And, he was required to earn his sovereignty by experience. Michael would complete his bestowal career on the world of Urantia. He would be enthroned as the supreme sovereign of the universe of Nebadon. This final bestowal would coincide with the Fourth Epochal Revelation on our world.

# 36. The Fourth Epochal Revelation
## *Michael's Bestowal*

*In each of the prior six bestowals, Michael of Nebadon yielded to the wills of the persons of the Paradise Trinity. He gladly did this of his own free will.*
- *On his first bestowal, Michael was subject to the will of the Father-Son-Spirit.*
- *On the second bestowal, he was subject to the will of the Father-Son.*
- *On the third, Michael aligned himself to the will of the Father-Spirit.*
- *On his fourth bestowal mission, he followed the will of the Son-Spirit.*
- *On his fifth bestowal, Michael submitted his will to the will of the Infinite Spirit.*
- *And, on his sixth bestowal, he was subject to the will of the Eternal Son.*

*Michael's Urantia bestowal, his seventh, would have a double purpose. Michael would embrace the final sevenfold will of Paradise Deity He would also embrace the creature viewpoints of time and space. Michael would fulfill his commission of bringing God to man and man to God. He would earn the supreme power and authority of his universe.*

*Michael had the usual prebestowal meeting with Gabriel. Then he presented himself to Immanuel. Immanuel is his elder brother and counselor. Immanuel confirmed the earlier completion of Michael's six perfect bestowals. Michael chose Urantia for his last mission. Urantia was a chaotic and disturbed planet. Immanuel pointed out that Michael would appear as a helpless baby. This would be a new and untried experience for him. All the beings in Nebadon depend upon Michael during their universe careers. Likewise, Michael would be fully dependent on the Paradise Father.*

*The Ancients of Days would prevent all spiritual danger in Nebadon while Michael was gone. Immanuel would again be responsible for Nebadon until Michael returned. Michael could focus on his mission. This last bestowal was to be the enhanced revelation of the Paradise Father.*

*Then Immanuel offered counsel regarding the final bestowal. Michael was to be born like all mortals. He was to grow up like all children of the realm and complete his human education. He was to live his life as he chose while subject to the will of the Paradise Father. He would finish his life as a man, just like all men. Then, he would ascend to the Father to receive the supreme sovereignty of his universe.*

*At some point, Michael would become conscious of his divine identity. Then he was to end the Lucifer rebellion in the system of Satania. He should do this as the humble Son of Man. He should do this as a weak mortal made powerful by his choice to follow the will of the Paradise Father. He was to meet and judge Caligastia and Lucifer. He should forever end their shameful actions. After this and the close of the mortal bestowal, Michael's authority would not be challenged again.*

*Great turmoil had been caused by the Caligastia betrayal and the Adamic default. Michael should make up for that confusion. And, after ending the Urantia secession, he should accept title of "Planetary Prince of Urantia." Gabriel and all concerned would fulfill Michael's wishes. His bestowal would end with a judgment roll call to awaken the mortal survivors. The dispensation of the bestowed Spirit of Truth would then begin. Immanuel advised Michael to assume the role of a teacher while on Urantia. Immanuel said that attention should first go to the liberation of man's spiritual nature. Next, shed light on the darkened human intellect. Heal the souls of men. Free their minds from age-old fears. Then, use your mortal wisdom to minister to the physical well-being and material comfort of your brothers in the flesh. Live the ideal religious life for the inspiration and instruction of your entire universe.*

*The will of the creature and the will of the Creator should become as one in Michael's earth life. This is how they are uniting in the Supreme Being. Michael was to bestow the Spirit of Truth. Then, all the normal mortals of Urantia would be fully open to the ministry of the Thought Adjusters.*

*Michael was bestowing his life on Urantia. But then, he was to live that life for every intelligence in his universe. His earth life was not to be lived in order to make an example for mortals to copy. Instead, his life was to be the inspiration for all lives, for all generations to come, for all Nebadon worlds. His life would serve to motivate and encourage all intelligent life. Michael's great mission would be done in one short lifetime in the flesh. He would reveal God to men through the wholehearted commitment to doing the Father's will. He was to show to the super mortal beings of Nebadon the potentials a God-knowing mortal can attain. Michael would show his entire universe: God seeking man and finding him; man seeking God and finding him.*

*As Michael lived as the Son of Man, he would still have his creative powers of personal divinity. After the arrival of his Thought Adjuster, he would have the power to end the bestowal by his own will. After awareness of his mission, Michael was warned against thinking of any super human desires. This was because his creator gifts could not be separated from his personal presence. Nevertheless, no super human events would happen apart from the will of the Father unless Michael made such a choice.*

*Immanuel further advised Michael about minor points of his mortal life. He thought that Michael might give some practical and immediate help to his fellow men. In his opinion, Michael should live his family and community life in line with the customs of those days. He should avoid politics and economics. Michael was not to interfere with the normal evolution of the races of Urantia. Nevertheless, he could leave behind an improved system of positive religious ethics.*

*It would be best if Michael worked within the religious and spiritual movements on Urantia. Michael's life and teachings were to become the common heritage of all religions and peoples. Thus, he should not set up any formal cult, or religion, or any special ethical groupings. Nothing that could become an idol should be left behind on the planet. Michael should leave no writings. He also should not allow his fellows to make any drawings of him. While Michael would live as a normal male, he should probably not marry. Such a relationship would be honorable. But one of the bestowal rules forbids the leaving of human offspring on any planet by a Paradise Son.*

*Lastly, Immanuel advised Michael to commit to the leading of his Adjuster. Thus, he would live the perfect life of a man on the planetary worlds. To any one man, in any one generation, on any one world, Michael's life might not be seen as perfect. Nevertheless, his life would be viewed as supremely replete on the perfected worlds of his universe.*

*Immanuel then assumed the status of acting sovereign of Nebadon. Michael left his place in Salvington.*

At noon, August 21, 7 B.C., Mary and Joseph became the parents of their first-born child. They named their son Joshua (Jesus) ben Joseph. Jesus was a normal, healthy, smart, and very curious child.

At an early age, Jesus learned many things from his mother. Mary taught him how to care for their animals, how to make cheese, how to weave, and how to care for flowers and plants. From his father, Jesus learned to read and write two languages before entering school. In school, he learned Hebrew, his third language. Jesus loved the study of nature and enjoyed long walks with his father. Joseph also taught Jesus carpentry. The family's carpentry shop was located at the crossroads to the caravans. This gave Jesus a chance to meet the people traveling from all over the world. Often Joseph took Jesus with him on business trips. Jesus got to meet even more people to study and learn about how men earned a living. And, Jesus learned from other family members as well. One uncle taught him farming and another taught him fishing.

Joseph was a thriving carpenter and contractor. He was able to provide many extras for his growing family of eight children. The children enjoyed travel, music lessons and instruments, as well as things like slates for writing. Both Mary and Joseph were devoted parents who provided an enriching home life for their children.

Graduation from the synagogue schools meant Jesus could go to his first Passover in Jerusalem. Slowly the realization unfolded that he was destined to perform a mission on earth. It would be for the enlightenment of man and the revelation of God. The day before the Passover Sabbath, Jesus' mind was flooded with spiritual light. His human heart was filled with pity for the spiritually blind and morally ignorant masses. That night, for the first time in his earth career, there appeared a messenger sent by Immanuel. The messenger said, "The hour has come. It is time that you began to be about your Father's business." (UB 124:6.15)

> *As time passed, the mystery of incarnation became more and more profound. We could hardly believe that this lad of Nazareth was the creator of all Nebadon. We still do not understand how the spirits of our Creator Son and Paradise Father are linked with the souls of mankind. Over time, we could see that his human mind was more and more sensing that, "while he lived his life in the flesh, in spirit, on his shoulders rested the responsibility of a universe." (UB 124:6.17)*

No human has ever gone through adolescent problems with more crucial testing than Jesus did as a youth. While his parents truly loved him, they did not, could not, understand him. Nothing, certainly no miracles, ever happened; Jesus seemed like a normal, bright lad. But this discouraged them, especially Mary, since they both knew that Jesus was special in some way.

Jesus maintained his advanced studies under the guidance of his synagogue teachers. He also continued with the home education of his youngest brothers and sisters. All the while, he formulated plans to "be about his Father's business." The future looked so bright. However, the affairs and plans for this Nazareth family were demolished when Joseph suffered an accidental death on one of his construction sites.

Jesus was barely fourteen years old. Nevertheless, he took responsibility for his pregnant mother and his siblings, ages one through ten. Jesus was an excellent carpenter. But, the earning power of a youth could not support nine people and the baby on the way. They slowly slipped into poverty as Joseph's land holdings were sold off. Financial hardship was not the only problem. Before the age of 21, Jesus had declined an offer of marriage; he avoided political involvement, (which turned many in his community against him); and he again dealt with death when his youngest brother, Amos, died.

Jesus was a nurturing and loving father-brother to his siblings. With patience, he dedicated himself to their care and upbringing. Jesus followed the traditions of his father, Joseph. He took each brother at age thirteen to Jerusalem for their first temple Passover. He helped each to choose their lifework and gave permission for marriage when the time came. Jesus saw to the education of even his sisters, when girls were not educated or allowed to go to school. He also saw that each family member was trained in the care and running of a household. Raising a family was not an easy task. Jude was a very difficult teenager. Jude avoided his financial duties to the family. He ran away from home and was even arrested once. Jesus had every chance to experience the problems faced by earthly parents.

Finally, at age 26, Jesus was ready to leave home. Ruth, the youngest, was twelve years-old. The family was settled, some in their own households or careers. Jesus had worked hard all those years and had managed to buy back the family's old carpentry caravan shop. Before leaving Nazareth, Jesus passed the title of the shop to James, the next oldest son in their family. At that time, James assumed full financial duties and the position of "head and protector of Joseph's house." Jesus was then no longer responsible for his earthly family. However, he promised to send money each month until "his hour shall have come."

It was a rainy Sunday morning in January A.D. 21 when Jesus quietly left home. For a time, he worked with an old friend of his father's, named Zebedee, and his sons, James, John, and David. They worked together building boats in Zebedee's shop beside the Sea of Galilee.

Jesus again provided for the needs of his family as he had promised. He turned over his earnings to James Zebedee who agreed to send the monthly contributions to Jesus' family. Jesus had explained to James that he wished to travel before beginning his Father's work.

Jesus took a trip to Rome that lasted two years. Only the senior Zebedee knew about it. Jesus worked for a wealthy businessman from India. He was an interpreter for the man and a tutor for his 17-year-old son. During this trip, Jesus did a vast amount of personal ministry work. He gained an intimate understanding of all races and classes of men and learned their reactions to life. To each he said or did something that added meaning and improved their lives.

When he returned, Jesus visited with each member of his family. Although he was quite natural, they more and more perceived him as difficult to understand. Again, the chance to travel presented itself. The conductor of a large caravan became very ill. Jesus, being a linguist, volunteered to take the assignment that would last over one year.

These were the transition times. Michael, who began life as God, appeared as man; he was now preparing to complete his earth career as man appearing as God. Great progress occurred as he achieved harmony between his human mind and his Thought Adjuster. Michael-Jesus was preparing for his great change in attitude toward the world.

After the caravan job, Jesus wandered alone through Palestine and Syria. He spent his time working and learning about people. He watched people, studied people, and he visited and ministered to them. He was finding out how man lives, thinks, feels, and reacts to the environment of human existence. It was also during this period that Jesus lived alone with God for six weeks on the slopes of Mount Hermon.

# 38. Mount Hermon and Jesus' Baptism

Jesus had arranged to have a lad deposit food twice weekly at a place halfway up Mount Hermon. However, Jesus faced his last struggle with the reality of mortal existence alone. He went into the great test with only his indwelling Adjuster to guide him. During these weeks, he completed his mortal task of mind understanding and personality control. He became totally assured of his divine nature. Near the end of his stay, Jesus asked his Father to allow him to meet with his Satania betrayers. Permission was granted. Jesus, as the son of man, as a human mortal, would face the traitorous leaders of the Lucifer rebellion.

Satan came to represent Lucifer; he and Caligastia were made fully visible to Jesus. To their many Luciferian proposals Jesus replied, "May the will of my Paradise Father prevail, and you, my rebellious son, may the Ancients of Days judge you divinely. I am your Creator-father; I can hardly judge you justly, and my mercy you have already spurned. I commit you to the adjudication of the Judges of a greater universe." (UB 134:8.7)

Michael of Nebadon won the unquestioned sovereignty of his universe. This was in the silence of nature on Mount Hermon. No human could hear or see the great trial that took place. Michael, as Jesus, had completed the tasks set for him as a Creator Son. The Lucifer rebellion in Satania and the Caligastia secession on Urantia were effectively settled. "Jesus had paid the last price required of him to attain the sovereignty of his universe..." (UB 134:8.9) When descending the mountain, he saw the lad coming up with food and said, "The period of rest is over; I must return to my Father's business." (UB 134:8.10)

Back in Capernaum, Jesus again worked in Zebedee's boat shop. Then the day came when he laid down his tools saying, "My hour has come." Jesus soon presented himself to John the Baptist at the Jordan River.

Jesus was a mortal of the realm. He had attained the height of human growth—evolutionary ascension. In all matters related to the conquest of mind, he was successful. His human self identified fully with his spirit. Perfect balance, alignment, had been established with his Adjuster. Full communication followed.

Jesus' Adjuster had skilled practice. He had indwelt Machiventa Melchizedek during his Urantia mission. Jesus' Adjuster was qualified for this special bestowal. But then, all Adjusters are qualified. Jesus' Adjuster and those that indwell us are all the same but vary in experience.

Baptism for Jesus was a ceremony. Jesus had nothing to repent; he had nothing to be sorry for or to regret. Jesus was without sin. Sin is knowing what God's will is and choosing to carry out your own will instead. Baptism was to honor his devotion to carrying out the will of our Paradise Father.

John the Baptist laid his hands upon Jesus to baptize him. At that moment, the Adjuster left the perfected human soul of Jesus. The Adjuster soon returned from the Paradise Father; but he returned as a Personalized Adjuster. Only Jesus saw his own divine spirit descending on its return to him. However, John the Baptist and two of Jesus' brothers were able to hear this Personalized Adjuster as he spoke to Jesus. And, this fragment of God of Paradise origin said, "This is my beloved Son in whom I am well pleased." (UB 136:2.3)

As Jesus looked up and prayed, he was shown a vision. He saw a vision of himself as a Son of God before his incarnation. Then he saw himself, as he would be when his final bestowal life was finished. Only Jesus witnessed the heavenly vision. This vision ended his purely human life. The divine Son had found his Father; and the Paradise Father had found his incarnated Son.

Jesus then retreated for forty days. Alone, he made plans. He decided how he would proclaim the new kingdom of God in the hearts of men. While in the hills, Jesus had his first personal communication since leaving Salvington. It was with Gabriel, his universe chief executive. As they talked, the Constellation Father of Edentia appeared. He came on behalf of Immanuel, Michael's sponsor-brother. He declared the release for the Urantia bestowal. Michael's work was finished. Michael had earned perfected sovereignty of his universe; he had ended the Lucifer rebellion. Michael was free to end his bestowal. He could ascend to the right hand of the Father and receive sovereignty. Michael could assume unconditional rulership of Nebadon if he chose.

Michael chose a plan of world ministry. It was not only on behalf of the people on Urantia but for all the worlds of Nebadon. This was the period of great decisions.

1. Jesus was in constant contact with his Personalized Adjuster. His Adjuster showed him (a vision of) all the assembled legions of celestial hosts. They waited for their beloved Sovereign to exercise his will. Jesus decided he would not use even one such being unless it was Father's will. With this great decision, Jesus *chose to deprive himself of super human assistance* for the rest of his earth life.

2. Jesus' human body became hungry. He needed to decide if he would live as all men, in accordance with natural laws. As a Creator, he could easily turn a stone into bread. But, in this great decision, he chose to live as a man. He would not use his powers for his personal necessities. This decision has been described as a temptation by Jesus' "enemies." However, Jesus *chose not to seek self-preservation.* It had nothing to do with so-called enemies. (Lucifer, Satan, and Caligastia were Michael's children that had fallen into terrible sin, iniquity, but they were not his enemies.)

3. The third great decision was what he planned to do when confronted by personal danger. He *decided to take only normal human precautions.*

4. Next, Jesus had to decide if he would use superhuman powers to further his mission. Would he show "signs" or proof of his divinity? Jesus *chose to establish the kingdom of heaven just as any son of God.* That entailed ordinary and at times, difficult work. Jesus was going through the great test of civilized man. And, that test is to have power but faithfully refuse to use it for selfish reasons or personal gains.

5. Jesus then had to decide how he would proclaim the kingdom of heaven. He needed to select methods. He needed to plan a good way to organize his followers and disciples. *Jesus decided he would not portray himself as the expected Jewish Messiah. To further the revelation of God to man was his goal.* Jesus planned to return to Galilee and quietly begin his teaching of the kingdom. He would trust his Personalized Adjuster to work out the details day by day.

6. Finally, Jesus made his last decision as concerned his mission. *Jesus decided that in all other matters he would be subject to the will of his Father.* He chose to finish his earth career as he had so nobly begun it, always subject to the Father's will.

And, when he rejoined his disciples, his face shone with the glory of spiritual victory and moral achievement.

# 39. The Apostles and Jesus' Core Teachings

Jesus personally picked six apostles who in time would each select another. For the next four months, they lived with the "Rabbi" and learned not to be afraid of him or dismayed by his divinity. Jesus taught: "I have come to proclaim the establishment of the Father's kingdom. And this kingdom shall include the worshipping souls of Jew and gentile, rich and poor, free and bond, for my Father is no respecter of persons; his love and his mercy are over all." (UB 137:8.6) The apostles, although at first shocked, early learned that women also had equal rights in the kingdom.

---

### Suggested Reading

Paper 139, "The Twelve Apostles," is a detailed study of the apostles. It covers their strengths, weaknesses, and why each was drawn to Jesus. There was a leading psychiatrist involved in the beginning of the Urantia Papers. The doctor had doubts as to who wrote the Papers until he read Paper 139. You can read it and see what you think.

---

Many people did not understand the true "kingdom of God" teachings. They often confused the kingdom of God with Jesus' return to rule in power and glory. Jesus did not succeed in using the better term, "the will of God." In addition, the superior concept of the "heavenly family" did not work for the people of those days. One of the core teachings was about the relationship between God and man (or woman). There is a bond between the heavenly Father and his liberated (free willed) sons and daughters. Jesus also taught that the heavenly family shares in joyful service to their fellows and in the worship of God the Father. Jesus taught in various ways, using several methods. But all these ideas were summed up in the teaching of the "Fatherhood of God and the brotherhood of men."

The apostles learned of the kingdom of heaven. Jesus learned more about the kingdom of men—human nature as it lives on Urantia and on other evolving worlds. Time after time Jesus crushed the apostles' hopes and all their ambitions for personal glory. Jesus was not a mild, sweet, gentle, and kindly mystic. He was a robust, dignified, naturally good man; his teachings were exciting and dynamic. Rugged Galilean fishermen called him Master.

### The Gospel of the Kingdom: (UB 142:1.2-5)

1. The kingdom of heaven is at hand. (In Hebrew, this meant, "the kingdom is here, it has arrived.")

2. By faith in the Fatherhood of God, you may enter the kingdom of heaven, thus becoming the sons of God. In other words, if you believe God is your Father, you are then his child; this makes you a part of the family or kingdom of heaven.

3. Love is the rule of living within the kingdom—supreme devotion to God while loving your neighbor as yourself. (Love dominates the actions of God's devoted children. The "golden rule" is another way of teaching us how to treat others with love.)

4. Obedience to the will of the Father is the law of the kingdom. Following God's will produces the fruits of the Spirit in one's personal life. (We are free will creatures. We freely choose to obey God's will. In doing this, we spiritually grow.)

"God is *your* Father, and religion—my gospel—is nothing more nor less than the believing recognition of the truth that you are his son. And I am here among you in the flesh to make clear both of these ideas in my life and teachings." (UB 141:4.2)

Other religions had suggested the thought of the nearness of God to man. However, Jesus made the care of God for man like the concern of a loving father for his dependent children. Jesus made this teaching the cornerstone of his religion. Thus, the doctrine of the Fatherhood of God made the practice of the brotherhood of man essential. (see UB 159:5.7)

The concept of atonement and sacrificial salvation is rooted in selfishness. Jesus taught that service to one's fellows is the highest view of the brotherhood of spirit believers. Salvation should be taken for granted by those who believe in the Fatherhood of God. The believer's chief concern should not be the selfish goal of personal salvation. It should be the unselfish urge to love and serve one's fellows, even as Jesus loved and served mortal men. (see UB 188:4.9)

The "golden rule" is often expressed as, 'do to others that which you desire others to do to you'. However, the apostles had many questions. Jesus explained that there are levels to this rule of living. The level of the flesh would be the interpretation of the purely selfish person. The level of the emotions, or feelings, would take understanding up one level. Sympathy and pity would increase the understanding. The next level is that of the mind. This level contains the dignity of self-respect. (see UB 147:4.4-6)

Still higher is the level of brotherly love. This is the level of unselfish devotion to the welfare of others. This is the higher plane of wholehearted social service. It grows out of the consciousness of the Fatherhood of God; that results in the recognition of the brotherhood of man. A new and far more beautiful understanding of this basic rule of life is discovered at this level. Then when you attain the moral level of understanding, you have real insight. The rightness and wrongness of things becomes clearer. You begin to see problems as you imagine a fair and wise third person would see them. (see UB 147:4.7-8)

Greatest of all is the spiritual level. This is the level of spirit insight. Spiritual understanding drives us to see in this rule of life the divine command to treat all men as we sense God would treat them. Jesus said, "That is the universe ideal of human relationships. And this is your attitude toward all such problems when your supreme desire is ever to do the Father's will. I would, therefore, that you should do to all men that which you know I would do to them in like circumstances." (see UB 147:4.9)

Jesus taught that we should show *fatherly* love rather than *brotherly* love. Brotherly love would love your neighbor as you love yourself, an adequate fulfillment of the "golden rule." "But fatherly affection would require that you should love your fellow mortals as Jesus loves you." (UB 140:5.1)


### The Indwelling Spirit and Faith: (see UB 138:8.8)

Jesus taught his apostles on the subject of faith—the new birth. The Jews taught repentance. John the Baptist had taught them "repentance—to flee from the wrath to come." Faith, the new birth, was the price of admission to the kingdom. Jesus taught that *faith* was the only thing called for in order to enter the Father's kingdom. Faith is the open door to God's perfect and eternal love.

Jesus sought to help them find a real and personal experience with God. He wanted his followers to know the pleasure of the indwelling of God's spirit of love and saving grace. He taught that the kingdom of God is within. Jesus pointed out that after praying to the Father, they should remain silent and open. During this quiet time, the indwelling Spirit could better speak to their listening soul. "The spirit of the Father speaks best to man when the human mind is in an attitude of true worship." (UB 146:2.17)

Jesus instructed, "When men and women ask what shall we do to be saved, you shall answer, 'Believe this gospel of the kingdom; accept divine forgiveness. By faith recognize the indwelling spirit of God, whose acceptance makes you a son of God.'" (UB 150:5.2) Entrance into the Father's kingdom is free; but, progress—growth in grace—is essential to continue.

The Father will always "respond to the faintest flicker of faith." Some are honest but fearful souls whose faith is weak. They conform to a passive attitude of consent to the religions of authority. The Father honors and fosters even those feeble attempts to reach out for him. However, you have been called out of darkness into the light. You are expected to believe with a whole heart. Your faith should dominate your body, mind, and spirit. (see UB 155:6.17)

Instructions were often given by Jesus. He told his believers and teachers, "The world is filled with hungry souls who famish in the very presence of the bread of life; men die searching for the very God who lives within them. Men seek for the treasures of the kingdom with yearning hearts and weary feet when they are all within the immediate grasp of living faith. Faith is to religion what sails are to a ship; it is an addition of power, not an added burden of life. There is but one struggle for those who enter the kingdom, and that is to fight the good fight of faith. The believer has only one battle, and that is against doubt—unbelief." (UB 159:3.8)

## Forgiveness and Loving Service:

Jesus taught that God *has* forgiven; that we receive his forgiveness personally by the act of forgiving our fellows. When you forgive your brother, you create the capacity in your own soul to receive God's forgiveness. The Father in heaven has forgiven you even before you have thought to ask him. God's forgiveness in *fact* is not subject to your forgiving your fellows; but in *experience*, it is exactly so conditioned.

Righteousness is defined as morally good or correct; a righteous person acts in moral, good, or correct ways. Jesus taught that faith, simple childlike belief, is the key to the door of the kingdom. Once in the kingdom there are steps that every believing child must ascend. These steps of righteousness help us to grow up to become strong sons of God.

The righteousness of the kingdom is revealed in the method of *receiving* God's forgiveness. "Faith is the price you pay for entrance into the family of God; but forgiveness is the act of God which accepts your faith as the price of admission." (UB 170:3.3) To receive the forgiveness of God involves an actual experience. It consists in the following four steps, the kingdom steps of inner righteousness: (UB 170:3.3-7)

1. "God's forgiveness is made actually available and is personally experienced by man just in so far as he forgives his fellows.

2. "Man will not truly forgive his fellows unless he loves them as himself.

3. "To thus love your neighbor as yourself *is* the highest ethics.

4. "Moral conduct, true righteousness, becomes, then, the natural result of such love."

Jesus said that a wise man understands the inner feelings of his fellows and naturally loves them. And, when we love our fellows, we have already forgiven them. Our ability to know man's nature and forgive what we see as his misdeeds is Godlike. Wise parents love their children in this way.

When we refuse, resist, or are not able to forgive, it is a measure of our lack of maturity. Jesus explained it as a failure to attain adult understanding and love. He said we hold grudges and want revenge in proportion to our ignorance; a lack of knowledge of the inner nature and true longings of our children and fellows, blocks forgiveness. Love is an inner urge of life and the outward effect of the divine. Love is founded on understanding; it is nurtured by unselfish service; it is perfected in wisdom.

The true and inner religion of the kingdom reveals itself in social service. Jesus taught a living religion. It prompted its believers into acts of loving service. "But Jesus did not put ethics in the place of religion. He taught religion as a cause and ethics as a result." (UB 170:3.8) He was never concerned with morals or ethics as such. But, Jesus was concerned with the inner fellowship with God the Father. Such inner fellowship outwardly shows itself as loving service. Man develops his character by unselfish service.


**Family Life Teachings:**
The features of family life and how they apply to the relationship of God and man were discussed at length. Jesus stated that a true family is founded on the following seven facts: (see UB 142:7.5-12)

1. *The fact of existence.* Children inherit certain traits from their parents. The children take origin in the parents. Existence depends on the act of the parents. The relationship of father and child is basic in all living existences.

2. *Security and pleasure.* True fathers take great pleasure in providing for the needs of their children. Many fathers are not content with just meeting the needs of their children; many also enjoy providing for their happiness.

3. *Education and training.* Wise fathers carefully plan for the education and training of their sons and daughters. When young, they are prepared for the greater responsibilities of later life.

4. *Discipline and restraint.* Fathers also provide needed discipline, guidance, and correction for their young offspring.

5. *Companionship and loyalty.* The affectionate father has loving interactions with his children. Always, he is willing to listen. He is always ready to share their hardships and assist them over their problems. The father is extremely interested in the growing welfare of his offspring.

6. *Love and mercy.* A freely forgiving father has compassion. He does not hold vengeful memories against his children. Fathers are not like judges, enemies, or creditors. Real families are built upon tolerance, patience and forgiveness

7. *Provision for the future.* Earthly fathers like to leave an inheritance for their children. The family carries on from one generation to another. Death often ends one generation and marks the start of another. Death terminates an individual life but not always the family life.

Jesus addressed this subject for several hours. However, Thomas was still not clear. He said that it seemed that the Father in heaven did not always deal kindly and mercifully with us. Man often suffered on earth. And, God did not always answer prayers. Thomas wanted to know where he failed to understand Jesus' teachings. (see UB 142:7.16)

Jesus replied, in part, that the earth family was an illustration. His example was to help them understand divine relationships. But they were being literal, applying his teachings to material affairs. Jesus asked them to separate the spiritual realities from the problems of the age. Slavery, poverty, houses, lands, and human justice are material problems. These matters are the concern of the men of this world. Jesus stressed that he should be able to instruct them as full-grown men of the spirit kingdom. Then Jesus asked, "Must I ever address you only as children? Will you never grow up in spirit perception? Nevertheless, I love you and will bear with you..." (see UB 142:7.17)

---

### Suggested Reading

"A human being's entire afterlife is enormously influenced by what happens during the first few years of existence." Paper 177, section 2. "Early Home Life," provides amazing insights. Normal, loving, and wise parents greatly affect us. Our character and our relationship with God are shaped by our early home life. Our first eight years affect our whole afterlife.

---

## Counsel for the Apostles and Believers:

On one occasion with his apostles, gentiles who thought the gospel was fit only for weaklings and slaves claimed that men could not live that way. This disheartened the apostles. Jesus spoke at great length on this subject. In part, he said, "I have come into this world to do the will of my Father and to reveal his loving character to all mankind. That, my brethren, is my mission. And this one thing I will do, regardless of the misunderstanding of my teachings by Jews or gentiles of this day or of another generation." (UB 143:1.4)

Jesus went on to say that our Paradise Father does rule by the compelling power of his love. Love is the greatest of all spirit realities. Truth is a freeing revelation, but love is the supreme relationship. Jesus pointed out that no matter what mistakes men make in world affairs, in an age to come the gospel will rule. *The ultimate goal of human progress is the reverent recognition of the Fatherhood of God and... the brotherhood of man.* (UB 143:1.4)

'But who said my gospel is only for weaklings? Do you resemble weaklings or did John the Baptist look like a weakling?' (see UB 143:1.5) The Father is a God of love; he delights in the practice of mercy. But, do not think the service of the kingdom is to be one of ease. The Paradise ascent is the supreme adventure of all time. It is the achievement of eternity. (see UB 143:1.6)

Jesus continued, saying that the service of the kingdom on earth would require all the courage they had. People who did not believe the gospel might tease them for preaching non-resistance. They might be made fun of for living lives of nonviolence. Nevertheless, they were just the first of a long line of sincere believers who would astonish all mankind by their heroic devotion to his teachings. Jesus said that no armies had ever displayed more courage than would be shown by them and their successors. They would proclaim to the world, with courage and zest, the good news—the Fatherhood of God and the brotherhood of men. (see UB 143:1.7)

# 40. More of the Teachings of Jesus

Jesus taught what could be understood. He did not make the mistake of over-teaching and causing confusion. He did not present truth that was too far beyond the listener's capacity. He taught his apostles by questions and answers. He held hundreds of long and earnest sessions with them. Jesus' public teaching was mainly in the form of short talks and parables.

**Assurance:** Jesus gave a great sermon in Jerusalem; it answered a question about assurance. A man wanted to know how they could be sure that he was sent by God; how could they really know that they could enter the kingdom they were hearing about. Jesus replied that his message and teachings should be judged by their fruits. He said that if they proclaim the truths of the spirit, the spirit would witness in their hearts that the message is genuine. Jesus explained they could be sure the heavenly Father would accept them. He asked what father among them would keep his child in suspense regarding his status in the family. Do earth fathers like to torture their children with uncertainty about their place of love in your human hearts? Neither does your Father in heaven leave his children of the spirit in doubt as to their position in the kingdom. If you receive God as your Father, then in truth you are the children of God. And, if you are sons, then are you secure in the position of all that concerns eternal and divine sonship. If you believe my words, you believe in the Father; you have made your status in heavenly citizenship sure. If you do the will of the Father in heaven, you will attain the eternal life of progress in the divine kingdom. (see UB 142:5)

Thomas once asked how new believers could really be sure about the truth of the gospel. Jesus said that the assurance of eternal life is a matter of personal experience. It is faith in the word of truth. It is equal to your mental understanding of truth, plus your spiritual faith, minus your honest doubts. (see UB 146:3)

We survive life in the flesh because we are identified with the Father's living spirit. We cannot observe his spirit at work in our minds. But, we can see the degree to which we have yielded to the teachings of the indwelling Spirit of the Father; it is the degree of our love for our fellows. (see UB 146:3)

---

### Suggested Reading

*The Urantia Book* contains many of the personal teachings and ministry of Jesus. Papers 130 through 134 covers Jesus' two-year trip to Rome and his transition years. His teachings are as insightful today as they must have been to those who heard the Master.

---

**God's Nature is Enlarged:** A man named Jacob met with Jesus privately. This man could not understand Jesus' teachings. Jacob pointed out that Moses and the prophets taught them that Yahweh is a jealous God full of great wrath and fierce anger. They said that God hates evildoers; God takes vengeance on those who do not obey his will. Yet, Jesus and his disciples teach that God is a kind Father who loves all men; God welcomes them all into the new kingdom of heaven. (see UB 142:2.1)

Jesus agreed that Jacob well stated the teachings of the olden prophets. Jesus pointed out that the prophets taught the generation of their day according to the light of their day. Our heavenly

Father does not change; he is changeless. Man's concept of God's nature has enlarged. It has grown since the days of Moses. Jesus explained that he came in the flesh to reveal the Father in glory. Jesus was showing the people on all worlds God's love and mercy. As the gospel of good cheer and good will to all men spreads over the world, we will have better relations among nations. In time, fathers and their children will love each other more; this will result in a better understanding of the heavenly Father's love for his children on earth. Jesus told Jacob that a true father not only loves his family as a whole but also truly loves and cares for *each member*. (see UB 142:2)

Many of Jesus' talks carried this theme. Jesus wanted men to see God as a Father-friend and himself as a brother-friend. He made it clear that love is the greatest relationship in the world. (see UB 143:6.4)

Our forefathers feared God. To them, God was mighty and mysterious. Jesus taught that we would adore God because he is magnificent—in love, in mercy and in truth. The power of God prompts fear in men. But, God's noble personality leads to love and willing worship. Jesus said again that he came to put love in the place of fear, joy in the place of sorrow. He would replace dread with confidence. Loving service and worship would replace ceremony that had lost its meaning. "But," Jesus said, "It is still true for those in darkness that 'the fear of the Lord is the beginning of wisdom.' After the light has come to a man, he is led to praise God for what he *is* rather than to fear him for what he *does*." (see UB 149:6.5)

**The Scriptures:** (see UB 159:5) Jesus taught the positive nature of the gospel of the kingdom. He suggested that some parts of Scripture contain more truth than others. He cautioned his hearers to feed their souls upon the best of the spiritual food. At one point, James asked Jesus to suggest how they might choose the better passages from the Scriptures for personal learning. Jesus replied that when they read the Scriptures, they should look for those eternally true and beautiful teachings such as:
- "Create in me a clean heart, O Lord.
- "The Lord is my shepherd; I shall not want.
- "You should love your neighbor as yourself.
- "For I, the Lord your God, will hold your right hand, saying, fear not; I will help you.
- "Neither shall the nations learn war any more."

You must cease to look for the word of God only on the pages of the olden records of religious authority. Those who are born of the spirit of God should discern the word of God regardless of where it appears to come from. Divine truth must not be discounted because the channel of its bestowal appears to be human. (see UB 155:6.12)

**Evil, Sin and Iniquity:** (see UB 148:4) Jesus made it a habit to take time for personal and private meetings twice a week. One evening Thomas asked Jesus why men must be born of the spirit in order to enter the kingdom. He wanted to know if rebirth was an escape from the control of the "evil one." Thomas finally asked what evil really is.

Jesus warned against confusing evil with the "evil one." The "devil" or "evil one" was the iniquitous one. He was the son of self-love. With full knowledge, he deliberately rebelled against the rule of the Father and his loyal Sons. Jesus said he had already vanquished the sinful rebels. He wanted to make clear the different attitudes toward the Father's will.

- Evil is unconscious. It is the unintended wrongdoing of the Father's will. It is imperfect obedience of the divine law.
- Sin is conscious. It is the deliberate transgression of the Father's will. It is the unwillingness to be divinely led and directed.
- Iniquity is willful and it persists. It is the determined offense of the Father's will. It is the ongoing rejection of the Father's plan of eternal survival; it is the rejection of the Son's ministry of mercy.

By nature, man is evil; by choice, he can be sinful. The new birth—the baptism of the spirit—brings release from evil. It is essential for entrance into the kingdom. But, none of this detracts from the fact that man is the son of God. The presence of potential evil does not mean that man is estranged from the Father in heaven. Man does not need to seek adoption by the Father. Such ideas stem from two places. One is our misunderstanding of the Father. The other is our ignorance of the origin, nature, and destiny of man.

The Greeks and others taught that man fell from godly perfection. Jesus was here to show that entrance into the kingdom assured man that he would rise up to God and divine perfection. All beings who fall short of the ideals of Father's will are potentially evil. But such beings are not sinful or iniquitous.

On another occasion, Jesus taught his disciples that they must not only cease to do evil but must learn to do well. They should be cleansed from all conscious sin. This included harboring feelings of guilt. Jesus said that if they confessed their sins, they are forgiven. Thus, they must maintain a conscience free of offense.

**Prayer and Worship:** (see UB Papers 143 and 146) Jesus often talked about prayer and worship. He explained that iniquity in the heart of a person would destroy the prayer connection between man and God. If man will not listen, he turns the ears of spirit away from hearing his personal prayers. A selfish creature cannot receive the unselfish glories of Paradise.

Man can open the human end of the channel of communication. This instantly opens the stream of divine ministry. As a person hears God's spirit speak within their human heart, God, at the same time, hears that person's prayer. The forgiveness of sin works in this same way. The sincerity of any prayer is the assurance of its being heard. The spiritual wisdom in a prayer determines the time, manner, and degree of the answer. When you have become dedicated to the doing of the will of God, your prayers are answered. This is because your will and Father's will are in unity. The Father's will is always made manifest in his vast universe.

Prayer does not change the divine attitude toward man. However, prayer does change man's attitude toward the changeless Father. The *motive* of the prayer gives it right of way to the divine ear. Jesus taught that knowledge of the Father's will was the most important prayer. Next, we should pray for divine guidance; this means to pray for divine wisdom. Jesus never taught that human knowledge and special skill could be gained by prayer. But prayer helps to enlarge one's capacity to receive the presence of the divine spirit.

Jesus taught that **effective prayer** must be: (UB 144:3.13-18)
1. Unselfish—not just for oneself,
2. Believing—according to faith,
3. Sincere—honest of heart,
4. Intelligent—according to light,
5. Trustful—in submission to the Father's all-wise will.

Prayer is not a method for gaining unfair advantage over one's fellows. A totally selfish soul cannot pray in the true sense of the word. Guard against the great danger of becoming self-centered in your prayers. Avoid praying much for yourself; pray more for the spiritual progress of others. Avoid materialistic praying; pray in the spirit and for the abundance of the gifts of the spirit. (see UB 146:2.9-10)

When you pray for the sick, do not expect that it will take the place of loving and intelligent ministry to their needs. Pray for the welfare of your families, friends, and fellows. But, especially pray for those who curse you. Also, make loving prayers for those who persecute you.

Many resort to prayer only when in trouble. Such a practice is thoughtless and misleading. True, you do well to pray when harassed, but you should also speak as a son to your Father even when all goes well with your soul. Let your real prayers always be in secret. Do not let others hear your personal prayers. Prayers of thanksgiving are appropriate for groups of worshipers; the prayer of the soul is a personal matter. There is but one form of prayer which is appropriate for all God's children, and that is, "Nevertheless, your will be done." (UB 146:2.12)

Jesus said we should not always be over-anxious about our common needs. We should not worry about the problems of earthly existence. In all these matters, by prayer, in the spirit of thanksgiving, let our needs be spread out before our Father. Jesus said that he came forth from the Father. If we are ever in doubt as to what we should ask of the Father, he told us to ask in his name. He promised to present our petitions according to our real needs and desires, and in accordance with Father's will.

Believers were taught to employ prayer as a means of leading up through thanksgiving to true worship. After prayers to the Father, we should stay for a time in silent receptivity. This would give the indwelling Spirit a chance to speak to the listening soul. The spirit of the Father speaks best to man when the human mind is in an attitude of true worship. We worship God by the aid of the Father's indwelling Spirit. Worship, taught Jesus, makes one more and more like the being who is worshiped. Worship is transforming. It is the finite approaching the Infinite.

To contemplate is to consider and think about something deeply. Worship is the contemplation of the spiritual. Worship must alternate with service. (Service is contact with the material.) The strain of living should be relaxed by the restfulness of worship. Feelings of being alone should be cured by the worship of the Father and by trying to realize the Supreme.

"Prayer is designed to make man less thinking but more *realizing*. It is not designed to increase knowledge but rather to expand insight." (UB 143:7.4) Worship is meant to look forward to the better life ahead. Then, one should apply these new spiritual meanings to their current life.

"Worship is the technique of looking to the *One* for the inspiration of service to the *many*." (see UB 143:7.) Worship reflects the extent of the soul connection. It shows detachment from the material world. It shows secure attachment to the spiritual realities of creation. Prayer is self-reminding; it is sublime thinking. Worship is self-forgetting; it is super-thinking. Worship is effortless attention, true and ideal soul rest. Worship is the act of a part identifying itself with the Whole; the finite with the Infinite; the son with the Father; time in the act of striking step with eternity. Worship is the act of the human soul-spirit when in communion with the divine Father.

And many other truths did Jesus teach about man's communion with God, but few could fully absorb his teachings.

**True Religion—the Religion of the Spirit:** (see Paper 155.5 & 6) Religions based on feelings and fears were not belittled by Jesus. However, he deplored the fact that so much of this primitive form of worship endured, even in the religions of the more able races.

The religion of the mind is upheld by church authority; the religion of the spirit is based on human experience. True religion is the conscious relationship of a soul with the Creator. Organized religion is an attempt to worship as a group. The human race must advance to a higher level; there it will recognize the reality of spiritual experience. Until then, large numbers of men and women will prefer the religions of authority; they only demand mental assent. The religion of the spirit entails both the mind and soul in the faith adventure of human experience. The religion of the spirit means effort, struggle, conflict, and faith; it means determination, love, loyalty, and progress. The religions of authority require little or none of these from its believers. Tradition is a safe refuge and an easy path for halfhearted souls or those who are fearful. The religion of the spirit is a daring faith voyage upon the high seas of unexplored truth.

| The Religions of Authority: | The Religion of the Spirit: |
|---|---|
| Ties you to the past | Consists in progressive revelation |
| Divides men and sets them against each other | Draws men together; causes them to be more sympathetic with each other |
| Requires uniform beliefs (Impossible given the state of the world) | Requires unity of experience—uniformity of destiny. Allows for diversity of beliefs |
| Requires uniformity of viewpoints and outlooks | Requires uniformity of insight |
| Requires uniformity of intellectual views | Requires unity of spirit feeling |
| Crystallizes into lifeless creeds | Grows into noble deeds of loving service |

Be only concerned with the spirit of living truth and the power of true religion. It is not the fear of a dead religion that will save you. It is your faith in a living experience in the reality of the kingdom. Do not allow yourselves to become blinded by prejudice and paralyzed by fear. Do not permit traditions to pervert your understanding so that your eyes see not and your ears hear not. True religion not only brings peace, it insures progress. "There can be no peace in the heart or progress in the mind unless you fall wholeheartedly in love with truth..." (UB 157:2.2)

When the feelings of service for your fellows arise within your soul, do not stifle them; when the emotions of love for your neighbor well up within your heart, give expression to such urges of ministry to the needs of your fellows.

Never forget there is only one adventure that is more satisfying and thrilling than the attempt to discover the will of the living God; that is the supreme experience of honestly trying to do that divine will. And, fail not to remember that the will of God can be done in any earthly occupation. Some callings are not holy and others are secular. All things are sacred in the lives of those who are spirit led; that is, subordinated to truth, ennobled by love, dominated by mercy, and restrained by fairness.

Religion has, from time to time, approved all sorts of behavior. It has allowed practically all that is now regarded as immoral or sinful. Conscience, untaught by experience and unaided by reason, can never be a safe guide to human conduct. Conscience is not the Adjuster's voice speaking to the soul. Conscience is the moral and ethical content of the mores of any current stage of existence. It is the human understanding of the ideal reaction in a situation.

Many have minds that accept the theory of God while they spiritually fail to realize the presence of God. Because of this, Jesus taught that the kingdom could best be realized by attaining the attitude of a sincere child. It is not the immature mind of the child that he recommends; rather he recommends the *spiritual simplicity* of such an easy believing and fully trusting little one. It is not so important that you should know about the fact of God. But you should grow in the ability to *feel the presence of God.*

When you once begin to find God in your soul, you will begin to discover him in other men's souls. What chance does the Father have in the souls of people who give little or no thought to such spiritual realities? While the mind is not the seat of the spiritual nature, it is indeed the gateway thereto. But, do not make the mistake of trying to prove to others that you have found God; you cannot produce such valid proof. Even so, there are two positive and powerful displays of the fact that you are God knowing. They are:

1. The fruits of the Spirit of God showing forth in your daily routine of life.
2. The fact that your life is proof that you have risked everything you are and have, on the adventure of survival after death; it is all because of your hope in finding the God of eternity, whose presence you have foretasted in time.

**The Fruits of the Spirit:** (see UB 193:2.2) The fruits of the divine Spirit that are yielded in the lives of spirit-born and God-knowing mortals are:
- loving service
- unselfish devotion
- courageous loyalty
- sincere fairness
- enlightened honesty
- undying hope
- confiding trust
- merciful ministry
- unfailing goodness
- forgiving tolerance
- enduring peace

If professed believers bear not these fruits of the divine Spirit in their lives, they are dead; the Spirit of Truth is not in them. "My Father requires of the children of faith that they bear much spirit fruit." (UB 193:2.2)

**Spiritual Living:** (see UB 156:5) Living a spiritual life greatly increases true self-respect. But self-respect is not the same as self-admiration. Self-respect is always coordinate with the love and service of one's fellows. It is not possible to respect yourself more than you love your neighbor; the one is the measure of the capacity for the other. The measure of the spiritual capacity of the evolving soul is your faith in truth and your love for man. The measure of your strength of character is your ability to resist holding grudges and brooding in the face of deep sorrow. Defeat is the true mirror in which you may honestly view your real self.

As you grow older and more experienced in the affairs of the kingdom, are you becoming more tactful in dealing with difficult mortals; are you more tolerant in dealing with stubborn fellows? Tact is the fulcrum of social leverage; tolerance is the earmark of a great soul. If you possess these rare gifts, over time you will become more expert in your worthy efforts to avoid all social quarrels. Such wise souls are able to avoid much trouble; trouble brought about by those who suffer from lack of emotional adjustment, those who refuse to grow up, and those who refuse to grow old gracefully. (see UB 156:5.18)

"The God-conscious mortal is certain of salvation; he is unafraid of life; he is honest and consistent." (UB 156:5.20) He bravely endures suffering that he cannot avoid. He does not complain when faced with hardship he cannot escape. The true believer does not grow weary in well-doing just because he is thwarted. Difficulty whets the passions of the truth lover; obstacles only challenge the efforts of the undaunted kingdom builder. (see UB 156:5.21)

"Avoid dishonesty and unfairness in all your efforts to preach truth and proclaim the gospel. Seek no unearned recognition and crave no undeserved sympathy. Love, freely receive from both divine and human sources regardless of your desserts, and love freely in return. But in all other things related to honor and adulation seek only that which honestly belongs to you." (UB 156:5.19)

**An Experience is Good When:** (see UB 132:2.5)
- It heightens the appreciation of beauty.
- It boosts the moral will.
- It enhances the discernment of truth.
- It enlarges the capacity to love and serve one's fellows.
- It exalts the spiritual ideals.
- It unifies the supreme human motives with the eternal plans of the indwelling Adjuster.

All of these lead directly to an increased desire to do the Father's will. Such experiences promote the divine passion to find God and to be more like him. Although the apostles understood only a few of these teachings, other worlds did, and other generations on earth will.

**Self-mastery:** (see UB 143:2) John the Baptist taught the practice of self-denial. Jesus taught that we should strive for self-control. Jesus explained that John taught based upon the light and laws of his fathers. That was the religion of self-examination and self-denial. But Jesus brought a new message of self-forgetfulness and self-control.

Jesus said that he who rules his own self is greater than he who captures a city. Self-mastery is the measure of man's moral nature; it indicates his spiritual growth. In the old order, you fasted and prayed; as the new creature of the rebirth of the spirit, you are taught to believe and rejoice. In the Father's kingdom you are to become new creatures; old things are to pass away; behold I show you how all things are to become new. And, by your love for one another, you are to convince the world that you have passed from bondage to liberty, from death into life eternal.

Your secret of the mastery of self is bound up with your faith in the indwelling Spirit, which ever works by love. Even this saving faith you have not of yourselves; it also is the gift of God. As the children of this living faith, you are no longer the slaves of self; rather you are the triumphant masters of yourselves, the liberated sons of God. You show the fruits of the Spirit in your daily lives. The fruits of the Spirit are the essence of the highest type of dignified self-control; they are even the heights of earthly mortal attainment—true self-mastery. The spirit dwells within you.

You are no longer slaves of the flesh but free and liberated sons of the spirit. The new law of the spirit gives you the liberty of self-mastery; it replaces the old fear of the slavery of self-denial.

The soil essential for religious growth assumes a progressive life of:
- self-realization
- coordination of natural tendencies
- the exercise of curiosity
- the enjoyment of reasonable adventure
- the experiences of feelings of satisfaction
- functioning of the fear stimulus of attention and awareness
- the wonder lure
- and a normal consciousness of humility

Growth is also based on the discovery of selfhood along with self-criticism—conscience. Conscience is really the criticism of oneself by one's own values, habits, and personal ideals.


**Superstitions Regarding God's Gifts:** (see UB 166:4) For ages people believed that, wealth and success were the signs of divine approval; hardship and suffering were proof of God's displeasure. Jesus taught that such beliefs are superstitions. The Father causes his rain to fall on the just and the unjust; the sun likewise shines on the righteous and the unrighteous. In the matter of sickness and health, you should know that these bodily states are the result of material causes; health is not the smile of heaven neither is affliction the frown of God.

There are three groups of events that may occur in your lives: (see UB 166:4.5-8)
1. You may share in those normal happenings that are a part of life you and your fellows live on earth.
2. You may chance to fall victim to one of the accidents of nature. Know that it was in no way prearranged or otherwise produced by spiritual forces.
3. You may reap the harvest of your direct efforts to comply with the natural laws governing the world.

When it comes to the bestowal of spiritual gifts, the Father is limited by man's capacity. The Father is no respecter of persons. In the bestowal of spiritual gifts, God is limited by man's faith; he is limited by man's willingness to abide by his will. (see UB 166:4.11)


**Fear and Pride:** "Few persons live up to the faith which they really have." (UB 48:7.4) Unreasoned fear is a master fraud practiced upon the evolving mortal soul. Jesus said, "Let not your heart be troubled, neither let it be afraid." (UB 140:5.18) Jesus also said that "fear is man's chief enslaver and pride his great weakness." (UB 142:0.2) "Much of man's sorrow is born of the disappointment of his ambitions and the wounding of his pride." (UB 149:5.3) Jesus said, Seek not for false peace and temporary joy. Rather seek the assurance of faith and the security of divine sonship that yields composure, contentment, and supreme joy in the spirit. (UB 149:5.4)


**Anger:** (see UB 149:4) Anger denotes the failure of the spiritual nature to gain control of the mental and physical natures. Anger points to a lack of tolerant brotherly love, plus a lack of self-respect and self-control. Anger depletes the health, debases the mind, and handicaps the spirit teacher of man's soul. Jesus said to let our hearts be ruled by love; then our spirit guide will not have trouble keeping us from outbursts of animal anger that conflicts with divine sonship.

**Intolerance:** (see UB 146:3.2) Jesus and the apostles met with a Greek philosopher. The apostles were a bit confused by the open manner of Jesus' assent to many of the Greek's proposals. Jesus later told them that they should not have marveled at his tolerance of the Greek's philosophy. Jesus said that true and genuine inward certainty, does not fear outward analysis. Truth does not resent honest criticism. Intolerance is a mask; it covers up secret doubts as to the trueness of one's belief. No man is ever disturbed by his neighbor's attitude when he has perfect trust in the truth of what he believes. Courage is the confidence of complete honesty about those things one believes. Sincere people do not fear critical study of their convictions.

**Peace:** (UB 140.5.18) Personal peace integrates the personality. Social peace prevents fear, greed, and anger. Political peace prevents rivalry amongst the races; it prevents national suspicions, and war. Peacemaking is the cure of distrust and suspicion.

---

### Suggested Reading

One week, Jesus enjoyed complete rest while most of the apostles went home to visit their families. Nathaniel and Thomas were busy having discussions with a Greek philosopher named Rodan. Paper 160, Rodan of Alexandria, covers his views on such subjects as "the art of living" and "the balance of maturity." Rodan was noted as one of the greatest of his race who had become a believer in the gospel of Jesus. His ideas are well stated and quite helpful.

---

**Judgment:** (UB 159:1) You cannot pretend to sit in judgment on the souls of your fellows. You may not forgive sins. Nonetheless, you should maintain order in the kingdom on earth. Although you cannot determine the eternal fate of a person, you may set rules for the conduct of the group. Jesus taught about the dangers and unfairness of judging others. Discipline must be maintained; justice must be administered. But, in such matters, wisdom of the brotherhood should prevail. Jesus gave authority to the *group,* not to the *individual* in such matters. The authority of the group must not be used as personal authority. There is always the danger that an individual may be prejudice or distorted by passion. Group judgment is more likely to remove personal bias. Jesus sought to reduce unfairness and revenge.

### How to Handle Relationship Problems within a Group: (see UB 159:1.3)

- If your brother sins against you, (offends you), go to him alone. With tact and patience, show him his fault. Do this between you and him alone. If he will listen to you, then you have won your brother.

- However, if your brother will not hear you, if he persists in the error of his way, go again to him. This time, take one or two mutual friends. Thus, you will have two or even three witnesses to confirm your statements. This will establish the fact that you have dealt justly and kindly with your offending brother.

- Now if he refuses to hear your brethren, you may tell the whole story to the community. If he refuses to hear the brotherhood, let them take such action as they deem wise. Let such an unruly member become an outcast.

**<u>Spiritual Unity:</u>** (see UB 141:5.1) We do not have to see alike, feel alike or even think alike in order to *be alike* spiritually. Spiritual unity is derived from the consciousness that each of us is indwelt by the spirit gift of the Father. Uniformity is the earmark of the physical world. "Spiritual unity is the fruit of faith union with the living Jesus." (UB 195:10.11)


Jesus taught and answered nearly every question we can imagine. He sowed seeds as he passed by and ministered to the multitudes. However, nothing was more important than an individual in need.

# 41. Ending of the Fourth Epochal Revelation
## *Celestial Activity*

Jesus had chosen the first six apostles in February A.D. 26. They lived together and were trained by Jesus. By the end of July of that year, the six each selected another apostle. Thus, Jesus prepared twelve men to carry on his work. The twelve apostles were ordained Sunday, January 12, A.D. 27.

John the Baptist had also ordained twelve apostles, led by Abner. After John's execution, both sets of apostles remained with Jesus for two and a half months. They worked together until November A.D. 27. Abner continued to teach and train many disciples.

For five months in A.D. 28, an enormous camp, a tent city, was set up. It had a changing population from 500 to 1,500 people. Peter was in charge of the school of the evangelists. Seventy evangelists taught and preached the gospel. The first hospital of the kingdom was set up just south of the tented city. A Syrian doctor ran the hospital. Twenty-five women and twelve men assisted him.

In January A.D. 29, Jesus did an amazing thing. He set up a women's corps of evangelists. It began with ten devout women but two more were added. The ten women had worked at the tent city and hospital. They had heard all the teachings given to the male evangelists. The apostles were stunned; the whole country was stirred up.

Jesus set women free. Never again was man to look upon woman as his spiritual inferior. (Despite the fact that the later Christian leader, Paul, accepted this in theory, he just could not practice this truth.) The women's corps was allowed to travel on tour with Jesus and the apostles. These women could go places that righteous men could not. Mary Magdalene, a prostitute, heard the teachings from these sisters. She became a believer and member of the women's corps. She became the most effective teacher of the gospel among that group. Rebecca was the twelfth member of the women's corps.

In November A.D. 29, many groups met together. Present were Jesus and the twelve apostles. Abner and about fifty disciples were there. The seventy evangelists taught by Peter attended. The women's corps was included. About one hundred and fifty true and tried disciples from all parts of Palestine were also there.

Jesus and the apostles began a course of intensive training. Jesus gave a talk to the students each morning. Peter taught methods of public preaching. Nathaniel instructed them in the art of teaching. Thomas explained how to answer questions. Matthew taught them how to handle group finances. The other apostles also helped with training. From this well-trained group, Jesus selected seventy. He ordained them as the "seventy messengers of the kingdom" and put Abner in charge. Thus, there were many well-trained ministers and preachers to carry the gospel of the kingdom to the whole world.

The political tides began to turn; the Jewish rulers listened only in the hope of trapping Jesus. Then Jesus began to teach by the use of parables. (The Urantia Papers have at least thirty of Jesus' parables.)

The Jews clung to the idea of a wonder-working deliverer. Jesus refused to stoop to requests for miracles. When he healed the sick, he told them to tell no one, even though most did; they called it a miracle. When 5,000 people gathered to hear Jesus and stayed long past mealtime, he wanted to feed them. When he did, because of their limited thinking, they attempted to make him king. Jesus criticized them for wanting a king in order to have free bread. What he wanted to give them was spiritual food for their souls. Without miracles, all but 500 refused to follow him.

Lazarus and his sisters, Mary and Martha, were close friends of Jesus since childhood. Many times Jesus and the apostles stayed at their home. Upon the death of Lazarus, and with the Father's consent, Jesus did exhibit his power over life and death. His actions were partly for the benefit of the scribes and Pharisees of Jerusalem. Jesus wanted them to have one more chance to accept his teachings. Jesus brought Lazarus back from the dead on Thursday, March 2, A.D. 30. That was four days after he had died. This assured every person that Lazarus was truly dead. Jesus called Lazarus out of his tomb. Jesus said that all who believe the gospel would also experience what had happened to Lazarus. But they will be resurrected in a more glorious form. Jesus said, "You shall be a living witness of the truth which I spoke—I am the resurrection and the life." (UB 168:2.7) Lazarus was of great interest to many, both believers and the curious. After the death of Jesus, Lazarus had to flee the wicked Sanhedrin.

The Sanhedrin was the supreme court of the Jewish nation. They felt threatened. Many believed in Jesus as a result of raising Lazarus from the dead; others only hardened their hearts to reject him. The alarmed Sanhedrin quickly called a meeting to determine what should be done. It was suggested that Jesus be put to death without a trial. This was unheard of and fourteen members resigned then and there. Five other members were thrown out because it was believed they had friendly feelings for Jesus. The remaining members were against Jesus.

Over the next few weeks, the Sanhedrin worked to get rid of Jesus. Lazarus and his sisters were required to appear before the Sanhedrin. There was no doubt that Jesus had raised Lazarus from the dead. However, the Sanhedrin insisted that Jesus was in league with the prince of devils. Yet, no matter what the source of his power, if Jesus was not stopped, the common people would believe in him. Many Jewish believers already saw him as the Messiah.

Jesus knew what was happening. He was unconcerned. He and his apostles finished their teaching tour. It was dangerous to go to Jerusalem. But Jesus insisted he was going for the Passover. He and his apostles arrived in Bethany. This was just outside of Jerusalem where Lazarus and his sisters lived. It was Friday, March 31, A.D. 30. Jesus had been preparing them for what would happen. He had told them as plainly as he could that he would be put to death and return to the Father in Paradise. Still, the apostles just could not accept this truth.

A warrior king always enters a city riding a horse. A king on a mission of peace and friendship enters riding a donkey. Jesus chose to enter Jerusalem riding a donkey. Several thousand visitors heard of Jesus' nearing arrival; they went out to see him approach the city. More visitors joined the crowd waving palm branches and singing. Some of the Pharisees reported back to the Sanhedrin; they were afraid that the ignorant common people all over the world would believe in Jesus. Although, Jesus knew better. He knew these people did not have a deep belief in the gospel of the kingdom. He knew that most would stand against him when they realized he would not establish the material kingdom they wanted. Most would support the Sanhedrin later in the week.

In the temple, Jesus became upset with the banking and trade that took place. Animals for sacrifice were sold. Moneychangers were there; they changed regular money for special Jewish coins. The coins were for temple dues, animals, and payment of vows and offerings. The moneychangers collected a fee for their banking service. None of these activities was respectful in a place of worship. Jesus is well known for his act of cleansing the temple.

The rest of Monday and Tuesday, Jesus taught through parables. Nevertheless, the Jewish rulers tried to slow down his teachings with questions. They hoped to trick Jesus into breaking Jewish law. Jesus gave answers that even managed to win some of the hearts of these Jewish rulers. Tuesday was the last discourse Jesus gave in the temple. He said good-bye to Lazarus that day; gave parting advice to the women's corps. He gave personal counsel to each apostle. The Sanhedrin often talked about stopping Jesus. That Tuesday night, April 4, A.D. 30, they voted to impose the death sentence upon Jesus and Lazarus. It was official. The order for the arrest of Jesus went out the next morning.

Wednesday, Jesus called for a day of rest. He wanted to go into the hills alone. David Zebedee wanted to send three armed guards to protect Jesus. Jesus said he did not need anyone to defend him. No one would lay hands on him until he was ready to lay down his life. But, John Mark, a young lad, wanted to go with Jesus. It was permitted because John Mark craved to go along. They compared their early childhoods, talked, and had a nice day together.

Thursday was Jesus' last free day on earth as a divine Son. He spent it with his apostles and devoted disciples. In the morning, he gave a farewell address to the camp group of about fifty. He spoke of sonship and citizenship. He tried to prepare the group for what was about to happen. Jesus told the apostles they would celebrate Passover one night early. That Thursday evening was the Last Supper. Jesus again explained the necessity for his leaving. He told them that life in the Father's kingdom is not an endless rest of idleness and selfish ease; rather it is unending progress in grace, truth and glory. He promised to return for a short time after his death. Jesus assured them that soon after returning to the Father he would send a new spirit teacher, his Spirit of Truth. Jesus established the remembrance supper. He said, "This is the new Passover which I leave with you, even the memory of my bestowal life, the word of eternal truth; and of my love for you, the outpouring of my Spirit of Truth upon all flesh." (UB 179:5.9) Jesus talked of love. He gave a new commandment: Love one another even as I have loved you. He gave last words of comfort before they returned to their camp.

In the last hour before Judas would betray the Master, Jesus called for a messenger. The messenger was to go to Abner at Philadelphia. Jesus wanted Abner to know the time had come that he would be delivered into the hands of his enemies. He would be put to death. However, he will rise from the dead and appear to Abner before he goes to the Father. He will give Abner guidance as to the time when the new teacher will come.

Jesus waited in the garden for the soldiers. He even stepped forward and said he was the person they came to arrest. This was to give Judas a chance to avoid betraying him. Judas did not have to kiss the Master but he did anyway. Judas expected a great reward from the Sanhedrin. The Sanhedrin rewarded him the price of a healthy slave. He was stunned. He realized his sin and tried to give back the thirty pieces of silver. They refused and threw him out. Judas was a onetime ambassador of the kingdom. He walked the streets alone, forsaken. In despair, Judas killed himself.

Jesus was dragged before Annas, the single most powerful Jew. At three in the morning, Friday, April 7, A.D. 30, Jesus was taken to the Sanhedrin. He would have a special trial. Normally a trial is in two parts if it is a death sentence. The first day is a trial. Then the Sanhedrin would fast and mourn until the second part of the trial held the next day. The Sanhedrin could not wait. Only one hour passed before the second part began. During that hour, the soldiers and servants brutalized Jesus. They beat him, spit in his face, and abused him for fun. The second part of the trial found Jesus guilty. (1.) He was found guilty of perverting the Jewish nation; he deceived the people and incited them to rebel. (2.) He was found guilty of teaching the people to refuse to pay taxes to Caesar. (3.) Jesus claimed to be a king and founder of a new kingdom. Thus, he was found guilty of treason against the emperor.

Next Jesus was taken for trial before the governor of Judea, Pontius Pilate. Pilate said that Jesus was a Galilean and should go before Herod Antipas. Herod had ordered the death of John the Baptist. Herod knew that Jesus was Pilate's problem. He was glad that Pilate would be the one to put Jesus to death. He had Jesus returned to Pilate.

The Son of God stood again before Pilate. He was arrested without indictment; accused without evidence; judged without witnesses; punished without a verdict; and was about to be condemned to die by an unjust judge. Pilate admitted he could find no fault in Jesus. But Pilate was afraid of a riot. He feared the crowds at Passover in Jerusalem. Pilate appealed to the crowd saying that Jesus was a religious offender; he should be judged by Jewish law. Pilate was about ready to release Jesus but a high priest stepped in. He threatened Pilate in a loud voice so the crowd would hear him. He shouted that Pilate was not Caesar's friend and he would make sure the emperor was told. Jesus was brought out before the crowd. Pilate told them to behold their king. They screamed, "Crucify him! We have no king but Caesar." Then Pilate ordered a basin of water. He washed his hands in front of the crowd. He said, "I am innocent of the blood of this man. You are determined that he shall die, but I have found no guilt in him. See you to it." And then the mob cheered and replied, "His blood is on us and on our children." (see UB 185:8)

Just before 3:00 p.m. Friday, Jesus, in a loud voice, said his final words from the cross. He cried out, "It is finished! Father, into your hands I commend my spirit." After he spoke, with bowed head, he gave up the life struggle.

The death of the Son of Man has no connection with the Jewish system of sacrifice. His death was managed by men. It was man, not God, who executed the death of Jesus on the cross. The Father refused to interfere with man's free will. The Father did not decree, demand, or require the death of his Son as it was carried out on Urantia. The gospel that man may, by faith, become spirit-conscious that he is a son of God, is not dependent on the death of Jesus. The gospel has been illuminated by the Master's death but it is *greatly* enlightened by his **life**.

Michael of Nebadon as the bestowed human, Jesus of Nazareth, was born like all humans; he lived like all humans; he experienced death just like all humans must do. At some point, he would have divested himself of his mortal body but that could have happened in any number of ways. The Father never planned or willed the death of Jesus on a cross. Death was part of Michael's mortal career but it did not have to be violent. All of that was man's doing.

Lazarus fled and joined Abner after Jesus' death. Mary and Martha sold off their lands and joined their brother. Lazarus became the treasurer of the church in Philadelphia. He supported Abner in his controversy with Paul and the Jerusalem church. Lazarus died at age 67 by the same sickness that had killed him when he was a younger man.

There were strict laws against the burial of a crucified person in a Jewish cemetery. The Jewish rulers had planned to throw Jesus' body in an open burial pit south of the city. All victims of crucifixion were disposed of that way. The wild beasts took care of remains. Joseph of Arimathea had been a member of the Sanhedrin. He was one of Jesus' supporters who resigned membership. Nicodemus was also a member of the Sanhedrin who had resigned. The two men boldly claimed Jesus' body. They had obtained a permit order from Pilate.

The Jews did not really bury their dead; they embalmed them. Joseph wrapped the body of Jesus with bandages soaked in aloe and myrrh. They tied a napkin around his face and wrapped his body in a linen sheet. Then, with reverence, they placed his body on a shelf in the tomb of

Joseph. The men had to hurry back to the city to prepare for Sabbath. The women had secretly watched. They were not allowed to be present with the men at such a time. They decided to return after the Sabbath with spices and ointments to better prepare the Master's body for the tomb.

*The celestials gathered at the tomb could do nothing. The creature can do nothing to resurrect the Creator. Michael had laid down his own life and he had the power to take it up again. The Personalized Adjuster of Jesus spoke. He told the anxious celestials that they could not assist their Creator-father in his return to life. As a mortal, he had died a mortal death. As the Sovereign of a universe, he still lived. They were observing the mortal transit of Jesus from life in the flesh to morontia life; he would attain to the status of true spirit life. They would see part of this but could not participate.*

*Sunday morning, April 9, A.D. 30, the resurrected morontia form of Jesus came out of the tomb. The body in which he had lived for almost 36 years was still in the tomb as it had been placed. The stones in front of the tomb were not disturbed. The seals of Pilate were unbroken. The soldiers were still on guard.*

*The chief of the archangels of resurrection asked Gabriel for the mortal body of Jesus. They planned to invoke the process of accelerated time. It was enough that they had seen the Sovereign live and die; the hosts of heaven would be spared the memory of seeing the slow decay of the human form of the Creator of Nebadon. Permission was given; the body disappeared; it returned to dust.*

*The secondary Midwayers of Urantia had rolled away the stones from the entrance to the tomb. One was a huge circular stone that moved in a chiseled groove. It could go back and forth to open or close the tomb. The second had been placed in front but was smaller.*

In the dim light of the morning, the guards saw the stones move. They were seized with fear because no one was there; they fled. The Jewish leaders bribed the twenty Roman soldiers and guards. They were paid to say that while they slept at night, the disciples of Jesus came and took away his body. The Christian belief in the resurrection of Jesus is based on the fact of the "empty tomb." It is a *fact* the tomb was empty but that was not the *truth* of the resurrection. This led to a belief that was not true—the teaching that the mortal body of Jesus was raised from the grave. Jesus took on the morontia form like all resurrected mortals.

Jesus made 19 visits in his morontia form. The morontia Master was part of the personal experience of almost one thousand people. The human eyes that saw the morontia Jesus had help. It was the special ministry of the personalities with Jesus that made it possible to see him. (Transformers, Midwayers, and morontia helpers were there.) Most, at first, saw a stranger. They recognized Jesus by his voice and words. No one was allowed to touch him. When he finished speaking, he would just vanish.

Five women went to the tomb to better prepare Jesus' body and found he was gone. Then they saw a stranger; when he spoke, they recognized it was Jesus. Mary Magdalene went to embrace his feet but Jesus told her not to touch him. He explained he was in a new form. He said he would be with them for a while before he ascended to the Father. He instructed them to go tell the apostles that he had risen and they had spoken with him.

Peter and John ran to the tomb. The other apostles did not believe the women. Peter and John found the tomb just the way the women described. They left confused. Mary Magdalene returned to the tomb and Jesus again spoke to her. Mary really did see Jesus; it was not a vision.

He told her not to have doubt, to have courage. He told her to go back to the apostles and tell them again that he had risen. She was to tell them that he would soon go to Galilee as he had promised them. Mary did this but the apostles still did not believe her. When Peter and John returned, they reported the tomb was empty. The other apostles stopped their ridicule of Mary.

David Zebedee had organized messengers that served to keep the teachers of the gospel informed. He gathered twenty-six messengers to herald the good news that Jesus had risen. David was met with resistance from others but the twenty-six runners began to spread this news far and wide. It was their last volunteer act of messenger service.

Jesus' third appearance was with his brother, James. James was in the garden near the tomb when he became aware of a near-by presence. It was as if someone had touched his shoulder. He turned to look and slowly he saw the appearance of a strange form by his side. He was too shocked to talk and too scared to run. But the strange form spoke. When he heard the words, he knew it was Jesus.

Jesus soon met with his earthly family and friends, twenty in all. The fifth visit was with twenty-five women believers. The sixth was with forty Greek believers. Jesus then visited two brothers. Next, he spent time with his apostle, Peter. On the ninth morontia appearance, Jesus met with ten of his apostles. (Thomas was not with them and Judas was dead.) On April 11, Jesus showed himself to Abner, Lazarus, and about one hundred and fifty believers.

The ten apostles told Thomas all about seeing the risen Master. Thomas refused to believe unless he saw Jesus with his own eyes and put his finger in the nail marks of Jesus' hands. The eleven apostles were eating dinner in a locked room when the Master appeared right before Thomas. When Jesus finished speaking with them, Thomas said, "I believe!" (But, like everyone, Thomas was not allowed to touch the morontia form of the Master.) Jesus said that Thomas believed because he really had seen and heard him. Blessed are those who will believe even though they have not seen with the eyes of the flesh or heard with mortal ears. Early the next day the apostles left for Galilee.

David Zebedee led the messenger service. Messengers were relay runners. It took five runners to go from Jerusalem to Alexandria. On Tuesday evening, April 18, the last runner arrived at Rodan's home. The message was given to Rodan and about eighty other believers. Even as the messenger spoke, Jesus appeared in morontia form in full view of all. After he spoke, as with each appearance, he vanished. That was the twelfth morontia visit.

As the eleven apostles got close to Galilee, Simon Zelotes grew sadder and more hopeless. He left the apostles and went to his home. In Galilee, the ten went fishing. They caught nothing by dawn so they decided to return to shore. A stranger on the beach shouted to them to cast their net on the right side of their boat. The net was so full they could barely haul it in. John Mark, the lad that had spent the last day of rest with Jesus in the hills, had tagged along to Galilee. He came upon the eleven men on the beach. He saw that it was the ten apostles and the risen Jesus. Jesus stayed and talked. They made fish for breakfast. After breakfast, Jesus strolled the beach with the apostles, two at a time. He told them to contact Simon. He arranged to meet them all the next day, Saturday, April 22, at noon where he had ordained them. Then he vanished from their sight.

The fourteenth visit was with the eleven apostles. Jesus repeated the words he said when he had ordained them. He re-enacted the scene. But, the morontia Jesus spoke in tones of majesty and with words of power like they had never before heard. The Master spent an hour with them, said farewell, and vanished.

No one saw the morontia Jesus for a week. They did not know it but Michael-Jesus was quite busy. He was going through the morontia experience. However, word spread that Jesus had appeared, that he had risen. More than 500 people gathered to hear Peter preach. It was his first public sermon since the resurrection. At the end, few doubted that the Master had risen from the dead. Just as Peter finished his statement of faith, Jesus appeared by his side. He was in full view. Jesus said, "Peace be upon you, and my peace I leave with you." Then he vanished.

The apostles left for Jerusalem. They preached along the way. John Mark arrived home just after his father died. All were sad. Elijah Mark had hosted Jesus and the apostles; had become very close with them. It was at the Mark home that they had many events and it was there that they had the Last Supper. The apostles could not go to the funeral and had to remain in seclusion because of the Sanhedrin. Nevertheless, they made their headquarters there until Pentecost.

It was at this time that most of the apostles took the first steps to change the gospel. The real gospel was sonship with God and brotherhood with man. The new gospel proclaimed the resurrection of Jesus. Thomas, Simon Zelotes and the Alpheus twins did not agree. Nathaniel was at first opposed. However, he could not overcome Peter, the disciples, and the women believers. Under Peter's leadership, the well-meaning agents of the gospel slowly changed it. The *religion of Jesus* turned into a new form of religion *about* Jesus.

Jesus next met with the apostles, women's corps, and over fifty disciples. It was the sixteenth appearance. Jesus gave them instructions. He told them the gospel message was not changed by his resurrection.

Jesus had spoken years ago to a woman at Jacob's well concerning the water of life. On May 13, the morontia Jesus appeared to the same woman. About seventy-five believers (Samaritans) were also there. He again taught the gospel—the Fatherhood of God and brotherhood of man. He again taught that faith sons would live eternally. His eighteenth appearance was with a group of believers. Again, he taught the gospel. He said the fruits of the Spirit would show in their lives. (He named these qualities.) Further, he spoke of the Spirit of Truth.

The Master's last visit was Thursday morning, May 18, A.D. 30. It was on Mount Olivet with his eleven apostles. They were silent and somewhat bewildered. His last words to them were, "Love men as I have loved you and serve your fellow mortals even as I have served you. By the Spirit fruits of your lives, impel souls to believe the truth that man is a son of God, and that all men are brethren. Remember all I have taught you and the life I have lived among you. My love overshadows you, my spirit will dwell with you, and my peace shall remain upon you. Farewell." (UB 193:5.2) When the morontia Master had finished speaking, he disappeared from their sight.

*By way of Jerusem, the Master went to Edentia. There, the Most Highs released Jesus of Nazareth from the morontia state. Through the spirit channels of ascension, Michael proceeded to the right hand of the Paradise Father. From the Paradise Father, he received his sovereignty as a Master Michael Son.*

*Master Michael of Nebadon was welcomed home on Salvington. He was received as the supreme and unconditional sovereign; the universe of his own making, serving, and complete understanding.*

*On none of Michael's bestowals did he reveal God the Supreme. However, the total of all seven bestowals in Nebadon was a new revelation of the Supreme Being. Michael is a sevenfold Master Son. He has identified himself forever with the Supreme. It is speculated that in the next universe age, he will work with the Supreme Being in the universes of outer space.*

*Master Michael of Nebadon continues his unending progress in grace, truth, and glory. All the Father's faith children do.*

*Urantia is the sentimental shrine of all Nebadon; it is the mortal home of Christ Michael.*

*Christ Michael is:*
- *The supreme sovereign of all Nebadon*
- *A Melchizedek minister to the realms*
- *A system savior*
- *An Adamic redeemer*
- *A seraphic fellow*
- *An associate of ascending spirits*
- *A morontia progressor*
- *A Son of Man in the likeness of mortal flesh*
- *The Planetary Prince of Urantia*

*And this same Michael has promised to return to the world of his final bestowal, the World of the Cross.*

Michael's unrevealed plans for the future are of great interest to many. Michael's promise to return is thrilling, more so if it happens in our lifetimes. We might even witness—all at the same time—the appearance of Christ Michael, Machiventa, Adam and Eve, a Magisterial Son or Trinity Teacher Sons. (see UB 93:10.8)

The seventh and final bestowal of the Paradise Son of Nebadon was fulfilled; thus ended the Fourth Epochal Revelation on Urantia.

# 42. The Spirit of Truth on Urantia

At the time of Jesus' ascension, there were thousands of visitors in Jerusalem. That was because it was the Jewish festival of Pentecost. Pentecost was the celebration of baptism; it was especially for the baptism of the gentiles who wanted to serve Yahweh. One hundred and twenty of the leading disciples of Jesus were there. They gathered to hear the report of Jesus' farewell message and ascension. Jesus' mother, John Zebedee, and Jesus' brother, James, were among the group.

As the group prayed, they became aware of a strange presence in the room. All became aware of a new, powerful sense of spiritual joy; they felt secure and confident. This new sense of spiritual strength was followed by a strong urge to go and publicly proclaim the gospel of the kingdom. They wanted to share the good news that Jesus had risen from the dead.

The gospel was the Fatherhood of God and the brotherhood of man. These men had been taught the gospel. But, at the moment of their spiritual ecstasy, the greatest news they could think of was the fact of the risen Master. With power from on high, they preached glad tidings—even salvation through Jesus—but they stumbled into error. They substituted some of the facts *connected with* the gospel *for the gospel* message itself.

Christianity developed from that day forward as the fact of God as the Father of the Lord Jesus Christ. This was in relation to the experience of believer fellowship with the risen Christ.

Jesus always taught "the Fatherhood of God and the brotherhood of men." Still, it is not hard to understand how they came to preach a new **gospel about Jesus** in place of the **gospel of Jesus**. More than two thousand listeners followed the apostles to the river. They were baptized in the name of Jesus.

Not just the gathered disciples received the Spirit of Truth. It was bestowed upon all sincere believers and the honest of heart worldwide. The Thought Adjuster is the presence of the Father, but the Spirit of Truth is the presence of the Paradise Son. The Spirit of Truth is not the letter or law of truth. It also does not function as the form or expression of truth. The new teacher is the conviction, the certainty, of truth. It is the spirit of living and growing truth.

The Master lived in the hearts of those evangelists. God was not a doctrine in their minds; he was a living presence in their souls. Even today, the stagnant soul drags the living truth to the dead levels of exalted knowledge. The true child of spiritual insight looks for the living Spirit of Truth.

These three spirit gifts work together to establish a spirit personality:
* Faith-insight, or spiritual intuition, is the gift of the cosmic mind along with the Thought Adjuster.
* Spiritual reason, soul intelligence, is the gift of the Holy Spirit.
* Spiritual philosophy, the wisdom of spirit realities, is the gift of the Spirit of Truth.

The Spirit of Truth comes freely; no ceremonies, sacred places, or special behavior is needed. The Spirit of Truth is designed to reduce the assertiveness of a mortal, whole groups, nations, and races. Assertive behavior increases tension; that leads to wars. Mankind can only be united by the spiritual approach. The Spirit of Truth is a world influence assisting us. It is leading the way towards peace.

The coming of the Spirit of Truth purifies the human heart. It leads the receiver to make a life purpose aligned to the will of God and the welfare of men. The joy of this spirit may be consciously experienced; when this happens it is a tonic for health, a stimulus for mind, and energy for the soul.

A Paradise Son must be bestowed on a world in order for the Spirit of Truth to be poured out upon that world. Michael was the Paradise Son bestowed on Urantia. Not until the Spirit of Truth is present can the Thought Adjusters indwell the minds of *all* normal humans on that world. Pentecost was the day that the Spirit of Truth was poured out upon Urantia. Since that day, the divine Adjusters have been bestowed on Urantia worldwide.

Dwelling within the human mind is the fragment of God. The Spirit of Truth sojourns with the human soul. These two spiritual forces work together to assist mortals. They help people to grasp the reality of spiritual values. They help us to understand universe meanings. They help us to apply truth to our personal religious experiences.

The proof of your fellowship with the Spirit of Truth is not found in an awareness of this spirit. The Spirit of Truth does not create such an awareness of himself. This spirit creates a consciousness of enhanced fellowship with Christ Michael.

The Spirit of Truth is chiefly concerned with the truth revelation of the Father's love and the Son's mercy. These are the truths of divinity that people can understand the best. The Spirit of Truth reveals the Father's spirit nature and the Son's moral character. "The Creator Son, in the flesh, revealed God to men; the Spirit of Truth, in the heart, reveals the Creator Son to men." (UB 194:3.1)

The Spirit of Truth leads us into new areas of spiritual reality and divine service. We are not given truth to shape into concrete or safe, honored forms. Truth is living. Our revelation of truth must be enhanced by passing through our personal experiences. Those who recognize spiritual fruits can see such spiritual gains. With the Adjuster and the Spirit of Truth, we are led to glorify the Father. Happiness ensues from the "recognition of truth because it can be *acted out*; it can be lived." And, "divine truth is best known by its *spiritual flavor*." (UB 2:7.6)

Nebadon has three distinct spirit circuits.

- The bestowal spirit of the Creator Son, Michael of Nebadon—the Spirit of Truth

- The spirit circuit of the Creative Daughter, Divine Minister—the Holy Spirit

- The intelligence-ministry circuit, including the activities of the seven adjutant mind-spirits

Michael may come and go; he may be present in his local universe or elsewhere. His location does not disturb his gift of the Spirit of Truth. The Spirit of Truth is centered in the person of the Divine Minister. Our Mother Spirit (Divine Minister) never leaves the headquarters world. The Holy Spirit of the Divine Minister would stop functioning if she should be removed from Salvington. Because of her fixed presence and focus, Michael is able to leave Salvington.

When the Holy Spirit ministers to mind, it has the capacity to choose the presence of the Thought Adjuster. This choice may be conscious or unconscious. But, when the Spirit of Truth functions, all normal minds are prepared automatically for the Adjusters. The Spirit of Truth and the Holy Spirit work as one. The two spirit gifts are linked; it hovers over the world, seeking to teach truth and enlighten the minds of mortals. It inspires the souls of mortals and leads the people towards their Paradise goal of divine destiny.

In part, the Holy Spirit is conditioned by the choices and cooperation of the will of man. It is partly free of human attitude. Even so, the Holy Spirit is more effective when a mortal *obeys* the divine leadings. The Spirit of Truth is more limited in function and power. A mortal's reception and understanding of the mission of the bestowal Son affects those limits.

In or with an evolving mortal can be:

- The Holy Spirit—of the Universe Daughter—of the Infinite Spirit
- The Spirit of Truth—of the Paradise Father and Creator Michael Son—of the Eternal Son (UB 194:2.16)
- The Adjuster-spirit—of the Paradise Father

The presence of all three denotes the balance of spiritual endowment and ministry. It enables a mortal to consciously realize the faith-fact of sonship with God.

You begin your eternal life in the flesh by faith. Accept your orders to advance. Do not fear your human forgetfulness or uncertainty. Do not be troubled with doubts of failure or by confusion. Do not falter and question your status and standing. For at every crossroad in your forward struggle, the Spirit of Truth will always speak, saying, "This is the way." (UB 34:7.8)

# 43. The Development of Christianity

There have been seven outstanding, purely human, teachers on our world; they were Sethard, Moses, Zoroaster, Lao-tse, Buddha, Philo, and Paul. The early Christian doctrines were based mostly on the religious experiences of three people; they were, Philo of Alexandria, Jesus of Nazareth, and Paul of Tarsus.

Philo made a great effort to combine Greek thinking, Roman Stoic doctrines, and the Hebrew religion of laws. He led the way for Paul to restore the concept of the Paradise Trinity and other truths. However, some of Paul's teachings of original sin and atonement were his own ideas.

During this time, the worship of Mithras was the mystery cult with the greatest number of followers. It competed with the newly forming Christian religion. Mithraism began in Iran. It was influenced by the teachings of Zoroaster, especially his ideas of good and evil. Like all religions, Zoroaster's teachings grew from Melchizedek's teachings; all were altered to various degrees.

Mithras supposedly came from a great rock and was a militant god who made water gush from rocks hit by his arrows. It was believed he caused a world flood and only one man survived because he had built a special boat. Also, Mithras had a last supper with the sun god before ascending into heaven. Followers believed that at the end of the world, Mithras would judge the living and the dead; the wicked would be destroyed by fire and the righteous would rule forever with Mithras. On this judgment day, the Mithras keys of heaven would unlock the gates of Paradise for the faithful. The unbaptized would be destroyed when Mithras returned to earth.

Followers of this cult worshipped in secret places including caves. They chanted hymns, mumbled magic, ate the sacrificed animals, and drank their blood. They worshipped three times a day and had special weekly ceremonies. They had their biggest event on December twenty-fifth. Men could join one of seven different orders. Later, wives and daughters of believers were allowed to attend adjoining temples of the Great Mother.

In the third century after Christ, both the Mithraic and Christian churches looked the same on the outside. Each had altars with backgrounds showing their suffering savior who had brought salvation to a sin-cursed world. Both religions baptized believers; both practiced the sacrament of bread and wine. Mithras worshipers dipped their fingers into holy water when they entered the temple. The Christian churches around Rome took up this custom from the people who, at the time, belonged to both religions.

The two cults competed. One religion had Jesus as their savior and the other had Mithras. Mithras followers were quite militant; Christians were very peaceful. The Mithraic cult was tolerant of all religions except for the Christian religion. The deciding factor in their struggle came when the Christian faith fully allowed women to join.

In the end, the Christian religion dominated the West. Mithraism supplied the rituals; Greek philosophy supplied the ethical values. The Christian religion was the technique for saving moral and social values. In addition, it should be noted that Paul and his successors were willing compromisers and keen religious traders.

The Christian religion was founded almost solely on the spiritual events and beliefs of Paul. Mithraism was the dominant religion of Tarsus when Paul was in his teens; Mithraism must have influenced him. Most of the New Testament is not devoted to the inspiring religious life of Jesus; instead, it is a discussion of Paul's religious experience and his convictions. The letters that Paul wrote to his converts were much later regarded as the "word of God." But then, Paul had no way of knowing that would ever happen.

Many, many of the earliest Christians were Jewish converts. A lot of the Hebrew religion was blended into the Christian religion; their morals, belief in the hereafter, and their belief in Yahweh were merged. Much influenced how the Christian faith developed; the teachings, cults, personal beliefs, and the fact of Jesus' life all had an effect.

The gospel of Jesus spread westward. But, as it spread, his teachings changed. They began to lose their universal appeal. Over time, Christianity became a "white man's" religion.

The Christian religion contains more of Jesus' teachings than other religions; but it also contains much that Jesus never taught. The Christian atonement doctrine is the teaching that Jesus was the sacrificed Son who paid for the sins of the world. God the Father's stern justice would then be satisfied and his divine wrath appeased. It was an early effort to connect the gospel teachings to the Jewish practice of sacrifice. It was supposed to win converts of the disbelieving Jews. These efforts failed to win Jews. It did however succeed in confusing and pushing away many honest souls in all the centuries that followed.

The second great blunder was the focus on the person of Jesus. Jesus founded the religion of personal experience in doing the will of God and serving each other. Paul founded a religion in which the glorified Jesus became the object of worship; the brotherhood comprised fellow believers in Christ. Paul's doctrines made Jesus the *Redeemer* of the children of the church. Early Christians were too concerned with whom they thought Jesus was; they overlooked what Jesus said about his mission to bring man closer to God and God closer to man.

The East and West will have difficulty sharing in the worship of the Paradise Father as long as Christianity, (1.) Promotes a religion *about* Jesus, and, (2.) Stresses the differences in world religions. Both Western and Eastern religions can accept the true religion of Jesus. It is their common thread, if only they were more willing to recognize it.

In the minds of the world, Christianity suffers under a great handicap. This religion has become identified with:
- the social system
- the industrial life
- the moral standards of Western civilization

And thus has the Christian religion seemed to sponsor a society that staggers under the guilt of tolerating:
- science without idealism
- politics without principles
- wealth without work
- pleasure without restraint
- knowledge without character
- power without conscience
- and industry without morality

Still, the Christian faith is a beautiful religion *about* Jesus. But, it has for the most part, forgotten the personal religion *of* Jesus. At the heart of Jesus' teachings is the ***Fatherhood of God and the brotherhood of all people.***

# 44. The Fifth Epochal Revelation

The word "epochal" (ep'-ek-al) is used to denote an important and often long period of time. The word "revelation" means that divine truth is made known. There have been many events of revelation on Urantia; but only five are deemed epochal revelations. These are as follows.

1. *The Dalamatian* (dal-ah-may'-shan) *teachings, See Chapters 24-27.* Prince Caligastia with his staff of One Hundred corporeal (physical) members arrived. This was about five hundred thousand years ago. They taught the true concept of the First Source and Center worldwide. This expanding revelation of Deity went on for more than three hundred thousand years. Then the teachings suddenly stopped. Our celestial prince and part of his staff joined the Lucifer rebellion. Urantia was then isolated from the system. Except for the work of Van, the Dalamatian revelation was nearly lost to the whole world. Even the Nodites had forgotten these truths by the time of Adam's arrival. Of all who received the teachings of the One Hundred, the red men held them longest. The idea of the Great Spirit grew hazy in Native American religions. But, contact with Christian beliefs greatly strengthened them.

2. *The Edenic teachings, See Chapters 28-31.* Adam and Eve arrived almost thirty-eight thousand years ago. They again portrayed the concept of the Father of all to the evolving peoples. The default of Adam and Eve stopped the course of the revelation before it had fully started. The Sethite priests carried on the teachings of Adam. Some of these truths have never been entirely lost to the world. The evolving religions of the Middle East were influenced by the teachings of the Sethites. But, by 2500 B.C., mankind had largely lost sight of the revealed teachings from the days of Eden.

3. *Melchizedek of Salem, See Chapters 32-35.* About 3000 B.C., this Son of Nebadon launched the third revelation of truth on our world. His central teachings were *trust* and *faith*. He taught trust in the all-powerful goodness of God. Melchizedek proclaimed that faith was the act by which men earned God's favor. His teachings slowly mixed with the beliefs of the religions of evolution. They evolved into the religions present on Urantia one thousand years after Christ.

4. *Jesus of Nazareth, See Chapters 36-43.* Christ Michael gave, for the fourth time to Urantia, the concept of God as the Paradise Father. His teachings have mostly carried on ever since. The essence of his teaching was *love* and *service*. A creature son offers loving worship in response to the loving ministry of God his Father. The free will service of creature sons to their brethren is a joy because they are also serving God the Father.

5. *The Urantia Papers, The Urantia Book* is the most recent gift of revealed truth to the mortals of Urantia, Earth. This revelation differs from all the others, for it is not the work of one universe being. These papers are a combined presentation by many beings. It is not complete; only the attainment of the Paradise Father is complete. All other celestial ministry is partial; it is adapted to the local conditions of the times. Such admissions might detract from the force and authority of this revealed truth. But its time has come. Frank statements are wise, even though there is a risk that they might weaken the influence of this, the Fifth Epochal Revelation.

Our planet needs the narratives found in *The Urantia Book*. This is because there is great confusion about the nature of God and the vast orders of beings that serve on his behalf. The priests and prophets of the past failed to see the difference between personalities. Also, our sacred books fail to distinguish between the persons of the Trinity and the local universe creators. Even messages from lower orders like angels are recorded as coming straight from God.

If a Paradise Son arrived on our world today, who would recognize him? If the Lucifer rebellion quarantine was lifted, how would we react? What would happen if we were to meet our brothers and sisters that inhabit other worlds? Would we be wise enough to know that advanced technical skills are no measure of spiritual growth?

For most people, the Urantia Papers are hard to grasp. But the Revelators know that the Father fragment, the Spirit of Truth, and other spirit helpers, will assist us. They are able to help us understand and experience God-consciousness.

The Revelators are the Orvonton corps of truth revealers. They were allowed to put into English the presentations given to us as *The Urantia Book*. Their mandates required that they were to make use of the highest and most advanced human spiritual knowledge. They could only use pure revelation when there were no adequate human concepts. More than one thousand human sources were used in the Urantia Papers.

The Urantia Papers do not claim to be perfect. Anything that human hands or minds touch is open to imperfection. What *The Urantia Book* does claim, what it does reveal, will not fail to enhance your spiritual growth. But you must integrate the new truths with an open heart and mind. Still, new revealed truths are always contaminated by the older beliefs. Evolved religions are based in fear; revealed religion is based in love. Mankind has yet to shed all his fears. Mankind has yet to experience the real gospel of Jesus—the Fatherhood of God and the brotherhood of all men and women.

The laws of revelation are very clear about what may be told. Unearned or premature knowledge is not allowed. Human wisdom must evolve. For these reasons, science in *The Urantia Book* will stand in need of revision as new discoveries are made. Science that was current in the 1920s and '30s was used. This already has resulted in errors as we have learned much more. Such errors may tempt students to disregard the whole revelation. But, remember that science deals with facts; religion deals with values; the mind tries to unite both into a concept of complete reality.

The strength of Islam has been its clear-cut and well-defined presentation of Allah as the one and only Deity. Its weakness has been the use of military force in spreading its teachings and its degradation of women. But Islam has firmly held to its teachings of the One Universal Deity of all. 'He is the merciful and the compassionate.' 'Truly God is plenteous in goodness to all men.' 'And when I am sick, it is he who heals me.' 'For whenever as many as three speak together, God is present as a fourth.' (UB 95:7.6)

Buddhism holds that the Buddha (divine) nature resides in all men; that man, through his own endeavors, can attain this inner divinity. This teaching is one of the clearest truths of the indwelling Adjusters ever to be made by a world religion.

Much of Asia rests its hope in Buddhism. The disciples of the great teacher in India once listened to his proclamation of new truth. Will this noble faith, which so valiantly carried on through the dark ages of the past, once again receive expanded truth? Will this ancient faith respond once more to new concepts of God and the Absolute for which it has so long searched?

All of Urantia is waiting for the uplifting message of Michael—without the added doctrines of evolved religions. The hour is striking for presenting to Buddhists, Christians, Hindus, even to the peoples of all faiths, the living spiritual reality of the gospel of Jesus. The Fifth Epochal Revelation paves the way.

*The Urantia Book* holds the promise of a deeper personal relationship with God. Mankind needs to understand religion as **the Fatherhood of God and the brotherhood of mankind; this is sonship with God for each individual**. Sonship with God is the true religion of personal experience. This is the gateway to divine love.

Urantia is now quivering on the very brink of one of its most amazing epochs. It is a time of social readjustment. It is a time of moral quickening. And, it is a time of spiritual enlightenment. Mankind is on the march! We are headed toward a new and unknown planetary destiny. There is need of preparation. There is need of deeper understanding.

# Closing

*The Urantia Book* is a revelation. It is the fifth epochal revelation to our world. It takes over a million words to expand our understandings. We are taught who God the Father is and our relationship to him. We learn how the universes are structured and how they are governed. The narratives provide a history of our origins as well as show us our future. We learn what becomes of mortals after death, our glorious destiny. It corrects misunderstandings. It tells us the source of myths. It gives us new facts, new meanings, and new values. It moves us beyond global thinking to cosmic citizenship. The Papers inspire us to become our spiritual best, to love, and to serve. So, what can be said after all of this? What is the closing to such teachings?

*The Urantia Book* sums it up in the final two paragraphs. Rephrased, the Revelators have the following parting thoughts.

The great challenge today is to achieve better contact with the divine Adjuster. A mortal's greatest quest consists in the wise effort to expand the borders of self-consciousness; then, it is to move through the dim realms of soul-consciousness to reach the borderland of spirit-consciousness. Such contact with the divine presence is God-consciousness; it is the religious experience of knowing God. It is the basis of actual sonship with God. Otherwise, the assurance of sonship is based on faith.

Only the spirit content of any value is eternal. That which is true, beautiful, and good in human experience will not perish. If a mortal does not choose to survive, then the Adjuster saves those realities born of love and nurtured in service. "And all these things are a part of the Paradise Father. The Father is living love, and this life of the Father is in his Sons. And the spirit of the Father is in his Son's sons—mortal men. When all is said and done, the Father idea is still the highest human concept of God."

# Glossary

*The Urantia Book* introduces new terms, names, and applies unique definitions to some words. This Glossary lists these types of words that appear in more than one chapter.

**Adjuster**: *See Thought Adjuster.*

**Adjutant mind-spirits**: The adjutant mind-spirits are not personalities; they are more akin to circuits. There are seven adjutant mind-spirits in each local universe. They function through the Universe Mother Spirit. These adjutants represent the mind ministry of the Infinite Spirit, as does the Mother Spirit. The adjutant mind-spirits are called the spirit of intuition, understanding, courage, knowledge, counsel, worship, and the spirit of wisdom. All seven must be functioning in a person before the Thought Adjuster can arrive. *See Chapter 14.*

**Amadon**: (am'-ah-don) Amadon was a descendant of Andon and Fonta (the first humans) who donated his DNA to the Caligastia One Hundred. He was the assistant to Van and remained loyal during the Lucifer rebellion. Amadon is considered the human hero of Urantia for his loyalty and service. *See Chapter 25.*

**Andon and Fonta**: Andon and Fonta were the first human beings. *See Chapter 23.*

**Andonites**: (an'-don-ites) Andonites were descendants of the first two humans, Andon and Fonta. They are the aborigines or original evolutionary humans. *See Chapters 23 and 27.*

**Caligastia**: (cal-i-gas'-chah) Caligastia was the (invisible) celestial Planetary Prince of Urantia. He betrayed us by joining the Lucifer rebellion about 200,000 years ago. *See Chapters 24-26.*

**Circuit**: The term circuit, in the spiritual sense, denotes a path for the flow of spiritual energies. A circuit is not a personality or being. The source of the flow of energies or gifts is of a divine nature. A circuit serves to provide the channel whereby the spiritual flow from the divine source reaches and connects with mortal man and other lower orders.

**Cosmic mind**: The Seven Master Spirits fully represent the Infinite Spirit and are the source of cosmic mind, Infinite mind, the mind of God. The mind of man is an individualized circuit, an impersonal portion, of that cosmic mind as it is bestowed in a local universe. *See Chapter 8.*

**Dispensation**: A dispensation is an age or period of time in which sleeping survivors are unconscious. These mortals have died but have not been resurrected due to insufficient spiritual growth during their physical lives. When a dispensation is terminated, a roll call ensues, a judgment is made, and the sleeping survivors are resurrected all together. A new dispensation is then initiated. It is unclear what brings about the closing of a dispensation. Michael-Jesus closed a dispensation. The sleeping survivors were from the times of Adam and Eve until his bestowal mission was complete. Therefore, we cannot assume that epochal revelations earmark dispensations. (Adam was the second epochal revelation and Jesus was the fourth.)

**Edentia**: (e-den'-chah) Edentia is the headquarters of our local constellation. The Garden of Eden on each world is named in its honor.

**Fusion**: Fusion is the union of the evolving mortal soul with the eternal and divine Adjuster. Fusion with a fragment of the Paradise Father is the divine validation of eventual Paradise attainment. Such Adjuster-fused mortals are the only class of human beings who all traverse the Havona circuits and find God on Paradise. *See Page 3, and Chapters 16 and 17.*

**Havona**: (hah-vohn'-ah) Havona is also known as the central universe. It is eternal. The Infinite Spirit created this perfect universe of one billion perfect worlds.

**Immanuel**: Immanuel is an ambassador of the Paradise Trinity. He is a Union of Days, a high Trinity Son. He functions as advisor to our Creator Son. Michael of Nebadon refers to Immanuel as his elder brother. *See Chapters 14 and 36.*

**Isle of Paradise**: The Isle of Paradise, also called the Isle of Light and Life, is the dwelling place of God. Paradise is at the center of creation and is stationary. *See Chapter 7.*

**Jerusem**: (jeh-roo'-sem) Jerusem is the headquarters world of our local system of Satania.

**Lucifer**: Lucifer was the System Sovereign until he started a rebellion about 200,000 years ago. *See Chapters 25 and 26.*

**Master Spirits**: There were just Seven Master Spirits created by the Infinite Spirit. Each works primarily with one of the seven superuniverses. *See Chapter 8.*

**Melchizedek**: (mel-kizz'-uh-deck) Melchizedeks are a descending order of Sons created by a local universe Creator Son and Creative Daughter Spirit. *See Chapters 10 and 14.* Machiventa (mack-ah-ven'-ta) Melchizedek incarnated on Urantia about 2,000 B.C. His was an emergency mission during the times of Abraham. *See Chapters 32-35.*

**Michael**: Michael is the name of an order of Paradise Sons (Creator Michael Sons), that go forth into time and space to create local universes in partnership with the Creative Daughter Spirits. Michael of Nebadon is the Paradise Son that created our universe. Since his incarnation on our world, he has the earned title of Master Michael of Nebadon.

**Midwayers**: Midway or halfway between mortals and angels are the midway creatures. There are two types of Midwayers, primary and secondary. They are just beyond our range of sight. Midwayers are permanent to a planet until that world reaches the age of Light and Life. *See Chapters 14 (at end), 15, 24, and 26.*

**Morontia**: (moh-ron'-chah) Morontia is the long phase between the material life and the spirit life. After physical death, the soul is resurrected (with mind and identity) and given a morontia form. The morontia form is not flesh and blood and it is also not a spirit form; it is the phase of existence between the two. *See Chapters 16, and 17.*

**Nebadon**: (neb'-ah-don) Nebadon is the name of our local universe.

**Nodites**: (nod'-ites) Rebel members of the Caligastia One Hundred were led by Nod. Descendants were called Nodites and considered the eighth race. *See Chapters 25-27.*

**Orvonton**: (or-von'-ton) There are seven superuniverses. The seventh, to which we belong, is called Orvonton.

**Personality**: Personality is the unique bestowal of the Paradise Father. How the Father gifts personality and what exactly it is, remains a mystery. We are told that personality is changeless and a being either has personality or does not have personality. It should not be confused with such terms as character, nature, or disposition that can be changed. Personality is not body, mind, spirit or the soul. Personality is self-conscious and free willed. It is unique; there are no duplicate personalities in creation. *See Chapters 1 and 2.*

**Reflectivity**: Reflectivity is a unique power. It makes it possible to see, hear, and sense everything as it happens. The mental, material, and spiritual is revealed at the same time. This knowledge can be directed and sent anywhere in the superuniverses. Reflectivity allows the universe rulers to know about remote events instantly. *See Chapters 4, 9, and 17.*

**Salvington**: (sal'-ving-ton) Salvington is the headquarters world of our local universe of Nebadon. It is home to Michael and Mother Spirit, our universe creators.

**Satan**: Satan was the first assistant to Lucifer, the System Sovereign. *See Chapters 25 and 38.*

**Satania**: (sah-tane'-ee-ah) A local universe is comprised of 10,000 systems for administrative purposes. Satania is the system we belong to in our universe. It was named in honor of Satan long before the rebellion.

**Thought Adjuster**: The Thought Adjuster is also called the Adjuster, the Father Fragment, and has various other names such as the Mystery Monitor. The Adjuster is a gift from God the Father. The Adjuster is an actual fragment of the Father that dwells within the mind (not the physical brain), of all morally conscious people. The Adjuster serves to adjust our thoughts Godward. The Adjuster *is* God the Father in our lives. *See Chapter 1.*

**Urantia**: (you-ran'-chah) Urantia is the celestial name of our planet.

**Van**: Van was one of the Caligastia One Hundred. He remained loyal when the Lucifer rebellion broke out. Van was the leader of the loyal angels, Midwayers, and mortals on Urantia. *See Chapters 25-28.*

# Resources

*The first two listings are the "main" organizations, followed by additional groups in alphabetical order, and last are [mostly YouTube] videos. This is not a complete listing, as new groups are always forming. Also, check Facebook for Urantia groups.*

**The Urantia Book Fellowship:** www.urantiabook.org
The primary focus of The Urantia Book Fellowship is the dissemination of *The Urantia Book*, but they also strive to bring together people who read and believe in the book. There is no official doctrine, viewpoint, or belief system promulgated by the Fellowship. They seek to coordinate the efforts of all readers to study *The Urantia Book*, to grow spiritually, to foster community, and to participate in the worldwide spread of the book and its teachings. Fellowship members seek understanding among all students of *The Urantia Book* and among the peoples of the world. They are committed to the ideal of spiritual unity, which embraces individual religious freedom and diversity, as embodied in the teachings of *The Urantia Book*. [This site allows you to search for a study group by country, province, or zip code. It also has the entire *Urantia Book* you can read online, a UB search engine, an audio Urantia Book you can listen to, topical studies, and a link to their Spanish Fellowship website. On the drop-down menu under Reader Resources, is Outreach Resources that is excellent!]

~**UrantiaNow:** http://urantianow.com
Sponsored by The Urantia Book Fellowship
UrantiaNow.com is an interactive community platform designed to foster worldwide spiritual unity through the positive free expression of personal religious experience as revealed in *The Urantia Book*. They seek to reach anyone interested in learning more about, becoming involved with, or staying involved with the community of Urantia Book readers. The content and aesthetic of the site is particularly meant to appeal to younger generations. The site is designed as a news blog. Featured posts rotate regularly, focus on personal religious experience, and encourage comments and discussion. The site also offers an opinion section and resources for study, support, socialization, service, and outreach.

~**YaYA:** http://urantianow.com/about/
This is the place to learn about the Youth and Young Adult committee. They formed in July 2010 with some great founding members. It is a one-stop shop for all things new and current in the world of Urantia Book readers, and, more importantly, a sounding board for this generation's commitment and contribution to the work at hand. They believe that their generation has a great advantage over all prior generations because of their ability to communicate through the world wide web. Hungry souls look every day for truth online and when they do find them, they make their commitment loud and clear. They believe their intentions and goals must shine like the sun. "Let us leave no doubt in their minds that the truths and ideals we hold are the kind that transform your life." [Very inspiring youth group!]

**The Urantia Foundation:** www.urantia.org
The mission of Urantia Foundation is to seed *The Urantia Book* and its teachings globally. Urantia Foundation is committed to producing high quality translations of *The Urantia Book* that faithfully represent the English text in all major languages. The book has been translated into Dutch, Estonian, Finnish, French, German, Hungarian, Italian, Korean, Lithuanian, Polish, Portuguese, Russian, Spanish, and Swedish, and the books are distributed in countries where these languages are spoken. Chinese, Japanese, and Farsi (Persian) translations are under development. [You can read *The Urantia Book* online in English or 18 other languages. It also has a search program for *The Urantia Book* on their website.]

### ~Urantia Association International [UIA] https://urantia-association.org
"Urantia Association International is a worldwide network of believing Urantia Book readers who have chosen to participate in our two-fold mission: *to foster the in-depth study of the book and the dissemination of its teachings* – teachings which have the potential to rejuvenate spirituality in this world and enhance the comfort, happiness and well-being of every person. People are welcome regardless of beliefs or background, race or nationality, faith or religion." They created an organization to serve as a central hub of information and outreach to people across the world. They recognize the value of teamwork in the projects and activities they undertake for the mutual benefit of those whom they serve – our fellow citizens of the world – by way of national and international conferences, reader services, publications, forums in various languages, and numerous other projects. [Be sure to check About Us/Services & Programs and Study Groups/Study Aids & Resources.]

---

**11:11 Progress Group:** www.correctingtime.org [Wonderful new website!]
- http://1111angels.net/index.php [Home of the 11:11 Progress group- English, Spanish, French]
- http://board.1111angels.com/viewtopic.php?t=345 [a message board/English forum]
- http://1111angels.net/old_files/archives.html [2,400+ communications from celestials]
- http://1111angels.us4.list-manage.com/subscribe?u=0db301c879183b1f2c566143f&id=22bd2e860d [You can subscribe to receive a daily, short message by email]
- http://www.1111angels.net/index.php/store [Of particular interest is the book, The Search for 11:11 by George Barnard. It details how George ended up working with a platoon of Midwayers years before he heard of *The Urantia Book!*]
- www.1111akashicconstruct.com/ [This site offers The Akashic Construct CD- very reasonably priced. The CD contains the secrets that George Barnard uses to reach the deep alpha levels needed to make contact. Together with the techniques of deep meditation, George takes you on a carefully structured guided meditation into the realm of your very own Akashic Workshop.]
- www.correctingtime.org [From their website, "Our Mission"] It is the mission of the 11:11 The Correcting Time Organization to reach the heart, mind, and soul of all those who are searching for deeper meaning in their life and in their relationship with Spirit. [Be sure to read their 7-step plan.] "We are dedicated to the awakening process—to enlighten with Universal Truth, to inspire with heart-centered Beauty, and to embody the Goodness and Higher Love of the Indwelling Spirit—to reach out to as many people as we can who desire to know who they really are, why they are here at this time on earth, and to discover their "inner" and "inter" connectedness to all life."

**The Boulder School:** http://theboulderschool.com
The Boulder School was founded in 1982 by John Hay and Merritt Horn. Between 1982 and 1988, the school served 114 students. While the mission and purpose of the school remained steadfast in the heart of its founders and many of its graduates, the opportunity for the school to again open its doors to students would not be realized until now. "We are excited that 2017 marks the time for The Boulder School to once again welcome and serve you as a committed reader and student of the Revelation!" [Their site offers insight into the type of Urantia Book reader that would benefit from the school, an overview of the curriculum, some of the challenges, and the many opportunities provided by Urantia Book scholars and mentors.]

**Center for Christ Consciousness:** www.ctrforchristcon.org
At the Center for Christ Consciousness, they believe that every person has a spark of God within them and a divine and sacred purpose to his or her life. They affirm that it is your divine birthright to recognize who and what your relationship to your Creator is and to come into conscious awareness of your higher purpose as a child of God and a citizen of the universe. Sometimes it is challenging to find the part of yourself that is connected to your Divine Source due to feelings of unworthiness, helplessness, hopelessness, and fear, yet these emotions can be transformed. They are dedicated to help you go within and connect with the inner assistance you have access to through their offerings and services. [The CCC offers personal healing and transformation, Generational Healing, and other services to assist you in connecting with your divine parents. An array of books and CDs are also offered with a Stillness (meditation) CD especially for teens. If you are familiar with spiritual healing, I see this as healing for healers. If you are not familiar with spiritual healing, you will be gently guided through the process.]

**The Christ Experiment:** https://soundcloud.com/thechristexperiment [This is a podcast with a very interesting recording, but I only found the first episode.] Episode One: The Christ Experiment... where we hypothesize that the plain and open teachings of Jesus of Nazareth, without added dogma and tradition, can change the world and usher in a new era of peace and liberty.]

**God's Gumshoe:** www.godsgumshoe.org
Just as a Food Critic looks for Truth, Beauty, and Goodness in the food he loves, so with the Spiritual Detective and the Religious Quest. Each religion makes certain claims about their belief system. God's Gumshoe is your agent, looking into the Truth, Beauty, and Goodness, of these various Religions and reports upon his findings on these pages. And, just as the Food Critic does his work for the improvement and love of Food, so too the Religious Detective for the Spiritual. Come see what he has discovered!!! [Although this site is under construction, it is loaded with information. Be sure to check 'About GG' and read his impressive Awards and Activities. I have also listed *The Urantia Book* for Dummies under YouTube videos.]

**The Harp of God:** www.harpofgod.org
The Harp of God serves as a means for disseminating information from the global network of sincere seekers of truth whose communion with our celestial helpers offers a contemporary path to learning and service for ourselves and our fellow human beings on earth. [Harp of God has published some beautiful little books based on celestial transmissions that are unique.]

**The Jesusonian Foundation:** http://truthbook.com

The Jesusonian Foundation believes that the worldwide promotion and distribution of *The Urantia Book* and its great teachings are critical to the eventual spiritual and cultural transformation of humanity. They believe that the time is here for the religion of Jesus, distinguished from the religion about Jesus, to be presented afresh to the world. They believe that the Master's appealing gospel will win the minds and souls of all people. The Jesusonian Foundation is devoted to working with the contemporary world religions while simultaneously contributing to the foundations of a dynamic new world religious and philosophical movement. The Jesusonian Foundation is fully dedicated to love, understanding and good will with all people. Furthermore, they are committed to cooperative work and loving association with all individuals and organizations advancing the insights, activities, and religious growth stimulated by the spiritual truth found in, or harmonious with, the Fifth Epochal Revelation (*The Urantia Book*). [This site is truly amazing and features *The Urantia Book* online in various forms and a search engine. However, what makes it unique are the topical subjects given in detail such as Life After Death (Heaven), Angels, Adam & Eve, and Life Challenges. What makes it exceptional is the incredible Religious Art Gallery! Also, under Urantia Book/Audio, you will find information on two BlogTalkRadio shows, The Cosmic Citizen and Symmetry of Soul.]

**Light and Life:** www.lightandlife.com

This exploration of the Spiritual Universe includes several years of Teaching Mission lessons and a complete download of the first edition of *The Urantia Book*. Also, sites for art, poetry, video, books, music, photography and links to Planetary Light-bringers. Their multi-media Exploration of the Spiritual Universe is for your enlightenment and entertainment. They will range from the exposure of corruptions that blight our world to the highest visions of goodness. They hope you will participate by sending your creative expressions that speak to spiritual values, including essays, videos, MP3 music tracks, podcasts, poetry, artwork, and photographs. They want to showcase your activist movements for social and spiritual progress. The planet is quickening with new energies and insights, even as we stand at the brink of catastrophes from war, corruption, and environmental crises. "Hope you will join us in showcasing paths to enlightenment, and in realizing our Oneness in the Spirit. - Jim Cleveland" [On the menu is Phenomena, an unusual but appropriate topic! This is an interesting site with many offerings!]

**Magisterial Mission:** www.magisterialmission.org

This site is being carefully assembled to announce the coming of a magisterial son of high divinity known by the name of Monjoronson. He is expected to manifest in adult form during our lifetime. The purpose of this website is to introduce him to the world as one whose mission extends to all who reside on Earth. His message will include and at the same time transcend all religious and spiritual affiliations. He will represent the way of the Father, the First Source and Creator demonstrating for us the one family that we all belong to. It is our goal to highlight certain communications we have received from him and to facilitate the mission he is currently leading on our behalf that will eventually bring our planet back to an orderly, peaceful and sustainable course. [This site is user friendly and without distractions.]

**Master Universe Almanac-Charting the Urantia Papers:** http://masteruniverse.org

Archaeological evidence shows that statistical tables have been used at least as far back as the Assyrian times. They likely were used in Eden and Dalmatia. The revelators use tables regularly throughout the 196 papers. They are printed directly or suggested in the narrative. This almanac presents a collection of tables and charts that describe matter, mind, spirit, and personality throughout the master universe. The intent is to faithfully recreate information from the papers in the form of tables, lists, and charts. [Fascinating!]

**Origin Press:** http://www.originpress.com

Byron Belitsos is a multiple award-winning author and book publisher, an editor and educator. He founded Origin Press in 1996. Origin Press has won three national awards for its titles. They publish books in practical spirituality, psychology, self-help, global religion, philosophy, progressive business and politics, ufology, visionary fiction, and related subjects.

> **~Evolving Souls:** http://evolving-souls.org
> Celestia, a non-profit, is an imprint of Origin Press that publishes books for readers who are fascinated by the Urantia Revelation and other mysteries of consciousness, planetary history, and cosmology. [This is] a community devoted to epochal revelation and inner illumination. Experience the heart of cosmic spirituality with their unique books, videos, teleseminars, and conferences—all based on the Urantia Revelation. [See their YouTube videos, at least a dozen, at www.youtube.com/channel/UCr7PGcNLBjRqf-rs8RcTOkw]

**Perfecting Horizons Institute:** www.perfectinghorizonsinstitute.org

'To live a life of meaning' is above their mission statement. It says: In everything we do, we believe in discerning, recognizing, and thinking critically. We draw a personal living philosophy out of an expanding relationship with true science and true religion. Dr. Chris M. Halvorson, Ph.D. teaches an expanded viewpoint of our horizons—in terms of our origin, history, and destiny. Register for Free Friday Night Webinars or attend the study group in Boulder, CO. The group serves inquisitive-minded people, challenging them to discover fresh big-picture insights and new ways of thinking for themselves, encouraging them to draw a personal living philosophy out of an expanding relationship with true science and true religion, and to apply it to everything they do. [From my days in Boulder, I will say that Chris is a natural teacher with an ability to take very complex topics and explain them in a way that the average person can grasp. New readers loved his group as well as some very brilliant minds!]

**Pipeline of Light:** www.urantiabook.org/urantia-book-store/contributions

The Pipeline of Light was launched in 2002 to address the enormous demand for *The Urantia Book* in countries where readers cannot afford them. It is a joint effort of the Urantia Foundation and the Urantia Book Fellowship. The Pipeline of Light project provides a flow of donated books in every available language to areas where readers can otherwise only dream of owning a personal copy of the revelation. In the first quarter of 2017, the Pipeline of Light volunteers placed 267 copies of *The Urantia Book* into nine countries. That brought the current efforts to an all-time total of 7,110 copies of *The Urantia Book* placed into 85 countries around the world. Every penny raised for the Pipeline of Light is used exclusively for books and shipping costs, and donations are tax-exempt.

**Square Circles:** www.squarecircles.com

SquareCircles.com is a place to learn as much as possible about *The Urantia Book*. Here you will find studies that delve into the Urantia Papers' human sources, historic documents that lead us deeper into the mystery of how the Papers came to our world, and works that help us to understand difficult concepts in the Papers. [This site is packed with Urantia Book sources and resources. It has an interesting history of the UB movement, human sources discovered and used in *The Urantia Book*, books, articles, and study aids. Also distinctive is a six-minute video, Ascent to Paradise, in 20 languages! www.youtube.com/watch?v=wtQHsxHvYHg]

**The Teaching Mission Network:** www.teachingmissionnetwork.com
[A new interactive site is under construction: www.teachingmission.org]
They call themselves a band of friends and kindred spirits who have been working with celestial teachers for over 25 years, as both listeners and transmitters. They were motivated to organize the Teaching Mission Network for sincere seekers who want to connect with the celestial teachers with whom they lovingly interact. This process is begun by devoting time to listening in the Stillness [meditation], prayer, and the development of a personal relationship with God, your Creator. Stillness practice can be an exhilarating and energizing spiritual experience in itself. It can also bring to you a new wave of celestial teachers assigned to our quickening planet. They will offer you personalized guidance and foundational spiritual insights for your soul growth. You can learn to transmit the celestial teachers orally, by written journal or keyboard. While they are all evolving students of spirituality, they would be pleased to be your friends, your advisors, guides, and facilitators in your individual journey. They charge no fees and accept no donations. [New Points of Light, offers new TM materials including the previously untold history of the Teaching Mission and the continuation in Volume II. Be sure to see the Video Links that have many great videos not seen elsewhere.]

**TheoQuest:** www.theoquest.com
"Our vision is to provide an online portal that assists individuals in their search for spiritual truth—for God—by providing a variety of resources embracing information on love, death, angels, family, science, religion, philosophy, God, prayer, Jesus, personality, revelation, universe, and the soul. The centerpiece of this effort is an introduction to and presentation of the teachings of *The Urantia Book*, a revelation of truth of epochal significance for our planet. It is our hope that exploration of these greater truths will lead seekers to an understanding that we are all children of a loving Creator, that we live in a friendly universe, and that an unending universal adventure of growth lies ahead of us."

**Truthseekers:** http://tsquest.org
Truthseekers is an event-oriented group for teens aged 14-19 (older alumni are always welcome too as leaders or facilitators) who spend quality time together, getting to know one another via wonderful adventures set in some of the most beautiful places on earth. It was started by Tom Choquette and Fred Harris in 2002. It is a growing community from all walks of life who devote themselves to a sincere search for meaning and values. The program provides support and encouragement in recognizing their own values and related meanings to assist them in their lives. While each Truthseeker ultimately discovers his or her own values, the shared Truthseekers experience begins with three values: love, forgiveness, and service. Truthseekers is dedicated to helping youth and young adults find and explore the meanings and values that will enable them to lead healthy and productive lives. [See their inspiring short video that will make you wish you had such guidance as a teen!]

**UBtheNEWS:** www.ubthenews.com
"The information in *The Urantia Book* remains the same. The contribution that new discoveries and scientific developments make to our appreciation of history and material reality is ever changing. The UBtheNEWS project systematically documents how we are catching up to *The Urantia Book*. Some issues are quite simple and/or are reasonably settled topics among scholars and scientists. Other issues regarding *The Urantia Book*'s relationship to scholarship and science are more complex and/or unsettled. If it is important to you that the writings you go to for inspiration and information about God and spirituality are in harmony with the facts of material reality, then *The Urantia Book* is the place to go for this type of satisfaction." [Be sure to check out their "List of Reports" and "Report Summaries" with an impressive grouping of topics.]

**The Urantia Book Historical Society:** http://ubhistory.org/index.html
"We cherish the teachings of *The Urantia Book*, and share its vision of unity among all people of faith. Our mission is to promote and foster an awareness and appreciation of *The Urantia Book* through its heritage, origins, background, development, and general history. Our hope is that this revelation, delivered to humanity and its history will remain an inspiration for generations to come. This library makes available to the public--the history of The Urantia Book Movement. The scope of the UBHS collection on-line digital library includes records of individual expressions about the teachings in *The Urantia Book* and organizations whose sole purpose is the study and dissemination of the teachings."

**UrantiaUniversity:** www.urantiauniversity.org
Urantia University Institute, (UUI), is a global center of study and service dedicated to training teachers and farseeing leaders and fostering a spiritual community with cosmic ideals based on truths in *The Urantia Book*. UUI offers an innovative series of online classes that introduce newer readers to some of the most important concepts, truths, and themes found in *The Urantia Book* and more in-depth studies of selected topics in the book for experienced students. They have a series of online forums designed to explore new directions and integrative thinking in science, religion, philosophy, and human systems. Fundamental to Urantia University Institute's long-range vision is the multi-stage development of a unique university that will encompass and foster academic study infused with cosmic ideals and dynamic training programs. Part of a long-range plan to develop a university grounded in cosmic wisdom, ideals and aspiration, UUI was set up to provide diverse learning paths for students in an online educational environment in which to explore, discern, and actualize the truths and knowledge found in *The Urantia Book*. Parallel to a track of academic programs, UUI plans to support the development of workshops and classes that effectively apply the insights of *The Urantia Book* to dealing with issues in relationships and everyday living in ways that foster soul growth and promote spiritual community.

**Urantology:** www.urantology.org
Urantology is an extensive program of learning offered through The Center for students of the Urantia Papers. It facilitates the search for self-knowledge and the discovery of truth. We trust your personal journey inspires faith in a loving God and encourages a desire to spiritually serve the human family. [This site provides an interesting course development. Also of interest is the Origin and History section.]

---

# **Videos/Movies/Documentaries** [many over 30 minutes]

### **A Three Sticks Film Production – James Leese**
~**The Urantia Book Trailer:** https://vimeo.com/162891253 Apr. 2016, 1:01
~**UrantiaUniversity Trailer:** https://vimeo.com/162892648 Apr. 2016, 2:05
~**Bethsaida 29 AD:** https://vimeo.com/163398180 Apr. 2016, 4:35
~**This I Believe; This I Live:** https://vimeo.com/162997338 Apr. 2016, 10:51
~**The Day Alone With God:** https://vimeo.com/170869895 June 2016, 26:06
[James Leese does beautiful video work. Many Urantian videos are his work but credit is given to the creator.]

## Deborah Goaldman Videos
~**Living in Divine Consciousness:** https://vimeo.com/220358310  Nov. 2013, 6:03
~**The Garden of Transformation:** https://vimeo.com/220359983  Nov. 2013, 5:41
[These are a sample.]


## Gary Tonge Videos
~**All One:** https://www.youtube.com/watch?v=F-PLtXkovvQ Mar. 2016, 2:06
~**Journey Through the Universe:** www.youtube.com/watch?v=9CkbbohKDoY 2010, 5:03
~**The Urantia Book Introduction:** www.youtube.com/watch?v=_wf21UbsdJ4 2014, 8:28


## God's Gumshoe: www.youtube.com/user/godsgumshoe
~**The Urantia Book for Dummies: Chapter 1, "Life Implantation"**
https://www.youtube.com/watch?v=LooIudKVG6c   June 2015, 35:35
~**The Urantia Book for Dummies: Chapter 2 section 1 "Civilization in Crisis #1"**
https://www.youtube.com/watch?v=HIEOY7peRfQ Feb. 2016, 30:04
~**The Urantia Book for Dummies: Chapter 2 section 2 "Civilization in Crisis #2"**
www.youtube.com/watch?v=ta9sI-2HkIM  Apr.2016, 46:15
"Here, in this series, we begin exploring the contours of an emerging worldview that has come to be called "cosmic." We need to think outside of the box in order to move forward and bring our civilization to the next step. These papers seem to afford us the only escape from the mechanical clutch of the material world and from the error distortion of the incompleteness of the intellectual world; it is the only discovered solution to the impasse in mortal thinking regarding the continuing survival of the planet. It appears to be the only passport to completion of reality and to understanding of the eternity of life in a universal cosmic creation of love, law, unity, and a progressive evolutionary wholeness to the future of the human race." [www.godsgumshoe.org] [This is only a sample of the first few. I particularly like that these videos are narrated because I can relax and enjoy the artwork, etc. They are all very high-quality productions.]


## Triniteit
~**The Urantia Secret:** www.youtube.com/watch?v=bbYGcGhMH4Y Jan. 2013, 6:27
~**Urantia and the Planetary Mortal Epochs:** www.youtube.com/watch?v=0-MnPnxQJT8 2012, 6:48
[Both of these videos will have particular appeal to young people.]


## UrantiaBookFilms:
Top films and videos produced by readers of *The Urantia Book*.
https://www.youtube.com/channel/UCdHer8wRcZCxdYIpZMNUS9Q
[Below is just a sampling. Note that they have a good selection in Spanish.]
~**Re-Imagining Jesus: Discovering the Human Hero:**
www.youtube.com/watch?v=rgp-RcgaJjU
Unlike any other Jesus film. Follow a revolutionary Jesus amidst the social, political, and religious turbulence of his time. Seldom seen ancient synagogues in Israel, excavated Greek cities in Jordan, and Phoenician cities of Lebanon. This historical drama unfolds in the unique ecological environment and exotic landscapes of the region, culminating in an inspiring view of the human hero of the Christian story. Published Oct. 2016, 1:17:48

**~What do we do now???** www.youtube.com/watch?v=-k7gYk-naxg
A 50-year veteran of the Urantia movement [David Kantor] assesses the current state of the movement and its primary organizations on the 60th anniversary of the publication of *The Urantia Book*. With almost 1,000,000 copies of the book now in circulation in 16 languages, the movement is crossing the threshold into a completely new phase of development unlike anything experienced by any new religious movement before it. A mixed media presentation produced for The Urantia Book Los Angeles Society, presented at the Unitarian Universalist Church in Anaheim, California. Published Oct. 2015, 1:07:10

**UrantiaFilm:** https://www.youtube.com/channel/UCbXrivV3I9Qua4GueLgzhxw
Videos inspired by the ideas and ideals in *The Urantia Book*. [Below is just a sampling.]
**~A Feast of Uncertainty:** www.youtube.com/watch?v=oSM7ggRhYE4
Filmmaker Richard Jernigan explores *The Urantia Book's* version of the life and teachings of Jesus against the backdrop of modern-day Israel and the Palestinian territories. Both meditative and informative, A Feast of Uncertainty, goes where Jesus lived and taught as described in *The Urantia Book*. Jerusalem, Nazareth, the Sea of Galilee, and other key sites are revealed with a fresh eye and sympathetic regard for the people living amidst 4000-plus years of history and ever-present random violence. The film is narrated with text from *The Urantia Book*, bringing to life the book's profound, universal viewpoint on the life and teachings of Jesus, teachings that step beyond Christianity, for all humanity. Published Jan. 2017, 1:46:39
**~Jesus: An Introduction:** www.youtube.com/watch?v=Cn1vHyJn7Ts
An introduction to Jesus in *The Urantia Book*. First shown at the 2015 Parliament of the World's Religions. Published Oct. 2015, 7:20

**Urantian Artist:** www.youtube.com/user/UrantianArtist
www.a-urantian-artist-shares.com/A_URANTIAN_ARTIST_SHARES/
This woman writes on her website, "As I approach my 80th year, I have created this website with a desire to share with those who will appreciate the simple thoughts of an everyday artist and lover of truth, one of the common people. (written in August 2009)" She goes on to say, "I call myself a Urantian artist because I have the desire to be an artist of life. There are many artists who are more accomplished and skilled than I am, but I am, never the less, a fellow Urantian artist." Finally, although her site is packed with information, I include these remarks from this wonderful artist of life, "I am a dedicated member of the Church of Jesus Christ, first of all, and have also received a degree in Religion from the University of Hawaii. Both my university study and reading *The Urantia Book* have strengthened my surety of my testimony that my church is a revealed church which was organized with a purpose to prepare a people to eventually receive the Fifth Epochal Revelation." [Note her YouTube Channel has an abundance of videos, some rather short, all the way to quality full-length movies.]

**UrantiaPapers:** www.youtube.com/channel/UC-RODElBFJE7s6lK_PtKFsQ
The "urantiapapers" YouTube channel enables you to listen to, and share portions of *The Urantia Book* on Facebook and other social media applications.
~Urantia Book – Paper 1 https://www.youtube.com/watch?v=ygE53m4oNhQ Aug. 2012 45:04
~Urantia Book – Paper 2 https://www.youtube.com/watch?v=KB6latUloL8 Aug. 2012 45:05
~Urantia Book – Paper 42
~Urantia Book – Paper 112 https://www.youtube.com/watch?v=h537lTIHN_A Nov. 2012 59:17

# Index

guilt · 95, 129, 140, 150

## H

happiness · 8, 108, 124, 146
harmony · 19, 28, 55, 60, 118
harp of God · 50
Havona · 13, 19, 21, 30, 33, 45, 46, 50, 52, 53, 58, 59, 60, 61, 63, 64, 77, 87, 101, 158
health · 84, 93, 94, 97, 98, 134, 146
heaven · 45, 53, 67, 86, 101, 102, 107, 108, 111, 120, 121, 123, 124, 127, 129, 134, 149
Hebrew prophets · 112, 113
Hebrew(s) · 80, 105, 108, 111, 112, 113, 117, 121, 149, 150
Hebron, Israel · 102
hell · 108
Hindu / Hinduism · 107, 152
history · i, iv, 41, 57, 64, 72, 100, 101, 113, 155
Holy Spirit · 2, 15, 23, 40, 145, 146, 147
home life · 65, 91, 94, 117
honest · 95, 123, 127, 129, 131, 132, 133, 135, 145, 150
hope · 8, 9, 46, 68, 84, 96, 98, 112, 121, 132, 152
hospital · 137
humanity · iv, 102

## I

Ice Age · 80
Iceland · 103
ideal
    of God's will · 129
    of government · 54
    of home life · 91
    of human relationship(s) · 122
    of self-government · 60
    prayer · 67
identity · 3, 4, 23, 47, 60, 76, 115
Immanuel · 75, 76, 77, 86, 115, 116, 117, 120, 158
    ambassador of Paradise Trinity · 37
    Union of Days · 34, 37, 158
impatient · 94, 95
incarnation · 12, 15, 29, 35, 77, 101, 109, 114, 119, 158
Incas · 99
India · 80, 81, 97, 99, 107, 108, 152

iniquity · 85, 120, 129
    persistent sin · 85
insight · 3, 7, 24, 40, 66, 122, 130, 145
intolerance · 50, 51, 135
invisible · 84, 94, 97, 157
Iran · 99, 108, 111, 149
Iraq · 97, 99, 102
Isaac · 103, 105
Islam · 108, 152
Isle of Light and Life · 21, 158
Isle of Paradise · 21, 34, 59, 158, See Paradise
isolate · 53, 76, 82, 85, 88, 94, 151
Israel · 102, 111, 112
Italy · 108, 118, 149

## J

Japan · 99, 103
Jehovah · 111
Jerusalem · 101, 118, 138, 140, 143, 145
Jerusem · 34, 49, 50, 53, 54, 79, 84, 85, 86, 87, 93, 96, 98, 143, 158
Jesus · iv, 101, 107, 117, 118, 119, 120, 121, 122, 123, 124, 125, 127, 128, 129, 130, 132, 133, 134, 135, 136, 137, 138, 139, 140, 141, 142, 143, 145, 149, 150, 152, 153
baptism · 119
chose not to portray himself as the Jewish Messiah · 120
chose not to seek self-preservation · 120
chose to be subject to the Father's will · 120
chose to deprive himself of super-human assistance · 120
chose to establish the kingdom of heaven as a son of God · 120
chose to take normal human precautions · 120
father-brother to siblings · 118
great test · 119
his life more important than his death · 140
last discourse in temple · 139
last supper/ remembrance supper · 139
Master · 143
Messiah · 113
new commandment · 139
of Nazareth · 12, 29, 35, 105, 140, 149, 151
sentenced to death · 139
the son of man · 119

Made in the USA
Monee, IL
02 February 2020

21221330R00111